Sometimes Orange Is Almost Gold

Morgantown's Misfits of the Diamond

Jim Antonini
Suzanne Reynolds

Pump Fake Press—Morgantown, WV

Paperback ISBN: 979-8-218-53050-1

Library of Congress Control Number: 2025917334

Title: Sometimes Orange Is Almost Gold: Morgantown's Misfits of the Diamond

Author: Jim Antonini & Suzanne Reynolds

Paperback | 2025

Dedication

For Ravi Shibley, Tom Moore, Sean Kelley, and Meatball

Foreword

Morgantown's Bad News Bears
Chico's Bail Bonds, More Social Club Than Softball Team

Editor's Note: The following is an excerpt from a story written by Dave Mistich and featured on an episode of West Virginia Public Radio's program Inside Appalachia. The episode focused on the impact of baseball throughout the region. To listen to this episode and others, subscribe to the podcast at www.wvpublic.org/podcasts/inside-appalachia.

It's an early August evening on Libertore Field at White Park in Morgantown. The orange prison jumpsuit jerseys of Chico's Bail Bonds are impossible to miss — and so is our play. But, that's not necessarily a compliment.

On this evening, the team loses in typical Chico fashion.

The team name, of course, comes from the 1976 film *The Bad News Bears*, in which a down-and-out and cheap beer-swigging Walter Matthau coaches a group of rag-tag Little Leaguers and tries to whip them into shape.

Morgantown's Chico's aren't too far off from their fictitious counterparts.

On this night, there are flashes of defensive greatness in the outfield from Chico veteran Sean Kelley and rookie Dave Lawson. A few Chico batters turn infield errors into a few runs, thanks to some heads-up baserunning.

We hold our own against an outmatched and much younger rival, Gene's Beer Garden, only to crumble when we needed to come through.

But all isn't lost, as it never is with Chico's. The night is still young. Win or lose, the team had yet to get to the best part of the Chico's game-night experience.

...A Staple of Morgantown Softball

With just one season under their belt as the Nyabinghi Dance Hall, the team took on the Chico-moniker 20 years ago — in 1998 — the same year the bar took on the name of its address, 123 Pleasant Street.

Morgantown native Louis "LJ" Giuliani took over ownership of the bar and sponsorship of Chico's. He says Chico's immediately embodied the open-minded identity of 123.

"It doesn't matter if you're white or black, straight or gay, or whatever. It's all kinds that take the field when Chico's takes the field," Giuliani said, noting that 123 has held the same values from the beginning.

Chico's part-time first baseman and the author of this article swings mightily at a pitch on June 16, 2017. His arms do not normally appear this muscular — although, they do in this photo because of pure grit, determination and zen-like focus.
Photo by Jesse Wright.

...After 20 years, many Chico's have come and gone from the team and from Morgantown. But even those who have moved on still stay connected to the team and look back on the early days with fondness.

"It was probably, really, to do something healthier besides sitting in the dark bar. I think to go out and do something that was more participatory and less spectator-driven — because, we all sat around and watch baseball together at that time. So, it was nice for us to go out and do something [and] get out in the sun and see the day together," said Greg Leatherman, a journalist now living in Florida who was around when the team began.

Morgantown's Music Scene and 123 Pleasant Street

Giuliani, now retired from the softball field, says Chico's was always rooted in Morgantown's music and art scene.

"A lot of the players that they grabbed on to just happened to be musicians. Brian Porterfield, Tom Batchelor, you've got Jeff Goodwin who is a musician. He's playing on the team now," said Giuliani, recalling some of the players who have exercised their musical talents from the stage at 123 and other local venues.

Softball wasn't their first talent — nor their second, third or fourth, Giuliani said with a laugh.

"It was a way to bring like-minded folks [together] that liked talking about music or art or how many shots of Jameson they had. It was based more on like-mindedness," he explained.

Following each Chico's game, as it has been since the beginning, the Bonders gather at 123 for cheap beers like Black Label and Pabst Blue Ribbon — and, as Giuliani mentioned, celebratory shots of Jameson.

...Creating the Chico Mythology: Game Summaries Recap the Misery

But, even after a few drinks at 123, a Chico's game night isn't over until it's been recapped and shared on the team's Facebook group.

Part comedy, part mythology, the game write-ups exaggeratedly highlight the ups-and-downs over an always hard-fought seven innings. If Chico's doesn't get clobbered into a 10 or 15-run mercy rule before getting through all 7 innings, that is.

"There's three of us that have kind of done this and that's myself, David Foreman and Jim Antonini," Greg Leatherman said. "And, basically, it is sort of like the literary connection to Chico's softball team — is that we've always captured the games win, lose or draw and written up how the game went — in both a serious, professional, sort of sportscaster way but also with a lot of humor."

Shortstop, team manager, Morgantown native and occupational health science researcher Jim Antonini has taken over the write-ups in recent years.

...Another Losing Record, But No Giving Up

Chico's finished their 2018 campaign with a record of 3 wins and 25 losses. Two of those wins came as a result of a no-show forfeit from the opposing team, while the third came on a gloriously executed 7 innings against Davis Cabinetry.

Such a pathetic record *should* make anyone reconsider their motivations to keep playing softball. But, if you can't tell, Chico's isn't about winning. Antonini says no matter what happens over the course of a season, it's hard to imagine hanging it up.

"I think every year there's a point in the year — probably after you've played 18, 20 games and it's like 'Why are we doing this?' We come out and sometimes we really get humiliated," Antonini said. "But, then, the game ends and then you get together everybody has a few beers and then it doesn't seem that bad. It's a pretty good way to spend a night."

Giuliani, despite having not played in recent years, feels the same.

"Chico's is kind of a state of mind in the sense that we're not here to judge, we're here to support and we're here to spend time with each other. And that's the bottom line. We're a softball team that's more of a social club than an actual softball team," Giuliani said.

So, if you ever find yourself around 123 Pleasant Street surrounded by orange softball shirts, you'll know you're hanging out with the Chico's. Buy a few of them a drink and strike up a conversation. After all, we assuredly just got beat

—Chico Dave Mistich, September 12, 2018

At 123 Pleasant Street, Dave Mistich, Jim Antonini, Jon Vehse, Aaron Hawley, Jeff Ryan

2004 Chico's: (standing) Tim Nelms, Greg Leatherman, Matt Cross, Jim Manilla, Skinny Miller, Jordan Nelms, Jim March, Unknown, Robert Raese, (kneeling) LJ Guiliani, Dave Krovich, Fred Baer, Clayton Neal

Preface

Nobody loses better than Chico's.
— David Foreman, former Chico's pitcher, team manager, July 2000

This book has been a work-in-progress since 1998. David Foreman had the keen foresight to document the highlights (and lowlights) of Chico softball games from the first pitch of the very first game ever. The postgame write-ups have continued until this day. No one could have predicted that this team would still exist 27 years later. And no one could have ever imagined that over 400 game recaps (>100,000 words) would be penned and nearly 5,000 photos would be collected. In recent years, there has been growing pressure by former and current team members, Chico supporters, BOPARC (Morgantown West Virginia's Board of Park and Recreation) league officials, opposing players, and curious outsiders to document the Chico softball experience in a book.

We have tried our best to capture the spirit, togetherness, and silliness of Chico's Bail Bonds softball. Because of space limitations, we couldn't include every write-up. As most people know who have followed the team, the Bondsmen have lost a large majority of their softball games through the years. It is believed that the Chico's Bail Bonds have lost nearly 74% of the games they have played in their 26-year history—a dreadful winning percentage of only .264. That is a lot of losing, my friends.

And sadly, nearly all the write-ups from 2003–2006 have been lost—a period in their long existence when the Bonders were actually capable of winning some games. I've been told the missing write-ups were because of lost computer files, multiple hard drive crashes, and defunct websites where the early Chico write-ups were stored. Others, however, who shall not be named, insist there is another reason as to why the 2003–2006 seasons are considered the 'lost years.' They believe the inclusion of the details of those seasons in this book would go against the 'brand' that has made the Chico's Bail Bonds infamous—a somewhat lovable but pathetically bad softball team.

According to a few folks who played on the Chico teams during the 2003–2006 seasons, the Bonders won more games than they lost. It has been confirmed that the 2004 Chico team was the top performing squad of all time with a record of 14 wins and 9 losses (.609 winning percentage). For the seasons from 2003 to 2006, Chico's Bail Bonds reportedly had a glorious stretch of four straight winning seasons, winning 51 games and losing 40 during that period. And in that stretch, the reporting of Chico's greatest victory was lost. In 2005, a drunken Bonders squad drubbed a cocky and physically fit team of local police officers in a late-night affair, knocking them out of playoff contention on the last game of the season. It would have been nice to read about that game and others from the winningest seasons in the long, colorful history of Chico softball. Nonetheless, we tried our best to choose the most popular write-ups available (many in their unedited, original form). We hope you enjoy.

This historical collection of softball stories and photos would not be possible without the continual support and sponsorship from LJ and Lisa Guiliani of 123 Pleasant Street. We also must acknowledge Morgantown's best bartender and the heart and soul of 123 Pleasant Street, Donnie Duppee. We thank Tom Batchelor for the wonderful book title and for the photos of the team on the field and about town, we want to thank Jenny Roberts, Jesse Wright, Dave Carson, Aaron Hawley and everyone else who's posted a great photo of a Bonder online or contributed photos and artwork to this project.

x

Introduction

If there wasn't a softball game scheduled tonight, none of this would've ever happened. And that would have been such a shame. There can't be too many people in this world who had more fun than we did tonight. And we got slaughtered in two softball games.
—Jon Vehse, Chico's catcher, June 2023

The first season of what would become Chico's softball was 1997. The team was sponsored by the players and went by Nyabinghi, the name of the bar before it was purchased by LJ Guiliani and changed to 123 Pleasant Street. The team competed in the BOPARC Men's AA softball league in Morgantown, WV, that year. The original team wore baby blue shirts with brown letters. Team members included Rob B, Adam Koicuba, JP Carney, Meatball, Jeff Shilling, Matt Burtner, Jeff Hindal, Eddie Freedom, and others. The Chico roster then and now has been mostly composed of bartenders, musicians, and regular patrons of the bar.

In 1998, the team's name was changed to Chico's Bail Bonds, inspired by the sponsor of the Bad News Bears little league team in the 1976 movie starring Tatum O'Neal and Walter Matthau. Eddie Freedom originally suggested the name, which was quickly adopted. The team shirt color also changed. Although some have referred to the color scheme as "creamsicle," the correct terminology is "county orange and white," as in, "When I appeared before the judge, I was in my county orange."

The county orange scheme was first drawn up on a napkin at the since-closed Falstaff's bar and hamburger joint that was across the street from 123. The design included the now defunct sombrero-wearing mascot designed by Paul "Hermit" Baird and introduced for the Fall softball season in 1998. The new shirt and color choice competed briefly with an alternate design (grey shirts and purple letters), but orange soon won the hearts and minds of all Chicodom.

After the postgame beers and whiskey shots at 123 Pleasant Street, the Chico game night isn't complete until it's recapped and shared. Since their inception in 1998, Chico games have been reported and uploaded for public consumption, first onto the 123 Pleasant Street website, then to a Myspace page, a blog site, and eventually to a Facebook page dedicated to all things Chico's softball. The game recaps originally began as brief one- or two-line summaries of the game's highlights. They have since morphed into much larger commentaries of a paragraph or two about the night's event that oftentimes describe the psyche of the team and postgame hi-jinks in more detail than the actual softball game itself, usually a Chico loss. The postgame recaps were originally written by David Foreman and Greg Leatherman. In more recent years, Jim Antonini has handled the late-night write-ups. Others who contributed game recaps have included Jon Vehse, Ken Price, Dave Mistich, Tom Batchelor, and Chad Koury.

As of this writing, the Chico's softball team will begin their 27th season in the summer of 2025. These days it seems the actual playing of the games is only a formality. The celebrations in the parking lot and at 123 Pleasant Street after the game have become the real attraction for the team members and their legion of loyal supporters. And that's not a bad thing.

A Confession

We, the authors of the postgame write-ups, have a confession to make. We have written about our softball team, the Chico's Bail Bonds, for over 26 years, and it's time to come clean. In some cases, not all, we have embellished a little about what happened before, during, and after games.

We never lied about who won or lost. We may have reported an incorrect score here and there, but we never said we won a game we didn't win. And we never *lied, per se.*

We may have stretched the truth a little bit, and we may have taken liberties with some details, but for the most part, we can say that about 80% of the reportage has been true, and the rest of it is our imaginations—*filling in the blanks.*

No harm, no foul, right? We hope we haven't made anybody angry. And we hope we don't lose any readers with this confession. It's just something we felt we needed to get off our chests.

—Dave Foreman, Greg Leatherman, Jim Antonini

Contents

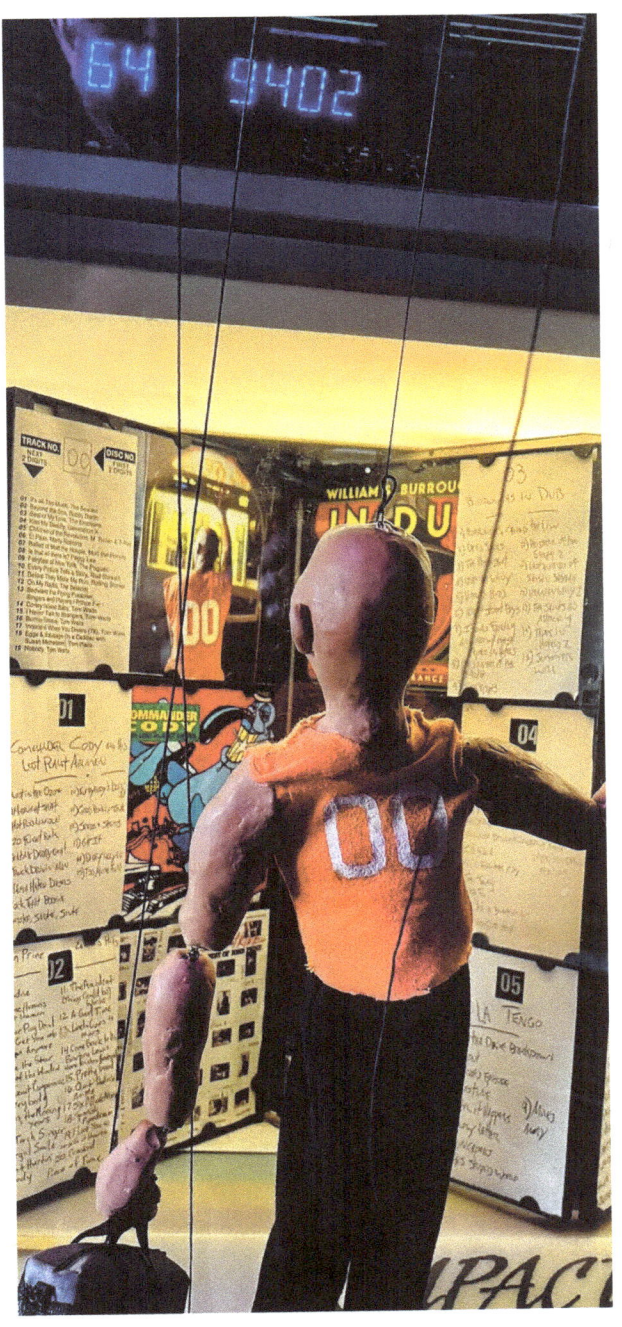

Chico softball brings us together and that's all that matters.
—Jon Vehse, Chico catcher, June 2023

Orange is the color of poison
—*overheard at a party, spoken by a young painter*

1998 CHICO'S GETS THE JOB DONE

1998 SUMMER SOFTBALL AA-LEAGUE (10 WINS / 12 LOSSES)

MAY 29–CHICO'S (3–4) VS MUNDY'S Hostile crowd doesn't make it any easier for anemic Chico's offense. Chico's tie it twice late but can't come up with key hits in final frame of heartbreaking 15–16 loss.—DF

JUNE 14–CHICO'S (4–6) VS JAMMERZ MVP Butler turns 36, and Chico's endure a bizarre and ridiculous interpretation of the infield fly rule in the 15–17 loss.—DF

JUNE 21–CHICO'S (4–7) VS BOAZ Chico's blow another lead and loses 12–16 to arch-rivals. Chico's eat BOAZ's food and promises them a keg as reparations.—DF

JUNE 28–CHICO'S (5–7) VS PURPLE COW AA Chico's break losing streak, dominate opponent 15–9 with major-league defense and indominable spirit.—DF

JUNE 30–CHICO'S (6–7) VS MT INFO Freedom overcomes debilitating pain and makes fantastic grab to shut down extra inning rally. Chico's otherwise spotty D makes it close, and Giuliani walks away in a good mood, nonetheless. Chico's wins 12–11.—DF

JULY 6–CHICO'S (6–8) VS BACKDOOR Chico chokes, giving up another lead, this time losing 10–11 on a bases-loaded walk in the bottom of the seventh.—DF

JULY 8–CHICO'S (6–9) VS CLASSICS Buenos Dias, Chico's! A hungover team gets clobbered (14–30) by a bunch of hicks. Giuliani skipped mass for this?—DF

JULY 19–CHICO'S (6–10) VS MARIO'S FISHBOWL Do not ever put your bats away against Chico's. It looked like a rout, but Chico's bounce back with 12 runs in the third to make it respectable. Can Chico's finish with a winning record? Can Chico's do better than last year's Nyabinghi team (6–15)? Chico's loses 16–26.—DF

JULY 20–CHICO'S (7–10) VS MARCH-WESTIN CO Chico's get the job done against the worst team in the league. Losing streak snapped! Chico's best 1997 Nyabinghi record! Double play combination (1–5–3) wows crowd! Chico's wins 19–9.—DF

JULY 20–CHICO'S (7–11) VS VFW POST 826 At 'em balls galore. Chico's can only scrounge up three runs against the veteran VFW juggernaut. Chico's loses 3–20.—DF

JULY 30–CHICO'S (8–11) VS ARCHIES Chico's look awesome against a hapless team (only 2 wins this year). Excellent glove work on the right side by Shilling and Leatherman. Chico's creep closer to .500 record. Chico's wins 24–0.—DF

AUGUST 6–CHICO'S (9–12) VS X-MEN Cursed. A pathetic display. "It was the worst game I have ever played, and I apologize to my teammates for doing so poorly," says shortstop and strikeout victim Foreman. Chico's loses 8–18.—DF

AUGUST 6–CHICO'S (10–12) VS GILLS Chico's overcome early deficit to rout a playoff contender. Boaz cheers on the team, Gills' loss = Boaz playoff berth! Free beer courtesy of BOAZ! "It's like shooting a 95 all day and then birdieing the 18th," quoted Carney. Chico's wins 22–15—DF

1998 SUMMER CHICO'S BAIL BONDS TEAM MEMBERS: Shilling, Burtner, Koicuba, Carney, Rob Borowitz, Brostman, Foreman, Brown, Kurkendal, Hindal, Butler, Giuliani, McMillen, Peterson, Leatherman

---

CHICO'S MVPS: Butler, Borowitz

1999 A GREAT LOVE OF THE GAME

1999 Chico's: (standing) Rob Borowitz, Adam Koicuba, Unknown Chico, Eddie Freedom, Jeff Schilling, Bob Butler, Matt Burtner, LJ Guiliani, Jim Manilla, Hollis Brown, JP Carney, (kneeling) Meatball, Dave Foreman, Clint Mahle, Jeff Hindal

1999 SUMMER SOFTBALL AA-LEAGUE (4 WINS / 14 LOSSES)

APRIL 30–CHICO'S (0–1) VS BLACKSVILLE DAIRY MART Good hitting performance subsumed by poor fielding. Six runs in the top of the first and, a 1–2–3 bottom of the frame quickly turned sour; Blacksville bats exploded for well-placed hits and Chico's fielding gave up some untimely errors. Late start (10:30!) did not help, nor did Carney's injured leg, low temperatures, unstretched hamstrings, wet grass, collectively plummeting self-esteems, and un-cleated sneakers. Chico's loses 14–24.—DF

MAY 19–CHICO'S (1–3) VS GLENMARK Chico's fall apart late. Glenmark "wins," 14–18 proving that they were the least bad team, not necessarily better. Poor fielding by both teams made for a sloppy game. Technicalities called by umpires (stepping on the plate, throwing bats, not sliding) get costly. Carney and his knee sorely missed. Foreman pitched again in relief. Leatherman walloped ball like there was no tomorrow. New shirts livened up an otherwise morose Chico's crew.—DF

MAY 20–CHICO'S (1–4) VS EG&G Chico's players and fans alike hope that this is rock bottom. No fielding, no hitting. Nothing clicked, nobody got in a groove against a team that we should be able to beat. Foreman pitched from start to finish. Carney back in the lineup and also acted as manager. Multiple strategic moves, including shuffling Brostman, Borowitz, Carney, Demco, March, Burtner, Leatherman, and Hindal around the field defensively did not work. Chico's poor play was reflected in the number of spectators. Sloppy play does not put people in the seats as only the die-hard fans come out to witness an embarrassing performance. Even the cicadas did not want to watch. An individual who shall discreetly remain anonymous struck out twice (Note: This is slow pitch softball). Chico's loses 11–22.—DF

MAY 28–CHICO'S (1–5) VS SPORTS PAGE After storming back to erase a seven-run deficit in the bottom of the sixth, Chico's saw its surge abated by a well-coached Sports Page crew who scored big in the top of the seventh then made three stellar defensive plays to close Chico's down. Pitcher Carney drinks more beers than Chico's score runs. Chico's loses 16–24.—DF

JUNE 15–CHICO'S (2–9) VS IMPACT THERAPY The first 10 o'clock victory in the history of the Chico's franchise. Chico's wins 19–14. Quality glove work abounds from home plate to the right field and every nook and cranny in between. Everyone records a putout, including an over-the-shoulder grab in the dark left field corner in foul territory by Borowitz and a perfectly thrown strike and well-caught tag by the duo of Leatherman (oh-so aptly named) and March. Foreman's balls nearly knocked onto the women's field by scorching line drive ("It was like a dream. All the sudden the ball hit my glove, and it was on the ground before me.") Changing strike zone in the final inning nearly allows I.T. to challenge Chico's 8-run lead with a series of walks and well-placed hits. What happened? All agree: it was the bats, two Supercell mommas imported from York, Pa, courtesy of CBB Hall of Famer, Adam Koicuba. Oh, were he, former coach and left field mainstay, here to savor the sauce dripping from the moist flesh of Victory's lathered thigh!—DF

JUNE 22–CHICO'S (2–11) VS ACE/MARIO'S In the dim pantheon of great Chico's performances, this game shall stand out against the dark fabric of the night sky as one of our finest moments. It was a 9–2 team we had on our plates for the 6 o'clock meal, a club that regularly scores 30+ runs . . . in an inning. Like the desperate soldiers at the Alamo, CBB fights valiantly to keep the ACE/Mario's fellas at bay. The boys in orange looked like old pros, holding their mammoth opponents to only four runs. Alas! Chico's only manages to cross the plate twice! Carney flawless at short; Meatball and March brilliant at third; Hindal and Demco a pair of geniuses at second; Burtner without equal at first; Leatherman a prodigy behind the plate; Borowitz, Giuliani, Freedom, and Peters fantastic in the outfield; Manilla an incomparable AH. New bats or old, they all wither in the desert-like conditions of Liberatore in the afternoon. Chico's loses 2–4.—DF

JULY 8–CHICO'S (3–11) VS MARCH-WESTIN CO A witching hour victory for Chico's. The ten o'clock game does not start until 11 PM and is not over until midnight. Defense unimpressive for the most part (except for another 1–2 punch from March to Leatherman, this time from second base) but the offense is unstoppable. Carney knocks it deep, over March Westin's heads, three times. Borowitz hits for the cycle. Giuliani? Walks every time! Freedom, March, Mike, Burtner, Meatball, Leatherman, and Manilla all contribute. Foreman walks twice as a batter and strikes a chump out as a pitcher. High-quality Jim March karma in the seats is key to putting Chico's over the top. Chico's wins 26–18. Game over at 12? Chico's home at 5.—DF

JULY 14–CHICO'S (3–12) VS DAY MYLAN Some late hustle cannot redeem the Chico's crew. Sloppy play in the field, some poor pitching and effeminate bats allow the other Mylan team to steamroll CBB 8–13. Giuliani is the sparkplug in the field and on the base paths. Everyone else sits and applauds. Freedom needs new hardware. Hindal, Giuliani, and Foreman pour beer on their wounds and meander to 123 bar to sulk and eat Chinese food.—DF

JULY 21–CHICO'S (3–14) VS IMPACT THERAPY

The team we beat a few weeks ago gets even with Chico's. A Freedom-less CBB crew hangs their heads and drags their feet from start to finish and wind up getting skunked by ten in four innings. Borowitz and Foreman strikeout looking (how shameful). It's hard to play with only nine guys on the field and an automatic out at the bottom of the order. The highlight was finding a tough-looking insect near home plate after the game: Chico's mascot for the next millennium. Chico's loses 7–19.—DF

1999 SUMMER CHICO'S BAIL BONDS TEAM MEMBERS:

Burtner, Ball, Rob Borowitz, Brostman, Leatherman, Foreman, Carney, Hindal, Demco, Giuliani, Peterson, McMillen, Manilla, March, Mike, Butler, Shilling, Koicuba, Kurkendal

CHICO'S MVPS:

Butler, Shilling, Koicuba, Kurkendal

1999 FALL SOFTBALL AA-LEAGUE (7 WINS / 9 LOSSES)

SEPTEMBER 7–CHICO'S (0–1) VS K RAY

A typical Chico's game: great defense, but no hitting. Big sluggers held to single digits, and Freedom makes some fantastic plays. Heroic Rob B persists like Brian Giles with fantastic hitting and fielding. It was the dawning of a new day at Liberatore Field. The player-sponsored Chico's team feels good and plays well with high spirits and a great love of the game and each other. I'd rather lose with these guys with my chin up high than ride the bench and win with a bunch of ringers Chico's loses 7–9.—DF

SEPTEMBER 9–CHICO'S (1–1) VS CENTER ROCK

A fine performance by the Chico's crew. A Rob B-less Chico's outhits and outhustles the not-so-good men in black. The big highlight was Skinny's bases-loaded double with two outs in the 4th to put the Bondsmen up by three runs. Carney gets a mouthful of dirt in the process of making some fantastic plays on some grounders (pop-ups were a little more troublesome). Giuliani and Foreman team up for another outfield assist at the plate. Manilla carries the hot bat. Manager Freedom frustrated by at'em balls to second base. Leatherman skies balls to the stratosphere. Burtner quite admirable in left field. In an unprecedented move, one of the umpires suits up and plays for Chico's and at one point gets a homer. The brilliant mind of Jeff Hindal causes an infield fly rule double play. Hotly contested strike out total for the season: Hindal 1, Foreman 1. Chico's wins 17–11.—DF

SEPTEMBER 14–CHICO'S (1–2) VS CITY SLICKERS

Leatherman cranks a homer and a triple, but his efforts are not enough to rally his mates and provide victory. Chico's loses 10–20. Poor first inning defense ruins team attitude as Carney injures glove hand on lined shot to his palm. No clear leadership on the bench creates chaos. Fourteen players show up, but who plays when and who plays where? Who is in charge around here? Freedom? Carney? Burtner? Foreman? Widespread dissension among Chico's mainstays raises big question marks about the team's future. Someone needs to step up, or this ship is going down. Carney, Rob B, Skinny, and Peterson overcome by body odor and pachouli fumes during Burning Spear show—will they recover in time for Thursday's game?—DF

SEPTEMBER 23–CHICO'S (2–3) VS UNITED ELECTRIC

A classic BOPARC softball match-up. Chico's jump to a big lead, but the bats go dry. Good effort late is not enough, Chico's loses 19–20. Members of opposite team—who all participate in Devil worship—sacrifice a chicken to Apollo, God of the Sun, during pregame ceremony. It works. Leatherman at first and Hindal at second are baffled by long shadows and bright sunbeams in their eyes. Many potential outs lost in the folds of Apollo's cloak. Skinny "officially" joins the CBB fraternity by striking out. On the way home, all of Chico's are tuned into sad songs on the radio. Greg thinks about new babies, especially his own.—DF

SEPTEMBER 28–CHICO'S (2–5) VS MYLAN MIDNIGHT

Tragedy on the diamond. Late in the game, Skinny takes a great throw from Giuliani at the plate and in his attempt to tag out the guy from Mylan, he is kicked in the face. He spits some blood and nearly passes out on his way to Rob B's car. Bones broken in three places—surgery, pins, plates, and screws. The Bondsmen shocked. Mylan shaken up. Everyone goes through the motions for the final few outs and wonders how Skinny fares in the ER. True to the Skinny ethos, he holds on to the ball and gets the out. Chico's loses 7–22.—DF

OCTOBER 3–CHICO'S (4–5) VS MORGANTOWN TRAVEL

Wearing duct-tape armbands in first game of two to honor injured hall-of-famer Skinny, a bleary-eyed Chico's squad survives Saturday night to suit up against Dirty Fred and his globe-trotting bachelors in spikes. Dirty Fred employs the geostationary ionized hitch-pitch, but it backfires as Bondsman batters need stimulation to swing and get it from the herky-jerky motion of the erstwhile landlord and lady's man. The Travellers, on the other hand, have no solution for the new-look Chico's D of Carney on the mound and Burtner at short. Burtner kicks off two double plays with his steady glove, Carney induces weak pop-ups from everybody but Sluggin' Psycho, and in an out-of-body experience, Hindal catches a live bullet with his teeth. Offensively, Big Mike homers, Dan Ball swings like a veteran and Kurkendall goes 4 for 4. Chico's Fan Appreciation Day draws starstruck singles in skirts and diehard stragglers set on erasing hangovers. Chico's wins 12–9—GL

OCTOBER 3–CHICO'S (4–6) VS BLACKSVILLE DAIRY MART

The second half of a Sunday doubleheader found our Bondsmen wilting under the heat of an October sky. Meanwhile, the other team seemed fine. Red faces alert fans that Chico's may be running low on radiator fluid. Thin roster allows for zero substitutions at a time when the team needs a breather. Not even the presence of Skinny can rally an exhausted line-up. Several Chico's hitters struggle to get the ball out of the infield. Commenting on the disappointing absence of the

123

LJ GUILIANI

OUTFIELD, TEAM SPONSER

BATS: RIGHT   THROWS: RIGHT   SEASONS PLAYED: 18
HOBBIES: GARDENING, PARENTING, WINTER SPORTS
SOFTBALL CATCH PHRASES: "HIT THE CUTOFF MAN!"; "TAKE A PITCH!"
WALK-UP SONG: "REPEATER" BY FUGAZI

LJ is considered Chico's all-time best outfielder. He purchased the 123 Pleasant Street live music venue and began sponsoring Chico's in 1998; could outrun Jim March running backward up a hill; has been compared to the Bad News Bears movie character Kelly Leak (but without the cigarette smoking and motorcycle).

singer called Freedom, cotton-mouthed softballers jibe, "Hog-blast better be good." The flashing bulbs of photo-seeking fans distract the brilliant Rob B who is overrun by female admirers wanting to remove his shirt. Leatherman caps a 6 for 7 doubleheader by standing stranded at first for most of the game. Pitcher Carney puts a muzzle on whining D-mart, but they still score enough runs to win. Misinterpretation of rules shames umpire who allows winning Blacksville run to advance 3 bases on a ball through the backstop. Chico's last outs come on an unforced double play featuring poor baserunning with sluggers on deck. Chico's loses 7–8.—GL

OCTOBER 10–CHICO'S (5-7) VS THE PRESS BOX

The Press Box fellas wanted to play, so the game goes on in spite of: a) Chico's can only muster 8 guys; b) the umpire already officially called the game a forfeit; c) Josh, the victim of the unforgiving CBB press gang, is declared ineligible because he played in the 8 o'clock game for March-Westin. The ump (bless her heart) allows the game to proceed on one condition—nobody gets hurt. Josh, the newest honorary Chico, delivers big with his bat. Skinny joins his pals on the bench, a little swollen but heartily cheering on his teammates to victory. A large inning ties it up in the 5th for Chico's. CBB stays alive, benefiting from Press Box errors and softballs to the nuts late in the game. But, poor defense by the Bondsmen results in an insurmountable lead. Chico's loses 18–20. On the way home, we congratulate ourselves on doing well with only 9 boys in the lineup. At the bar, Captain Beyond pulls Foreman aside firmly by the elbow. "God bless us everyone," he says, and Foreman nods in agreement.—DF

OCTOBER 27–CHICO'S (7-7) VS ARCHIE'S

Despite the absence of Carney and Foreman, Chico's manage to play some of its finest infield defense of the year, most of it coming in the form of Jim Antonini who took a break from devouring novels and chili-dogs to suit up and man the shortstop hole. Chico's wins 19–9. Archie's looked more like Jughead's against Burtner's erratic "dead ball". A new look D, with Peterson at second and Hindal behind the plate for the first time since shattering

his nose, held Archie's in check until Chico's found its collective swing. LJ's comical rundown and slide into third woke up the offense and the entire outfield of Kurkendal, Freedom, LJ and Rob B showed sweet level swings and hustle on the basepaths. LJ was "hittin' 'em where they ain't" and running like a '63 Stingray.

For a moment, the team seemed to be sliding back into a negative funk, with Freedom berating our valiant Bondsmen, but all that fell away as the runs piled up, the mutts barked with glee, and Chico's took the first game of their playoff doubleheader 19–9. Clubhouse chatter: For some reason, Chico's drank Stroh's (a disturbing trend to some) instead of High Life . . . a situation later rectified by Dan Ball who ensured a drunken doubleheader by scoring another round of brewskies for the boys in orange.—GL

OCTOBER 27–CHICO'S (7-8) VS ARCHIE'S

A riled-up Chico's confidently saunters into the arena for game 2 but ultimately comes up short. Chico's loses 10–12. Some fine defense by Archie's and bloopy hitting by Chico's = loss! Kurkendal finally swats a big one over the left field fence. On the bench, Skinny educates potential bad karma hecklers who may have had their hearts in the right place, but who needed schooling on the ethics of employee-owned and operated Chico's Bail Bonds Softball. The contributions of new Chico Antonini should not be underestimated. Carney's shoes are quite big and very hard to fill. (We hope he doesn't lose them while playing the slots at the Golden Nugget.) Several Bondsmen get silly at 123, swatting new gloves on the counter to break them in, shooting Tuaca, arm wrestling, and making promises to all the twins and frontiersmen who come within orbit of their stool.

"Sure, Joe, you can play tomorrow. 6 o'clock. Bring your glove."

Almost forgot! They got most of their runs off 5 homers!—DF

OCTOBER 28–CHICO'S (7-9) VS ARCHIE'S

Old problems come back to haunt the crew: dropping easy fly balls, not calling pop ups, striking out, booting easy grounders. Chico's find new and creative ways to lose (8–15): pitching while the left centerfielder has his back turned to the plate. In spite of a multitude of errors and poor hitting, the fellas put up a good fight and bow out of the loser's bracket playoffs gracefully. Rumors that Pat Benatar had joined the team for their big game attract a huge crowd. "No, Benna. She's from New York," explains Giuliani. When she finally gets her turn at bat, Archie's 24-year-old dumb jock outfielder protests about gender issues. Kurkendahl threatens, wielding his bat "Michelle." Leatherman faints! Foreman buries his head in the sand. Burtner and Skinny prepare for violent confrontation as both teams converge at the plate. Dan Ball and Hindal strategically situate Big Mike between themselves and the opposition. Mr. Bob, BOPARC commissioner, allows Benna her turn in the lineup under the special popstar clause of the Official Softball Beer League Rule Book (Section IX, Article 66, paragraph 13). Benna ropes one down the third base line and ends up at second.

"Rock 'n' roll," scream the kids, "rock 'n' fuckin' roll!"—DF

1999 FALL CHICO'S BAIL BONDS TEAM MEMBERS:

Butler, Shilling, Koicuba, Miller, Burtner, Rob Borowitz, Leatherman, Antonini, Miller, Foreman, Carney, Meatball, Hindal, Giuliani, Peterson, Brostman, Kurkendal, Manilla, March, Big Mike, Benna

CHICO'S MVPS: Butler, Shilling, Koicuba, Miller

2000 ALMOST EVERY INNING

MAY 9–CHICO'S (0–1) VS MARCH-WESTIN A sluggish game at the plate for Chico's and March-Westin. Post-hibernation Bail Bonders score only one run, and it was on a sac fly in the 5th. The Westin crew manages only four runs, a testament to Chico's excellent defense. Carney, who shined at short, connects with new guy Robarts from left center and throws a winded runner out at the plate. Sure-handed Krovich is carried from the field on the shoulders of teammates after making the tag. A quick pitch actually works against a Westin batter, weathered pitcher Foreman finally mature enough from the rubber to apply sneaky tactics in game situation. Chico's lose 1–4.

> ## "IT'S NICE TO GET THAT FIRST LOSS OUT OF THE WAY"

"It's nice to get that first loss out of the way," says one Bonder during postgame chugging. Someone adds that it's good to escape with no injuries.—DF

MAY 12–CHICO'S (0–2) VS GIBBIES Friday night and Chico's finds itself playing with a keg of beer on the line. Carney keeps them in the game from the mound, but the Gibbie's crew pulls away late when the tardy Foreman shuffles the infield and takes over the tossing duties. A late comeback curtailed by a "double play" that let the steam out of an exciting and hopeful rally. Chico's lose 8–13. A record number of Bonders show up and take part in playing and postgame, back-of-LJ's truck drinking. Children, spouses, fans, and girlfriends accompany the boys as they stumble blindly through the weeds and among parked cars towards the keg.—DF

MAY 15–CHICO'S (1–2) VS BACKDOOR II Chico's bats erupt. Krovich leads the way with a back-breaking triple in the fifth. Kurkendal, Big Mike, Carney and the rest of the Orangemen rope it left and right across the diamond, pummeling the hapless Backdoorsmen into an early submission. Once again, Carney takes the mound and prevents hits. Freedom's First Amendment rights threatened by home plate umpire during second inning, but he perseveres at the plate and in the field. Fine arms in the outfield and fine gloves on the interior of the diamond prove stifling for the Backdoor. Last game was a keg game. This one was an ear game. Hindal removes left ear from an enemy outfielder and hangs it around his neck with a dirty shoelace, a horrifyingly vivid example of what is at stake when Chico's takes the field. Chico's win 14–4.—DF

JUNE 2–CHICO'S (3–2) VS MYLAN 9 Chico's win 12–7. Rain, thunder, and lightning threaten this game, but one dozen Orangemen in uniform ward off inclement weather. Dampness seems not to affect the Bonders as they score in almost every inning. Skinny "The Six-Foot Fan Club" Miller points out that Rob B is the game's hero, knocking in six with his hot bat.

"Don't rest on your fattened laurels," say the pessimists.

"The glass is half-full," say the mutton-chopped fellows who always walk on the sunny side of the street.

Both drink at 123, butting heads, mixing metaphors, and smelling like dirt, sweat, pine tar, and oiled leather. Kurkendal and Big Mike feel their performances are tarnished by old bats. They could benefit from a new one, the kind that goes Shazam when it strikes the ball. Jellyfish in the Cheat? No way. A three-game winning streak for Chico's Bail Bonds? Whoa, Nellie!—DF

JUNE 22–CHICO'S (6–3) VS PICKLE BARREL PENGUINS Ho-hum. Looks like the Bondsmen will waltz into another victory with a 13–2 lead in the 5th until BAM! CRASH! KA-BLAM! The diamond turns into a flimsy remake of the Batman TV show from the sixties. David "Adam West" Foreman allows a truckload of hits, and the lowly Penguins get within two runs. "Holy cow," says Krovich, picking apart the infield with his speed and daring maneuvers around the basepaths. A late "homer" from Big Mike to deep center and a baffling quick-pitch strikeout to lead off the 7th by pitcher Foreman seals it. A surprisingly sober Chico's claims victory in the season's only ten o'clock game. Chico's wins 17–14.—DF

JULY 17–CHICO'S (8–6) VS MUNDY'S

It was the kind of game you are proud to place on your mantel next to the spelling bee trophies and pictures of grandma. Chico's plays near flawlessly in the field. Bats pound out base hits, and courageous, fleet-footed men in orange hurtle around the bases and score lots of runs. Excellent leather in the outfield. Rob B and Giuliani shock Mundy's batters with fanciness. DiMaggio-like grace in right center quiets hecklers. Solid catching in right forces groans from Mundy's supporters. On the infield, it is a similar tale—Carney makes one of the best grabs in the history of the team, extending his body like a Ripken (Cal, not Billy). Good pitching helps. Little children pretend with Legos and X-Men in the dirt on the first base side, imagining rocket ships and laser guns. Jedis at the plate perform superbly as hyperbolic dads and uncles congratulate victorious teammates. This one's for you Buttermaker. Chico's wins 16–9.—DF

JULY 21–CHICO'S (8–7) VS SHADY LANE

An eclectic group of Chico's players gathers late for the 7 PM game against the best team in the league. At a time when game faces and oiled gloves are vital for a good showing, the boys stumble and find ways to refuse the big opportunity. Orangemen creatively lose 3–13 at the plate and in the grass, topping off the effort with a Sputnik-like orbital thrown from Foreman's hand in the general direction of New England. Shady Lane is a good team, having won the championship last year and returning to the AA brackets because it is easier than AAA. They prove their worth with solid performances. The Chico squad dissipates immediately upon losing, nobody's heart in the team like it was on Monday when all the dominos fell in place for CBB. Playoff hopes dwindling, but a winning record still in the cards. Skinny so upset, he nearly suits up and takes a stand behind home plate.—DF

JULY 27–CHICO'S (9–9) VS BREWER & COMPANY

Brewer and Company's first mistake—a university professor in right field. Chico's capitalize on poor pitching and worse fielding to run the poor fella ragged. B&Co. hit well, admit the boys, but they were not good defensively. On the other claw, Chico's shines once again in the field. Krovich leads two big double plays from behind the plate: the first on a bases-loaded grounder back to the box and the other on a slick catch down the third baseline near the fence. Why would the guy on first take a few steps toward second on a pop up in foul territory? Also, Carney playing like a pro with some fine grabs, like Siva the many-handed. Hindal contributes with a two-run double. Hollis provides the vocal support of a howler monkey, but a bit more articulate, especially when chumps try to take out Krovich's lungs. Foreman strikes out two. Chico's wins 23–11.—DF

JULY 28–CHICO'S (9–10) VS VFW POST 548

Again, the story we tell is a familiar tale—no hitting, good fielding. Jim Manilla uses his golden glove to contribute to a double play and an inning-ending snag in the first two frames. Old chums VFW appear to be stifled, but they recover. Chico's loses 6–11. Skinny conducts a detailed analysis of the team's offensive statistical profile. His 965-page data mining report reveals a curious fact—with one out in the second inning of every 8 o'clock game that Chico's has ever played with a right-handed pitcher on the mound and with both Foreman and Giuliani in the line-up, someone hits a homer! This time it's Todd G. Last time (5/19/99) was Rob B against Glenmark. Beer in hand, a full cooler next to him, Carney is overheard saying with papal seriousness that Chico's is the luckiest team on the face of the earth. The sun is setting for summer 2000, and the Bondsmen vow to go out swinging.

"Swinging, yes," retorts Burtner, "but hitting? We shall see."—DF

JULY 29–CHICO'S (9–11) VS BLACKSVILLE DAIRY MART

Chico's loses 5–9. Everybody leaves the field pissed and crestfallen. A veil of sadness has been drawn across the hearts of the Bondsmen at the conclusion of the summer season. Blacksville is no help, taking advantage of Chico's error-ridden third inning and putting up just enough runs to keep the boys down. Even the presence of Freedom is not enough. What solution to the losing ways of this franchise?

"Burn the shirts and change the name," offers Giuliani.

Are such radical gestures necessary?

"Let the boy simmer down, and he'll come around," reassures a former catcher and level-headed loyal fan.

Even with a triumvirate of sympathetic umpires (one lent us a bat in our time of need), the CBB crew falls short. Orange #8 is already washed and folded, stuck in the drawer. Does it dream of fall league when newly initiated Bonders like Raese and Krovich can further contribute in long sleeves and 7 o'clock games under lights? Is its nightmare a relegation to weekends working on the house, be splattered with paint? Will it exist as mere symbol of more active days in the sun, on the rubber, with the fellas out late in celebration of a nice win?—DF

2000 FALL SOFTBALL AA-LEAGUE (2 WINS / 6 LOSSES)

SEPTEMBER 16–CHICO'S (1–2) VS STAMM'S Stamm's hit the ball like Rod Carew. Chico's hit the ball like Gilligan-n-Crew. Stamm's ran the bases like Ben Johnson on steroids. Chico's ran the bases like Arte Johnson on a tricycle. Stamm's fielded like Brooks Robinson circa 1970. Chico's fielded like Brook Shields circa 1984. Black Label Moment[1]: Young girl in orange and black shouts from the bleachers, "Why didn't you catch the ball, Daddy?" Chico's loses 6–16.—GL

SEPTEMBER 23–CHICO'S (2–4) VS LAUREL HOME IMPROVEMENTS Chico's is ten-runned by ninja stoners in black leotards. Facing the tantalizingly inaccurate "Mezz" Mezzrow, Chicos could barely decipher the ball and strike count, let alone resolve the calculus of a two-out rally. Hitting stars were Dirty Fred B, Rick, and Jonny V, with the rest of the crew relying on bloop singles and muffed grounders. Defensively, Chico's showed flashes of infield brilliance, particularly from Mark at shortstop, but the new outfield gloves that the girls from Lugen Farms crocheted for our boys proved to be a warm Technicolor mistake. Black Label Moment: Dirty Fred B tumbling into home on a sac fly to extend it another inning. Chico's loses 10–20.—GL

SEPTEMBER 25–CHICO'S (2–6) VS TEXAS ROADHOUSE After back-to-back demolitions at the hands of perennial powerhouses, small-market Chico's appear to be looking ahead, bringing some of its top prospects in from the bleachers. Unfortunately, the absence of veteran bats has led to an anemic offense against the corporate interests of Mylan and the Texas Roadhouse, both of whom have massive television deals, weight rooms, and professional haircuts. The hitting slump is so bad that several veterans joined Smokestack Lee and Dishdog atop the 123 Weather Tower last night to pray for Tropical Storm Isidore to rain out Thursday's contest. —GL

With Raese's amputated arm, Nittany Rick's Mary Kay duties, and Papa Manilla's red-eye flight to Marrakesh, there is little hope that the Bondsmen will regroup for a playoff push. Considering we've already lost Big Mike to genetic manipulation, Freedom to Vegas cardrooms, and Burtner to the professional pinball tour, this is the most decimated team Chico's has ever fielded. This reporter wonders aloud whether this might be the final harvest for Le Grande Orange. —GL

Game Notes Clayton pitched, while rookies Evander and Kid Manilla played well for the boys in orange. Papa Manilla showed some nice glovework in center. Chico's failed to score until the final frame. Black Label moment: Mark "Kid" Manilla legs out triple. Chico's loses 3–20.—GL

---

1 Black Label Moment. The three most popular beers among Chico players through the years have been Black Label, Stoney's, and Pabst Blue Ribbon.

2001 SUMMER SOFTBALL AA-LEAGUE (6 WINS / 14 LOSSES)

MAY 1–CHICO'S (1–0) VS CREMASTERS Laundered, pressed, and smelling like mothballs, Chico's stride confidently onto the field. They are strengthened by the fine play of their shortstop, Carney. Five attempts and five flawless plays. Cremasters foiled by good glove work all over the place, from Carney's soft hands to the quick reflexes of Big Mike and the speedy legs of Rob B. As the sun set over the trees in right, Cremasters strike out and the Bondsmen get just enough hits and runs to drive home with a perfect record. No injuries, even from the taut legs of Big Jim March[1].

"I've been shot at and didn't even run that fast," March says, beaming like a schoolboy on good time. Chico's wins 10–4.—DF

MAY 4–CHICO'S (1–1) VS MORGANTOWN EXCAVATORS Chico's loses 6–10. With great maturity, the Bonders hold the line after giving up tons o' runs in the first. Some baserunning mistakes and fielding miscues are part of the difference in this well-played contest. Really—and let's not try to fool ourselves—it comes down to bad hitting. A slump has crept into the hearts and

1 Jim March. Jim operated a boxing gym named Jim's Gym for many years. It was located behind Black Bear Burritos on Pleasant Street. The Chico roster was filled with many players who worked out at the gym through the years, including McGinley, Batchelor, Koury, Nelms, Pintus, and Manilla, among others. Jim would later write a book in 2010 titled *If Oprah Reads This I'll be Rich*.

psychologies of the Bondsmen.

"Voodoo worked for me in college," says Hindal, with a little doll dressed like the umpires in hand. "Some beads, a little chicken liver, and ram's blood never hurt nobody."

To what lengths will the boys go? What tactic too low? What sacrifices too expensive? What incantation too dark? That night, two cats disappear in Greenmont . . . Foodland reports a missing crate of lard . . . Ralph's runs out of Stoney's . . . Clothes pins fly from the shelves of local thrift stores . . .—DF

MAY 17–CHICO'S (1–3) VS JOHN HOWARD SUBARU Chico's loses 10–11. The loneliest man on earth takes the rubber to begin the fourth inning and imagines his scoop: "Chico's hurler tosses first perfect game in franchise history." One walk later, he imagines a modified opening line: "The no-hitter wasn't perfect, but few pitchers are." Humbled by a few runs but comfortably

ahead, he ends the inning with thoughts of the season's first blow-out and ways to present it to his online audience: "Early runs and more top-shelf glove work prove insurmountable as the Chico's powerhouse rolls forth." In the 10th frame of an 11–11 nailbiter, he picks his clutch defensive MVP: "Hindal has reached a new level of expertise with his glove." As the winning run crosses the plate, lonely-no-more hangs his head and walks off into the fog surrounding Ogden Field: "Chico's blows 11–0 lead, falls to 1–3." A splendid time was had by all.

"Nobody lost that game," say the winners.

Everybody wins when Chico's plays. Woodpeckers buzzed third base. It drizzled during the whole game.—DF

JULY 6–CHICO'S (3–9) VS BOB SOLLY'S TEAM It was
our finest hour. Carney dove headfirst into second to get an out. Big Mike snagged everything his way. Jim March fought off pitches until he found one of his own. Hindal was flawless, casual with his glove at second. Giuliani and Raese were near perfect while Borowitz and Getto had fine days, exciting catches. Foreman turned a 2–3 second double play with The Eric Carter at first. And it all ended when Raese took the whole thing into his own hands and rounded the bases with some super-ballsy baserunning against a pretty OK team of hackers and sportsmen. Chico's wins 11–10.

Surrounding the boys, the groundhogs scurried. They collected bats, helped stretch muscles, lit cigarettes, and fetched foul balls. They adore Big Mike and he doesn't mind the attention or the service. A few have stuck around the bar, showing a talent for rock and roll.

"They smell OK, they don't drink much, they sleep in a hole in the ground down by the river, and as soon as we get Chuck L potty trained, I think we'll be alright. And criminy, they sound better than Dirtstar," comments Giuliani.

The sextet has a regular gig on Tuesday nights. Some local mainstays are interested in possibly 86ing their current singer—Freedom—and replacing him with the 5-octave talents of Mr. Chuck D of New York City.

"But there's only one condition," reports 123's owner in whispered tones. "They should change their name to Groundhogblast."—DF

JULY 19–CHICO'S (5–10) VS UNIVERSITY MOTORS
Everybody on the team shows up, the largest collection of Bondsmen in one place since the Boaz game of 1999. A handful of willing Chico's players bows out after three innings. One of them is March, who does his duty with the stick and allows Dr. T to run the bases for him. March is gradually turning his science at the plate into art.

The subs enter the contest with a lead, something that has rarely occurred this season. Raese and Giuliani contribute with homers. Foreman displays some fancy thinking with his feet and, even though he should have been out, makes it safe at home, hands up in salutation. He later begins a crisp 1–5–4 double play to stymie a rally. Was there trouble when he left the mound and Carney took over hurling duties? Not a chance. Borowitz displayed his typical leather pyrotechnics, but soured his otherwise fine game by making two outs in the same inning. Chico's wins 15–4.

Groundhogs? A few showed up. Ever since the mysterious disappearance of Chuck I, the one with the hopeless crush on Robin Dallas, and the sudden emergence of Barry the Black-Eyed Opossum, the groundhogs have been few and far between.

"He called it love," said Barry in between drags on his Chinese cigarette, "but that ain't love."

Nobody says a word as Manilla closes down the game by making his second impressive grab in right with a borrowed glove and the wrong glasses on. Barry slinks away into the forest to sleep until night falls, and Hindal notices his gold chain—the one he left on the bench next to Barry—is missing.—DF

AUGUST 2–CHICO'S (5–11) VS UNITED NATIONAL
BANK United has a very good team. From top to bottom, they are athletic: quick, strong, and smart at nearly every position.

They show up in the hot, hot sun expecting to draw and quarter the hapless Bondsmen in quick time, two or three innings at most. When the horses reach full speed and the ropes draw taut, United's riders are thrown from their steeds and knocked flat on their butts. Eventually, the cruel dismemberment occurs, but not before Chico's puts a healthy scare into a pretty good team.

The defense is superb, allowing only ten runs. A busy Rob B makes excellent grabs and avoids muscle tightening and death in the brutal heat. Hitting is sharp, finding holes where the fast legs can't catch balls. But it is not enough. The horses return and stomp the Orangemen with heavy hooves, bone-crushing good luck charms punishing the boys again, the 11th time this year. Chico's loses 7–10. Ouch.—DF

AUGUST 6–CHICO'S (6–12) VS WESTERN SIZZLIN'/FOP

It is about time. Chico's erupt for 22 runs. The highlight of the game—certainly one of the finest moments in Chico's history—is Vehse's two homers. One was not enough. He touches home twice standing up with excellent hits that roll to the Liberatore fence after eluding diving outfielders. Even the Pam Berry Field women applaud the newest addition to the Chico's pantheon, breathless and wet with perspiration.

We must not overlook other achievements and oddities in this contest—Carney is tagged out at home by a young man borrowing his glove. Skinny dons his customized jersey and takes right field. He hits and walks and scores some more runs. March is on a tear, playing this game with ever greater ease and comfort. Raese and Giuliani have good games on both sides of the ball. What more can we say except that Foreman played three positions, Hindal's leg is half-chewed by home plate, Manilla is the leader we need, The Eric Carter is oh so graceful under pressure, the Nelms family is a fine addition to the team, Jarrod can't be stopped once he gets started, and beautiful women abound on the sidelines. Chico's wins 22–9.—DF

11 DAVE FOREMAN
PITCHER

THROWS: RIGHT   BATS: RIGHT   SEASONS PLAYED: 14
HOBBIES: READING, DAVE PARKER, WRITING, TREES
WALK-UP SONG: "DREAM BABY DREAM" SUICIDE

Dave was one of Chico's most effective all-time pitchers; was the former president of Morgantown's unofficial Beatles club; wrote the first Chico post-game write-up on May 29, 1998; his beloved softball shorts retired before he did.

2002 FOR THE SAKE OF THE TEAM

MAY 2–CHICO'S (0–1) VS KEGLER'S Chico's loses 19–25. In the postgame prayer circle, Skinny thanks the Lord for a well-umpired and safe game. He praises God for the team's continued health in these troubled times and for his gift of camaraderie.

"And please," prays Skinny, his hands locked among the circle of teammates gathered around the pitcher's rubber, "find it in your infinite grace to help the left side of the infield make a few plays next time."

The team is rapt in each word. "Hallelujah," hollers new guy Dirty Fred. "Please Lord, keep my hand steady in wind in rain in snow and in sleet. "Come what may," he bellows, "this hand shall be strong and shall smite thine enemies in the batter's box!"—DF

JUNE 25–CHICO'S (1–11) VS BUSTER'S AUTO SALVAGE Chico's loses 0–15. It's clear the Bail Bonders are not a warm weather club. Playing Dirty Fred B's old team, Chico's mustered no offense and only a smattering of cheers, as fans stayed away due to the oppressive heat. Chico's never truly threatened in the contest, the lone blast being Leatherman's towering triple off the fence to lead off the 2nd. Afterwards, emergency medics confirmed that Leatherman was still alive, though severely dehydrated from trying to run in blue jeans.

"Several of our guys are suffering from chronic hangovers," LJ commented, "Throw in the heat, ankle deep dust, and a neurotic umpire, and you have a recipe for a good old-fashioned butt kickin.'"

LJ was warned by the new female umpire for protesting.—GL

JULY 24–CHICO'S (1–14) VS WILLIE'S PUB Chico's loses 1–11. Chico's hire a team of consultants to analyze their playing behaviors and recommend change.

"We want to establish benchmark data during this game and come back to you with a strategy for managing change in your team," says the head guy. He's likable but causes uneasiness among the boys.

"How much is this gonna cost?" asks Leatherman who is tired and dehydrated.

Later, he overhears them talking among themselves, sounding somewhat appalled:

"The second baseman is not running at all. No hustle," they say.

Angry, Leatherman takes matters into his own hands and rifles it down the third base line where the consultants have gathered, clipboards in hand.

He breaks a pinky and chases him through the parking lot, yelling, "You want hustle. I'll show you hustle."

Bail Bonders lose 11–1. Tatum O'Neal[1], where are you in our darkest hour?—DF

AUGUST 2–CHICO'S (2–14) VS TINA'S CATERING A rough-and-ready team of nine Orangemen come out to put up their dukes in desperate battle. They withstand a 12-run attack in the 3rd to accomplish sweet victory, winning 21–14. Fine hitting is the name of the game for this crew. Fine glovework by many is critical.

Krovich snagged a seemingly sure hit to record the putout and double up the guy on first. Manilla celebrated new fatherhood with a few nice at bats and a great grab on a weird pop up at short. Bachelor was establishing himself as an important defensive presence at second while not sliding into home for important early runs. Dirty Fred squashed opportunities with his pitching in the first few innings and then handled the hot corner like a phenom from Havana. Clayton and Raese covered a big outfield with grace and élan. Leatherman was his usual Mr. Fantastic at first. Vehse anchored the whole team on offense and defense with great fortitude. Everybody raised their game to a new level

---

1 Tatum O'Neal. She played Amanda Whurlitzer, the 11-year-old star pitcher for the Bears in the 1976 *The Bad News Bears* movie.

with a shorthanded squad and some of the team's all-stars absent.

Chico's continues to draw the best-dressed fans of any team, and this time the faithful are treated to victory. Foreman caps his day with a strike out of the final batter on his special optical-illusion-Ripley's Believe-It-or-Not-now-you-see-it-now-you-don't-get-back-lucky-charm-change-up. Works every time.—DF

AUGUST 7–CHICO'S (3–14) VS PICKLE BARREL BAR & GRILL

[Author's note: Names have been changed to protect team members.] Chico's wins 11–4. Chico's is flawless on both sides of the ball. The Bonders take their second game in a row, and the Bonders-shocked by their sudden success-wonder aloud about why they are blessed with excellence after so many weeks of futility.

What superstitions prop up this team? What magic animates the boys so late in this dismal season?

Conversation turns to patterns in the last two performances. As Franklin leaves early to tend to a perturbed girlfriend, Johnson realizes the common thread that runs through the lives of every Bail Bonder: girls. It turns out that Jones is having trouble with his second wife, and he is 7 for 10 in the last three games. Jackson just broke up with his live-in girlfriend, and he has not made an error in five games. Hamilton and his pregnant girlfriend are experiencing some rocky territory—he hit two home runs in today's game.

On the bench, the boys relax between innings, but there is a severe tension as they sit among their significant others. It turns out that nearly every player on the team is having some sort of difficulty with his mate, and everyone decides that this is what has provided the spark in their playing. They all agree under blood oath to burn a few bridges and stoke the flames of discontent for the sake of their team, but only until Saturday.

"Women," scoffs Jackson, "Bah!"

He is greeted by the steely gazes of girlfriends, mothers, mistresses, and wives as they look at their watches, waiting for this whole damn softball thing to come to a swift and quiet end.—DF

> **THEY ALL AGREE UNDER BLOOD OATH TO BURN A FEW BRIDGES AND STOKE THE FLAMES OF DISCONTENT FOR THE SAKE OF THEIR TEAM, BUT ONLY UNTIL SATURDAY.**

AUGUST 8–CHICO'S (3–15) VS THE DERBY

Chico's loses 17–22. August spends its gold like a dying Caesar as a modest win streak comes to a mortifying end. A third baseman to be named later sets a record for errors in a single game, inning, and yes, even a single play. Game halted in 6th inning as the umpire's call for a group hug to console the bloodied gloveman. Short on reserves, there is nothing to be done. Typically, after the game, all toasts are for our fallen comrade (okay, we did make one or two toasts to the incomparable Pia Zadora[2], who, after all, once won a Golden Globe).—GL

---

2 Pia Zadora. A popular actress in the 1980s. She won a Golden Globe in 1981 in the highly criticized, Butterfly. She also won the Golden Raspberry Award for Worst Actress that year for the same role.

2006 Chico's: (standing) Ravi Shibley, Jim Antonini, Andy Pintus, Jon Vehse, Jim March, LJ Guiliani, Greg Leatherman, Tim Nelms, Dave Krovich, Jeff Hindal, (seated) Dave Foreman, Meatball

404
Page not found.

We're sorry, we can't find the page you're looking for. The site administrator may have removed it, changed it's location, or made it otherwise unavailable. Some reasons why this error message has shown up might be:

- The page was removed and other pages still link to it
- Our server may be experiencing technical difficulties
- You typed an incorrect address in your browser's address bar
- We were told that every photo you uploaded and every word you posted on the internet would be visible for future generations, forever, and that turned out to be a lie

2007 THE BOYS IN ORANGE

2007 Chico's: (back row) Jim Antonini, Jeff Ryan, Brian Porterfield, Greg Leatherman, Robert Raese, Jon Vehse, (front row) Dave Foreman, Jim March, Mack McGinley, Dave Krovich, LJ Guiliani

MAY 2—CHICO'S (1–0) VS HIT N' RUN The happy victory was not without tragedy. Early in the contest, Porterfield was removed from the lineup after running to first on a grounder and pulling The Muscle. Nelms, team doctor, pitcher, catcher, and sometimes first baseman, explained Porterfield's injury.

"Anybody who has seen Porterfield in a pair of shorts will know that he has only two muscles in his legs. He pulled both of them. This explains his extreme pain. There is nothing he can do about it."

It was the right fielder's first full sprint in at least a decade of almost complete physical inactivity. As he gasped and writhed in pain on the first base line in short right field, his two young daughters comforted him with blankets, pillows, and stuffed animals.

"How cute," commented passersby, Porterfield moaning in misery.

"Instead of the blanket, they should get a shovel," March loudly commented, "and jus' bury him there. He's done."—DF

MAY 7–CHICO'S (2-0) VS GST Leatherman was nervous early, and he was fidgety as the wind gathered force and the skies darkened. In the third inning, lightning struck just as Krovich and Giuliani raced toward a well-hit ball that turned into a grand slam home run. The game was delayed for thirty minutes as the storm dissipated, and the lightning drifted east. During the delay, Leatherman asked Foreman to substitute a new player for him at first.

"He's solid in the field, a little slow on the bases, but a monster at the plate."

> **"HE'S A GREAT ADDITION, BUT I THINK JIM MARCH IS STILL THE SLOWEST GUY IN THE LEAGUE."**
> **-LJ GUILIANI, CHICO PLAYER/OWNER**

It was true. He was seven feet tall, green, stitched together from dead flesh, and recently reanimated because of the fierce lightning storm that delayed the game. Frankenchico's addition to the lineup was just what the boys needed. He hit two scorchers down the third base line and actually got a double in his second at bat, lumbering around the bases while GST misplayed several relay throws.

"That's heads up," said Krovich. "Exactly what this team needs in the clean-up spot."

"His intensity is infectious," said Foreman, bearing down on the rubber to strike out five batters, three in a single inning.

"He smells like roadkill," adds Jenny, sitting with the scorebook as far away as possible on the bench.

Leatherman, near tears of joy at seeing his creation play flawlessly at first, doesn't mind sitting on the bench and watching the Bonders pound out 23 runs and allow a mere 18.

"The business of predicting the future is a tricky adventure," he told his team as he put the iron collar back around Frankenchico's neck. "But I think tonight's signs—as provided by the heavens and its newly wrought creation for our team—bode well for this season."

"Chico good. Chico good," shouted Frankenchico, stomping his feet and clapping his hands awkwardly. The boys patted him on the back and invited him to the bar to celebrate and watch the band, Nashville Pussy.

"Frankenchico is a great addition to the team," said Foreman, contemplating the possibilities of an entirely fabricated starting lineup and possibly moving up to the more competitive AA league.

"He's a great addition," added Giuliani, "but I think March is still the slowest guy in the league."—DF

MAY 11–CHICO'S (3-0) VS CHESTNUT RIDGE CHURCH Chico's Wins and Wants Me for a Sunbeam. In a match-up reminiscent of the Roman Coliseum's humans-versus-lions contests of old, Chico's enjoyed the taste of liver, muscle, and flesh. Chestnut Ridge--in spite of all its earnestness, youthfulness, and hopeful pre-marriage celibacy--could muster little offense in the five innings they survived.

Chico's Bail Bonders is a team of fornicators, devil-may-care blasphemers, and pro-choice barbarians. Atheists and Democrats populate the line-up. Liberatore Field was a battleground of not mere teams, but of conflicting ideologies. Libertarianism and Catholicism won out in a 13-3 Bonders victory. Yee-ha!

It was a fine defensive performance for the boys in orange. Batchelor continued to amaze at second. He and Antonini were very busy on the infidel . . . er, I mean infield . . . dirt and nearly turned several 6-4-3 double plays. Batchelor went back on a difficult play toward the line, showing incredible range to shag a weak fly. Foreman has refused several offers of a trade him up to double-A teams.

Up and down the lineup, the Bonders managed to get on base, hustling out grounders, blooping pop-ups to all corners, and just plain whacking it hard. Nothing could stop the bats late as Krovich hit a homer, and Giuliani tripled in Antonini to make it a game in the bottom of the fifth with the ten-run lead.

When two Christians found themselves sharing third base, Foreman took a perfect throw from Antonini at short to tag out the runner near the plate, holding the Ridgers to a scoreless inning. It was another illustration of the team's steel reserve. Afterwards, many Chico's fellas relived great moments, aches and pains, and youthful memories of little league at the 123 bar. Feeling tired and beat-up, the team wondered if they could keep it rolling.—DF

MAY 31–CHICO'S (4–2) VS RIVERSIDE CHURCH

Chico's Spooked, Loses. Whiston Field is clearly haunted. Ghosts flit in and out of the stands, on and off the field. One-eyed cripples, mysterious ancient suicides, and headless apparitions regularly appear among the boys walking in from the field at the end of the inning. They sneak upon the consciousness, light your cigarette on the bench, say something mysterious before each at-bat, and disappear when you turn around to do a double take. There is something about this field that has cursed the Bonders, wrecked their fortunes on the dirty stone-ridden infield. And now we have an explanation: ghosts.

Tonight was more evidence. Mistakes abound on a night the boys needed to be flawless. No, instead Foreman was dragged from second by a ghostly 1700s frontiersman butchered alive on the banks of the Mon by Shawnee warriors, lost and wandering eternity among us, causing mischief when Chico's plays on Whiston.

"In our early years, only nights with a waning moon brought out these creatures to this field," said Leatherman, noting his game logs and lunar charts. "Something has emboldened them.

GREG LEATHERMAN

FIRST BASE

93

BATS: RIGHT   THROWS: RIGHT   SEASONS PLAYED: 15
HOBBIES: WRITING, BASEBALL, GUITAR, CONVERSATION
WALK-UP SONG: "GARBAGE MAN" BY THE CRAMPS

As a 12-year-old, Greg batted cleanup for the Purgitsville Giants; on nights before games, he was known to wear his jersey to bed and sleep with his glove; retired from Chico's as the all-time leader in runs batted in; always brought energy and positivity to the team even during long losing streaks; currently working on multiple creative book projects.

19

The moon is approaching full."

A pale shape of a girl aged 12 knocked the hat from his head and disappeared in an instant, sending chills down the spines of the Chico ballplayers.

"It's Apple Orchard Annie!" screamed Meatball, pale and clearly scared.

"Apple Orchard Annie disappeared in 1904 from the White Family Orchard near these parts," explained Krovich. "Her ravaged corpse was found in the creek nearby. The mystery was never solved."

A young prostitute murdered in a downtown brothel in 1925 whispered, "two outs," in Giuliani's ear to draw him off the bag late in the game. There was in fact only one out recorded, and the game ended on that play. The night echoed with her coquettish laughter

in all men's ears, her mysterious negligee-d shape barely visible by second base, stab wounds visible underneath her loosely wrapped garments. Giuliani hung his head and cursed her again.

There is no humor when even the afterlife is not on your side. The farmer struck by lightning bringing in the final grains of the harvest out near Grafton in 1877 rolled back on his heels and laughed, fingers in his overall straps. Every laugh an error, every guffaw a strikeout.

Dead soldiers from all America's wars sat solemnly in the bleachers on the opposition's side, staring blankly at the action, emotionless. As the game progressed, they gathered in numbers, heads hung between their knees, vacant stares barely following the action. By game's end, hundreds had gathered and lined the outfield wall, leaning, crouching, lying down. It was a motley militia of bad luck and mourning, camped out in endless exhaustion and grief.

A World War II GI approached Foreman after the game. He patted the pitcher on the shoulder, offered him a cigarette and told him, "It could be worse. At least you are alive and can enjoy the bitter taste of defeat. It's better than being dead or even being dead and winning. Just ask these fellas."

He gestured to the hordes breaking camp and shuffling off into the woods, M16s and muzzleloaders clanking against each other, camo helmets and tri-cornered hats side by side in a postgame march into the black line of trees beyond the cars.

A Vietnam-war soldier, a boy of 18, came near the manager after the game and asked shyly, "Where was Jim March?"

"I don't know," said Foreman, closing his eyes and hoping all this would go away when the Bonders spend June on Liberatore Field, away from these horrors.—DF

JUNE 14–CHICO'S (5–4) VS HMS Chico's Hit 11 Button. Thunderstorms threatened this game. Lightning crisscrossed the horizon to the south and west. Thunder rolled ominously from the heavens. But Mother Nature kept her fury at bay. The skies cleared and Chico's was able to put on a show for the dozens of fans who gathered to witness day two of this week's three-game set.

All 11 runs came in the first three innings for Chico's. A few big innings early were all they needed. Highlights included Meatball's triple and Vehse's two-out double, both of which produced some nice RBIs.

But this game was best characterized by more fine fielding. Antonini, Batchelor, and Leatherman teamed up for their second 6-4-3 double play of the year. Later, Leatherman came in toward the plate and dove for a pop-up. He threw to Foreman covering the bag for an out on the guy who got hung up off first base. Giuliani ranged to his right, to his left, and back to his right late in the game to squelch rally-inducing hits. Pintus basket-caught a fly ball in right. Batchelor and Meatball both made over the shoulder catches on bloopers that would have otherwise spelled doom. The coup de grace for Foreman—other than his 13th K on the year—was his catch of a blistering line drive up the middle to notch the second out of the 7th.

"It goes nice with a four-for-four night," he remarked, chilling his swollen glove hand around a nice cold one at the trunk of his car.

"Indeed," agreed Krovich, limping to his car.—DF

JUNE 25–CHICO'S (6–5) VS ISR Chico's Erupts for 17 Runs in Win. What a hit fest! The orange crush crossed the plate a whopping 17 times in 7 innings. Everyone got in on the act at the plate. Foreman hit a three-run round tripper on a tailing drive to shallow right that skipped to the fence. Batchelor stroked it solidly to left center. He was one of many in the zone. Krovich managed to churn around the base paths and get clocked in the head for good measure. Porterfield had a sound game. Antonini delivered in the clutch. Kelley was victim of a mystery tag at third. Pintus had his mind wrapped around the strike zone like Einstein around $E=mc^2$. Meatball made it look easy. Vehse wore little lightning bolts on his boots. And Leatherman showed he was not just glove and legs like a pair of extend-o-grip pliers. He could hit like a bad motherfucker.

Seventeen runs, can you believe it? I cannot, and quite possibly neither can the Chica faithful who packed the stands on this periodically soaked night, muddy and slick. There is two weeks off to heal up and grow our livers back. Take care, Chico.—DF

JUNE 30 FOREMAN'S SHORTS ANNOUNCE RETIREMENT Manager Foreman's tan shorts announced early today that the 2007 BOPARC single-A softball season will be its final year of competition. Foreman's shorts have participated in Chico's Bail Bonds competition for more than 8 years. For most of these seasons, they helped to pitch. The shorts have also played a major role batting and running. Chico's fans will probably best remember them for the important protective role they played in sliding.

"My pants have been a wonderful partner during most of my career in softball," said Foreman. "I wish them well in the next phase of their career and life."

When pressed for clues about what the future may hold for the apparel, Foreman admitted to not having spoken with his knickers about the retirement.

"They've been discussing this decision for a long time, so it's not unexpected," explained Foreman. "But I did not hear about the announcement, frankly, until I read about it in The Times."

Foreman's admission revealed a long-rumored estrangement from his shorts. Experts suspect that the rift between the pitcher and his pants started in 2004 when the bottom stitching of the right pant leg revealed a significant tear.

Foreman's shorts were not available at press time for an interview. In the written statement, the shorts revealed that they are "one hard slide away from a very embarrassing on-field situation." The statement appears to confirm speculation among fans and the media that the threadbare garment is approaching un-usability as a result of the rigors of athletic competition and years of circulation in the washing machine after each game.

The shorts' agent, in an e-mail, did not commit her client to any future plans, but she did not refute speculation that retirement may include being tucked away in the back of a closet or being used as rags in the garage.

Foreman's shorts made their debut in 1999 in an early spring game against BOAZ, a 15 to 9 loss. Since that day, the shorts have participated in more than 150 games for Chico's Bail Bonds and the WVU Foundation. The shorts have also made major contributions to cutting the grass, painting the dining room, and trimming the hedges.—DF

JULY 13—CHICO'S (6–6) VS MYLAN CRUSH Chico's Gets Laid. Winning ways returned for our beloved team. The Bonders beats Mylan Crush 15-10. The weather was absolutely gorgeous, warm and sunny. On the field, the boys looked rusty. It had been three weeks since the last game, a heartbreaker. After the dust was brushed off the gloves and bats, things started to click.

And in the bleachers, beauty was radiant in black shirts and orange letters—Chicas had new shirts courtesy of Mary[1], and quite possibly this was the emotional boost needed to focus the team's energy toward bedding that elusive mistress, Victory.

It seemed like every play somehow involved second base and Mr. Batchelor. Let's start at the end—game over on a line drive tailing off to his left. Nice catch. Earlier, he hit a long fly ball that turned into a bases-loaded triple. Nice hit. In between, he covered second on numerous occasions for force outs from Antonini, Meatball, and even Giuliani.

After the game, he and Vehse took the stage and played music. Nice show. Other than Batchelor's fine work, many others contributed to the team's success. Krovich set the hitting tone with hits and aggressive baserunning. Leatherman got back on track with the bat. A few big innings secured Victory's love for at least one more night this year.—DF

AUGUST 18—CHICO'S (9–10) VS B & C Bonders closes Out 2007 with a Win! Jeff Ryan strode to the plate with the bases juiced and no outs. A hit or a walk wins the game. Ryan had played only one other game, but because he had the wrong kind of shirt--a 123 shirt and not a Chico's jersey--he was forced to sit early in the season for his only at-bat and take an out. Damnable rules. This time, well clad in the number 7, sleeveless, and sweat-soaked, he took a pitch for a ball. Pressure was on the pitcher, but Ryan was relaxed and confident. Next pitch got stroked to center field. Leatherman made sure it cleared the gloves of the infield and landed safely in the grass. He trotted home, exuberant and joyful.

Victory was Chico's once Leatherman's cleated sole graced the dusty plate at Whiston. Chico's win! Chico's win! Cheers erupted. Chicas swooned. Game hero Jeff Ryan was lifted in the arms of his imagination and thrown to the skies, aloft on victory.

Sleep well Chico's. You earned it.—DF

CHICO'$
CHICA$

BAIL BONDS
and
E$CORT $ERVICE

---

1 In 2007 Mary Hinchliffe made Chica fan shirts that were worn by all the lady friends of the Chico players. That's Mary in the photos to the left, photos taken at a 2025 Chico's game.

23

2008 Chico's: (standing) Jim Antonini, Andy Pintus, Mack McGinley, Robert Raese, Greg Leatherman, Brian Porterfield, Tom Batchelor, (kneeling) Dave Foreman, LJ Guiliani, Dave Krovich, Sean Kelley, Jim March

JUNE 18–CHICO'S (3–5) VS DIMITRIS Chico's Looks Crisp Against Young Team. The opponent was young and brash, and Chico's overwhelmed them with class and character. Good fielding, especially up the middle, and timely hits—March, Vehse, Nelms stood out in this reporter's mind—put the opposition away. Pintus started on the mound and did well with two fielding plays up the middle in the first. Foreman relieved and struck out two.

Both Antonini and Foreman got lippy with the umpires and opposition. The boys on the opposite team were trash talking all night. They didn't understand the rules, including the rules about avoiding contact when running the bases. Poor sports and bad hitters, the kind of team we like to defeat. They will learn. But all in all, there was a consensus among the players and fans that tonight Chico's looked crisp, like a new five-dollar bill.—DF

JUNE 20–CHICO'S (3–6) VS SKELETON CREW Orange Men Lose Another Fucking Game. The Bonders lost another game to some ringers—ring around the rosy ringers. But everyone was somewhat happy because Ravi was back for a game. And everyone was permitted a glimpse of softball brilliance. Diving catches! A triple! Hitting to the gap! Slapping it here and slapping it there. Einstein in orange, our Ravi! But it was short-lived. And it was not enough. The Crew we played had a good night and we lost. Dammit we lost.—DF

JUNE 23–CHICO'S (3–7) VS NUTTY C'S Chico's Hung in There but Came Up Short. Greg Leatherman was back! Back like Jesus! Greg blasted a homer with two guys on. It was so great to have the Leatherman in the four-spot in the lineup and playing first base. And dammit he delivered. The best part of having him back—during the course of the game, he dispensed invaluable hitting advice to his teammates about hitches in swings and timing.

SINGLE A STANDINGS AS OF JULY 2, 2008	
Hughart's	11–0
Nutty C's	11–1
Good Times Lounge	10–3
Healthcare Associates	9–3
GST	9–4
WVGS	9–4
Hall's Hit N Run	9–5
Big Hitters	7–5
Dimitris	7–5
Honest Abe's Used Cars	7–6
Mylan Crush	6–6
Clear Mountain Bank A	5–5
Skeleton Crew	5–7
Chico's Bail Bonds	5–8
Bucket Head's Pub A	4–8
Nationals	4–8
Johnson Brothers Trucking	4–8
D P Dough	4–9
Lo Jaks	3–9
Westover VFD	2–8
Colasante's	2–10
Riverside Ministries A	1–12

Foreman has been hitting like a mother, and so has Antonini. Batchelor is the #1 hitter no matter what at this point because pound for pound there is no man better than he in Single-A softball. Guaranteed. And we have him. And he has us. March is perceivably faster. Pintus has found a home—third base. Vehse has stroked it well in clutch situations and is a fine catcher. Krovich anchored the outfield. I could go on and on, on and on with accolades for Porterfield, Raj (Raj!), Nelms, Kelley, Mac, Giuliani, Clayton, Raese, and all the dudes.—DF

JULY 2–CHICO'S (5–8) VS BIG HITTERS Chico's Wins One for Krovich's Birthday. Greg Leatherman hit a huge single over the head of Big Hitter's left fielder to score Antonini and Porterfield in the bottom of the seventh. The hit secured the 9–8 win for Chico's and added to the legend of Greg Leatherman: the big guy has come up HUGE since his return to the area. Lots of great fielding and hitting across the board against a tough opponent. Chico's owns a two-game win streak and is creeping up the standings.—DF

JULY 5 FOREMAN'S GLOVE DIES IN PLANE CRASH The baseball glove of Chico's pitcher D. Foreman died early this morning in a single-plane crash in rural West Virginia. The glove boarded the twin-engine plane at 11:30 PM EST in Morgantown, bound for the rural Tug River Valley on a mission to assist with flood-relief efforts. The plane, reported to have been overloaded with too much cargo, was spotted at approximately 5:30 AM on the ground in Braxton County. Air traffic controllers lost radio contact with the plane soon after midnight.

Foreman's glove recently helped Chico's secure its historic 99th victory. Sources close to the team report that the glove was heard to express disappointment with limited playing time as a result of Foreman needing a different, larger mitt for playing in the outfield. Foreman reportedly also experimented on the mound with a similar glove that Leatherman found at the field the previous week.

Foreman, Foreman's recently retired shorts, and his old Reeboks with the blown-out shoelaces were not available for comment at press time.—DF

JULY 25—CHICO'S (6–10) VS HEALTHCARE ASSOCIATES You're Not Going to Believe This, but Chico's is guaranteed a losing season. But the opponent in the darker orange shirts paid The Bondsmen the greatest of flatteries: "When we are old, we want to be like you guys." It warms the heart.—DF

AUGUST 6—CHICO'S (7–11) VS LOJAKS Orange Erupt at the Plate for Big Win. LoJaks lost as a result of a big inning by Chico's. They went all the way through the order, foiling the LoJaks plan to use a rover in shallow center; Antonini saw through it and whacked one to deep left center for a big hit. The first out in the big fifth inning occurred when Vehse popped up in his SECOND AT BAT OF THE INNING! Lots of hits. The boys are swinging through the ball and making solid contact, and it is working.

Good work in the field too. Antonini made some great stops, and Giuliani was exactly where he needed to be every time.—DF

AUGUST 8–CHICO'S (8–11) VS GST Chico's End Season With Come-From-Behind Victory. GST scored seven runs in the first, but the Orange chipped away and chipped away and kept the opposition's bats in check with some fine fielding. —DF

2008 Post-season Awards

Best Outfield Glove: LJ Giuliani

Best Infield Glove: Jim Antonini

Best Hitter: Greg Leatherman

Best Arm: Robert Raese

Best Baserunner: Jim March

Best Addition: Mac McGinley

Most Improved: Andy Pintus

Comeback Player: Greg Leatherman

Clutch Player: Tom Batchelor

MVP: Jim Antonini

Best Moment: The Final Game, after being down 7–0 in the first, Chico's stages a come-from-behind victory to beat a playoff team. kept the opposition's bats in check with some fine fielding. The game—and the season—ended on a strikeout swinging. Perfect.—DF

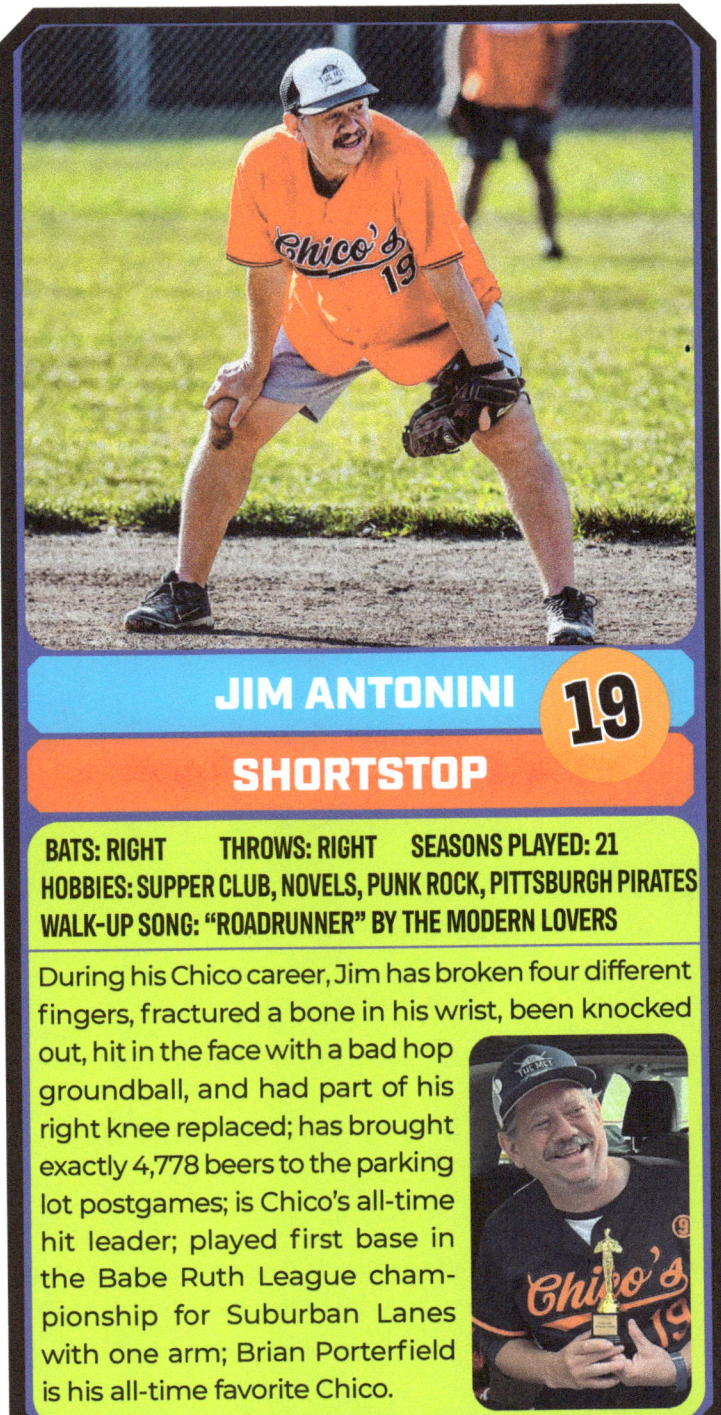

JIM ANTONINI · 19
SHORTSTOP

BATS: RIGHT   **THROWS: RIGHT**   **SEASONS PLAYED: 21**
HOBBIES: SUPPER CLUB, NOVELS, PUNK ROCK, PITTSBURGH PIRATES
WALK-UP SONG: "ROADRUNNER" BY THE MODERN LOVERS

During his Chico career, Jim has broken four different fingers, fractured a bone in his wrist, been knocked out, hit in the face with a bad hop groundball, and had part of his right knee replaced; has brought exactly 4,778 beers to the parking lot postgames; is Chico's all-time hit leader; played first base in the Babe Ruth League championship for Suburban Lanes with one arm; Brian Porterfield is his all-time favorite Chico.

2009 IT WAS A GOOD GAME

2009 Chico's: (standing) Brian Porterfield, Jim Antonini, Tim Nelms, Tom Batchelor, Greg Leatherman Ravi Shibley, Jim Manilla, Bob Butler, (kneeling) Jim March, Jon Vehse, Dave Krovich, Mack McGinley, LJ Guiliani, Meatball,

MAY 14–CHICO'S (0–1) VS BUCKETHEAD PUB Chico's opens with loss. Finally, the Chico's Bail Bonds team took the field for its first game of the 2009 season. The skies cleared and a cool breeze wafted over the squad, a full 15 men in orange, ready to play. It was a good game, but Chico's lost 10–3 against the Buckethead Pub.

The game started off on the wrong foot when Jimmy the Umpire declared the new, highly effective Beatles Club Revolver bat to be illegal. It has double walls. Who knew? After stroking a clean single to lead off the Bonders' hitting, Krovich's beloved Wombat was also deemed illegal because of the improvised duct tape handle. Not a good way to start the season.

Misfortune continued when the first Bucketheads batter of the game hit a grounder to the Chico's shortstop and he managed to knock

down the ball off an ugly hop with his upper lip. After stanching the blood, Antonini stayed in the game and managed to make some fine, super-smooth, digitally enhanced plays with both glove and arm. The Antonini-Batchelor axis of fielding prowess is Crosby-Malkin-like in its beauty and grace. Nothing lost in the off-season there. Krovich elicited the ghost of Freedom with an earnest "flop" on a sharp line drive. Foreman and Vehse turned a bang-bang double play off a sharp line drive to the box with a man on first.

But such minor inconveniences like illegal bats, busted lips, and bad hitting were overshadowed by the return of Meatball from California and Ravi from Evansdale. Both contributed mightily to the cause. Welcome back to the fold. Leatherman suited up and provided support, especially tips of hitting, "Back elbow up." Lots of wonderful fans with children and dogs in orange lifted spirits and enhanced the evening dusk with cheers, beauty, and loving adoration.—DF

MAY 29–CHICO'S (0–3) VS MRT Chico's loses in mud fest. It looked like Woodstock—so much mud, so many good musicians. Chico's took on a whole bunch of guys in baseball pants (always a bad sign). One guy even had that black stuff under his eyes. If you are wearing that stuff under your eyes, you should not be playing Single-A softball. Chico's plays Single-A softball

because there is no league that is lower in purported competitiveness. The team wants to have fun, win a few games, and get together with the guys. There are a number of teams who have deliberately entered into Single-A because they could not win it all in Double-A. That sucks.—DF

JULY 2–CHICO'S (0–8) VS WESTOVER VFD Westover VFD defeat the Bondsmen 14–8 on rain drenched Liberatore Field. Walks, walks, and more walks proved the downfall. Meatball lost command of the strike zone in an ugly 10-run VFD 4th inning. Chico's bats were hot early, but it was not enough. Ravi shined, going 4 for 4 with 2 triples. Jim March continued his hot hitting. Jon Vehse made several sparkling pick-ups at 1st base. There is rumor of conspiracy—assistant manager and pitcher Krovich's clock was mysteriously set back 30 minutes before the game and Foreman's magic and very lucky orange hat is missing. Chico team officials are investigating. —JA

5 — JEFF "NOLAN" RYAN

PITCHER

BATS: RIGHT   THROWS: RIGHT   SEASONS PLAYED: 19
HOBBIES: CURLING, E-BIKES, POTTERY, GARDENING, CIGARS, BOGO
WALK-UP SONG: "INDIVISIBLE" BY THE DIRT BOMBS

Jeff teaches kimchi-making classes in the off-season; was fluffed in a postgame by Yukon Jack shots; is known for selling eyes and hands; enjoys drive-in movies.

JULY 8–CHICO'S (1–8) VS PARADISE LAKE GOLF

Chico's (10 players, 9 gloves) beat Paradise Lake Golf (8 players). The game started normal. Meatball walked six in the 1st inning. Jim March debuted in right field without a mitt. It looked like it was going to be another long night for the Bondsman, but Paradise Lake showed up with only 8 players. After their 8th batter in the 1st, the umpires ruled Chico's the winners due to forfeit. Chico's win! Chico's win! CHICO'S WIN! There was much celebration in Chicoville on Pleasant Street in the postgame. —JA

JULY 22–CHICO'S (1–13) VS SHAVER CONSTRUCTION

Chico's play flawlessly but come up short, losing 8–6 in muddy battle on Liberatore Field. Not even a jug of Jeff Ryan's homemade wine-spodie-odie on the bench could lift the Bonders from the doldrums. A spodie-drunk Ryan misses his at-bat in the 6th inning for an automatic out. Pitcher Krovich strikes out eight. Several Bondsmen remained at the field for hours after the game – dazed, mud-stained, teary-eyed – their lips and tongues purple. —JA

JULY 24–CHICO'S (4–12) VS MR TROPHIES

Unable to win conventionally, Chico's put hex on opponent. To the amazement of everyone, all MR Trophies' players suddenly disappeared into thin air. It was a true Chico's miracle. Baffled and shaken, the umpires rule Chico's the victors by forfeit. Chico's win—finally.— JA

AUGUST 7–CHICO'S (4–13) VS RIVERSIDE APOSTOLIC CHURCH

Another Chico's nightmare. Because of a BOPARC scheduling error, Chico's were forced to wait for an extra 90 minutes before their game. That was just enough time for the Bonders to overload on cigarettes, beer, and leftover wine-spodie-odie. In the meantime, Riverside team members (with their bibles thrust high in the air) prayed, chanted, and prayed some more. Riverside's prayers were answered as they routed the Bonders 12–0 in a quick, clean five innings of action, leaving stunned Chico's members to wander around the darkened and deserted Liberatore field in search of answers—and more beer. —JA

AUGUST 13–CHICO'S (3–16) VS CUMBERLAND COAL Muddied and bloodied, Chico's lose again. With trumpets blaring, cannons exploding, Jim March ranting, and thunder rumbling, an inspired and slightly tipsy Chico's team roared into their game with Cumberland Coal. As the season neared its end, Chico's played with a newfound energy and passion— shortstop Antonini and second basemen Batchelor turned double plays, left centerfielder Raese threw out runners at the plate, Krovich struck out over-matched batters, Vehse made diving catches in left. After the dust settled, the scoreboard read Cumberland Coal 15 and Chico's 4. What? Wait a minute! There must have been a mistake! Who was keeping score? That can't be! —JA

AUGUST 17–CHICO'S (4–16) VS CLEAR MOUNTAIN BANK Chico's closes the book on another losing season, dropping the finale 9–0 to Clear Mountain Bank. Chico needs for the next season (not in order of urgency):

1. speed;
2. hitting;
3. better barber;
4. corrective lens;
5. bigger gloves;
6. more speed;
7. triple-walled bats;
8. fountain of youth.

Offseason workouts to begin tomorrow. —JA

2010 Chico's: (standing) Robert Raese, Mack McGinley, Greg Leatherman, Al Bonner, Andy Pintus, Tom Batchelor, Jim Manilla, Jeff Ryan, Hollis Brown, (kneeling) Dave Krovich, Brian Porterfield, Sean Kelley, Jon Vehse, Jim Antonini, Meatball

MAY 8—CHICO'S (0-1) VS T&B SERVICES Chico's Late Rally Falls Short in 18–16 Thriller to T&B Services in BOPARC Slugfest. Right fielder Porterfield led the way with 4 hits and 5 RBIs. Shortstop Antonini added 4 hits and scored 4 runs. Second baseman Batchelor had 3 hits. Jeff Ryan and Krovich added 2 more. First baseman Leatherman rattled the left center field fence with a moonshot. Hitting wasn't the problem. Beleaguered Chico outfielders were observed late into the warm spring night well after the game had ended, shagging flyballs in the dark.—JA

MAY 13—CHICO'S (1-1) VS COLASANTE'S BOPARC officials hate pitcher Dave Krovich as Chico's win ugly 12–10 to raise their record to 1–1. Krovich expertly worked the strike zone corners to no avail as the home plate umpire issued 12 undeserved

walks to Colastante's. Krovich did rebound to record 4 strikeouts and hit a key inside-the-park home run to put the Bonders out in front early. Game MVP goes to McGinley who saved the game with a running, diving, tumbling catch in right center with the bases full of Mylan Pill Pushers. McGinley also contributed a 2-run triple. Porterfield continues to pace all BOPARC leagues with 7 RBIs after only 2 games.—JA

MAY 23—CHICO'S (1–2) VS BUCKETHEAD PUB Chico's Embarrassed 12–1 by Buckethead Pub in BOPARC Blowout. Meatball and Pintus are thrown to the wolves as spot hurlers when Chico's star pitcher Dave Krovich (DK1) failed to show up for 1st pitch. A missing person report was filed with the Monongalia County Sheriff's office to the laughter of Buckethead players. DK1 was reportedly spotted drinking Jagermeister shots and lighting menthol cigarettes with $100 dollar bills at Buckethead's earlier that afternoon.—JA

MAY 27—CHICO'S (1–4) VS GRANITE Chico's drops both games in a twilight doubleheader to fall to 1–4 on the season. The Bondsmen late rally falls short in 11–7 loss to Granite in the first game. Chico's was led by Krovich's pitching and hitting. Guiliani and McGinley also provided big hits. In the 2nd game, Pintus hurled a gem as Chico's loses 4–3 in well-played pitchers duel. Several sparkling defensivce plays highlighted the nightcap—Manilla in the right, Kelly in the left, Batchelor and Antonini up the middle, and Pintus on the mound. The Bonders were so distraught with the doubleheader losses they wouldn't allow a hired professional photographer to take the team photo after the game—JA

JUNE 3—CHICO'S (3–4) VS SLACKERS Kelley and Leatherman Lead Bonders in Stunning 14–13 Comeback Victory. Outfielder Kelley delivered a bases loaded, walk-off single to plate the winning run in the last inning as Chico's rallied from an early 6–0 deficit. Leatherman paced the orange with 3 hits, including a majestic deep fly ball double that cleared the bases in the 5th. Important in the victory was when Batchelor aggressively slid into 3rd base with a snort and a grunt early in the game to avoid a tag— the Raging Bull was born. After the dust settled, the Slackers' third baseman was located after a short search in the parking lot across the street. The Slackers never recovered from that point on.—JA

JUNE 3—CHICO'S (4–5) VS BUSTER'S AUTO SALVAGE Chico's sweep. The Bonders returned to the diamond later that night to face the scrappy Buster's Auto Salvage in game 2 of the doubleheader. The postgame fireworks show was cancelled as Chico's bats exploded for 23 runs instead in the slaughter of Buster's Auto Salvage in six quick innings. BOPARC officials confiscated all three Chico bats to x-ray for cork, hemp, rocks, cement, whiskey, cum,

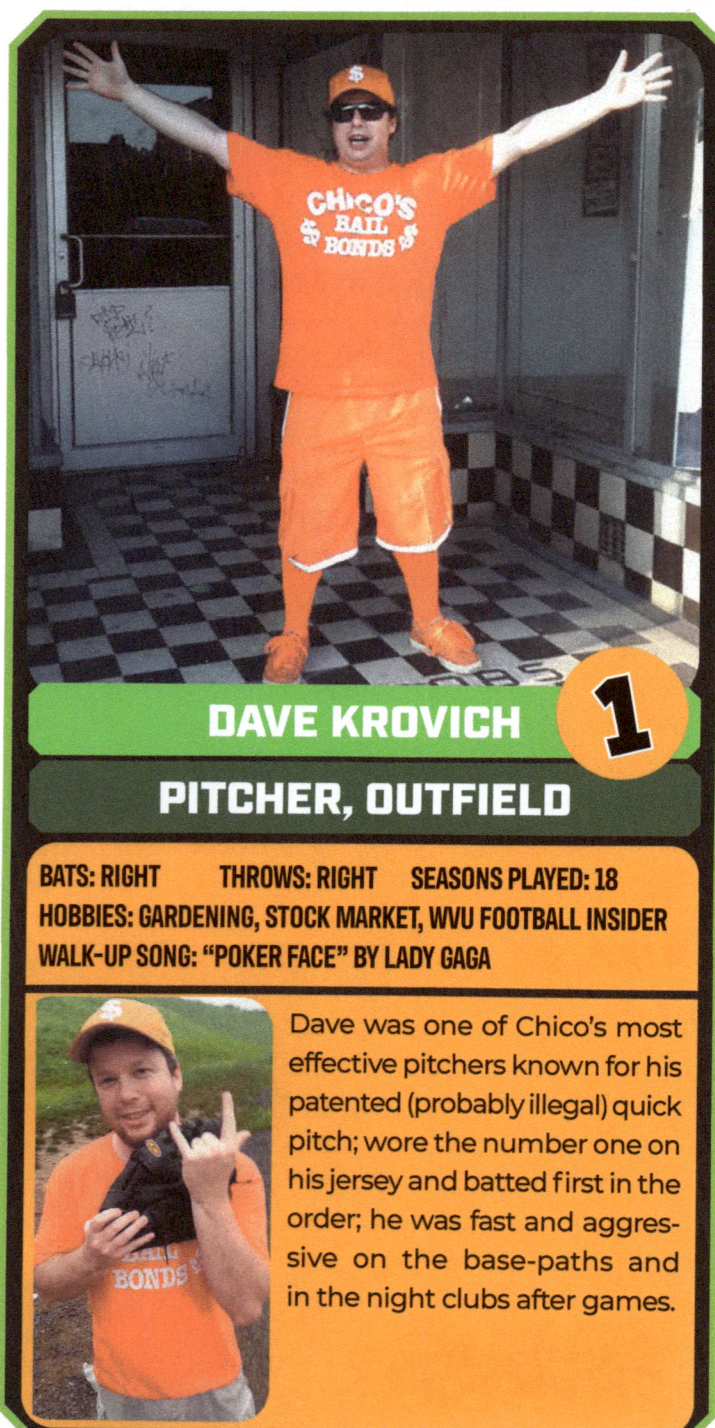

DAVE KROVICH

1

PITCHER, OUTFIELD

BATS: RIGHT **THROWS: RIGHT** **SEASONS PLAYED: 18**
HOBBIES: GARDENING, STOCK MARKET, WVU FOOTBALL INSIDER
WALK-UP SONG: "POKER FACE" BY LADY GAGA

Dave was one of Chico's most effective pitchers known for his patented (probably illegal) quick pitch; wore the number one on his jersey and batted first in the order; he was fast and aggressive on the base-paths and in the night clubs after games.

plutonium, and other possible fillers. Chico's banged out 31 hits as Leatherman continued to baffle opponent pitchers, reaching base in his last 16 plate appearances. Other notables: Raese drilled a 3-run triple, Antonini blazed around the bases for his 1st triple of the season, Leatherman, Pintus, and McGinley also added doubles. Krovich and Pintus pitched Chico's to victory. Early voting results indicate that Vehse leads all BOPARC catchers in early all-star voting.—JA

JUNE 23–CHICO'S (6–4) VS LEDO'S PIZZA Ledo's Pizza Stale as Chico's Romps 13–2 to Stretch Winning Streak to Five. Krovich twirled a gem allowing only 3 hits on the night. Porterfield delivered the big hit, a 3-run triple to put the Bonders in the lead for good. Bonner paced Chico's with 3 hits. BOPARC officials were asking, "What in the hell is up with Chico's? They keep winning." All Chico team members begrudgingly submitted urine and blood samples after the game, trying their best to conceal their new 30-inch biceps and 16-inch-long penises. It was a good time to be a Chico (and a significant other). "Playoffs? Don't talk about playoffs! Are you kidding me?! Playoffs?!"—JA

JULY 3–CHICO'S (8–4) HIT'N'RUN It was a total team effort as Chico's Bail Bonds extends their winning streak to six, raising their record for the season to 8–4. The Bondsmen got timely hitting, pitching, and fielding as they handed 2nd place Hit N' Run only their 3rd loss of the season. Chico's team members' spirits and morale are high as they celebrated the win and winning streak long into the holiday weekend. Look out Honest Abe's...

JULY 6–CHICO'S (8–5) VS HONEST ABE'S Honest Abe's Sell Their Soul in Stopping Chico's 6-Game Winning Streak in BOPARC Thriller 6–3. Chico team members were suspicious when Dave Parker, the 1979 National League MVP, showed up in a 1984 Cadillac Coupe de Ville swilling from a 40-ounce of bottle Schlitz Malt Liquor. A tipsy 350-pound Parker delivered the big blow—a majestic 3-run homer over the centerfield lights in the 6th inning to put Honest Abe's in the lead for good. To rub salt in the wound, Rollie Fingers came on in the 7th to pick up the save. Honest Abe's team members

rejoiced and boasted, knowing they are guaranteed their 1st (although tainted) winning season ever. Later that night, a barefooted McGinley was observed kicking Parker's ass in a parking lot behind the Great Wall Chinese restaurant.—JA

JULY 16—CHICO'S (8–6) VS SIDEWINDERS

Chico's Bail Bonds gets punched in the face and doesn't punch back in humiliating 18–0 thrashing at the hands of Sidewinders. Not much good to report for the Bonders except for two double plays turned by the middle infield, one of which was a near 6–3–2 triple play[1]. Chico's needs to break out of its recent slump in a hurry as the season winds to a close and the playoffs loom. A mandatory team meeting has been called for team building exercises and to finish off the last of the vodka-spiked watermelon.

JULY 21—CHICO'S (8–7) VS DP DOUGH

Chico's Humbled by Last Place DP Dough 8–5 in BOPARC Laugher. It was the 1st win of the season for DP Dough who started the game with one handicapped player and another wearing pleated slacks with leather dress shoes. After the 6-game winning streak in the middle of the season, Chico's sees its once promising season spiraling downward.—JA

JULY 22 BREAKING NEWS

In desperate attempt to correct the late season slump, Chico's Bail Bonds just traded star-hitting right fielder Brian Porterfield to DP Dough for an un-toasted plain bagel from the Blue Moose and six bottles of warm Stoney's beer.—JA

AUGUST 1—CHICO'S (8–8) VS CROCKETT'S LODGE

The Bonders can't recapture early season momentum, lose last game of the season, and are officially eliminated from the playoffs. There was little to report as the hitting, pitching, fielding, baserunning, and coaching woes continued. See you next year.—JA

---

1 A 6–3–2 triple play involves the shortstop fielding a batted ball, outing the runner headed from 2nd to 3rd, throwing to the first baseman, who outs the batter/runner, then throws to the catcher. to tag out the runner from 3rd and complete a triple play. This rare maneuver requires quick thinking, accurate throws, and baserunning mistakes by the opposing team. It almost happened on July 16, but didn't.

2010 Season Awards

Chico MVP: Dave Krovich

Chico All-Stars: Brian Porterfield, Meatball, Mac McGinley, Tom Batchelor, Jim Antonini, Greg Leatherman, Jon Vehse

Chico Rookie of the Year: Sean Kelley

Chico Most Improved: Andy Pintus

2011 IS THAT ALL THERE IS?

2011 Chico's: (standing) Robert Raese, Jim Manilla, Ravi Shibley, Mack McGinley, Tom Batchelor, Raj Chandran, Greg Leatherman, Dave Krovich, Andy Pintus, Meatball, Jeff Ryan, Hollis Brown, (kneeling) Jim March, Sean Kelley, Brian Porterfield, Jon Vehse, LJ Guiliani, Dave Foreman, Jim Antonini

APRIL 8—HEY CHICO SOFTBALLERS! Sharpen your spikes and oil your gloves! The roster has been turned in, and the forfeit fee paid. Organizational meeting tonight at the 123 bar for Supper Club. One new rule this year—all teams in Single-A will use the same type of bat provided by BOPARC. The Chico Buy a New Bat committee has been dissolved—JA

APRIL 28—CHICO'S (0–1) MASTER DEBATERS New BOPARC bat rule dooms Bondsmen as they can't shake off the rust in 12–2 drubbing at the hands of the Master Debaters in opening night softball action. Chico team members complained to BOPARC officials about a sticky substance on the bats shared with the Master Debaters to no avail.

Bonder Tom Batchelor complained, "What is this white shit on the handle? I ain't using this thing."

Bondsmen bats went limp from that point on. Swampy outfield conditions also didn't help. Chico team members are still searching for right fielder Brian Porterfield who went missing in the right field muck in the 4th inning—JA

MAY 5–CHICO'S (0–2) VS SKELETON CREW Chico shits bed in embarrassing 19–1 loss to archrival Skeleton Crew. There have been some low moments in Chico history, but tonight's loss was one of the lowest. Coked, stoked, and liquored up, the eager Bondsmen were informed by unapologetic BOPARC officials of a schedule and field change moments before the first pitch on a beautiful spring night. Unable to regain their edge at the later start time, Chico's looked old, slow, and tired in an uninspiring effort before 80 loud and energetic orange-clad Chico fans. It may be seasons before Chico team members recover from this one—JA

MAY 12–CHICO'S (1–2) VS SCOREGASM Bonders outlast the Scoregasms 3–2 in a defensive masterpiece to pick up their first win of the season. They say 2/3 of the earth is covered by water, then the other 1/3 must be covered by Tom Batchelor and Greg Leatherman. Patrolling the right side of the Chico infield, they caught every ball hit between Hite Street and Madigan Avenue. Guiliani was back to anchor the outfield. Krovich spun a complete game 5-hitter and scored the game-winning run with a daring base-running dash late in the contest. Pintus, Porterfield, and Kelley paced the Bonders with 2 hits apiece. It was a jubilant night in Chico Nation—JA

CHICO'S BAIL BONDS
2011 SOFTBALL SCHEDULE

W=Whiston
O=Ogden
L=Libratore

THUR., 4.28	9PM	@ MASTER DEBATERS	W
TUES., 5.3	10PM	MULTIPLE SCOREGASMS	W
THUR., 5.5	6PM	@ SKELETON CREW	O
THUR., 5.12	9PM	@ GRANITE CONCRETE	L
TUES., 5.17	9PM	PARADISE LAKES	L
WED., 5.25	6PM	THE LINEUP	L
THUR., 6.2	8PM	@ BO	L
TUES., 6.7	9PM	TROY SCHIFINO EXP.	L
THUR., 6.9	6PM	@ LANDSCAPE PLUS	W
THUR., 6.16	9PM	WESTOVER VFD	L
THUR., 6.23	6PM	@ HONEST ABE'S	L
TUES., 6.28	9PM	CLASSIC'S	W
THUR., 6.30	10PM	@ COLASANTE'S	W
THUR., 7.7	6PM	SIDEWINDERS	O
TUES., 7.19	9PM	@ BRICKS & STICKS	L
THUR., 7.21	7PM	MGTN. SURGICAL	L
TUES., 7.26	10PM	ALLIANCE REALITY	L
WED., 7.27	6PM	@ STEPHEN CAMPBELL	L

*Some games are subject to change whenever BOPARC deems it.

JUNE 7–CHICO'S (1–3) VS TROY SCHIFANO EXPERIENCE Despite their "mother being a mudder", Chico's Bail Bonds drop a close contest to the Troy Schifano Experience 7–4 in the mud, slop, and blood of Liberatore Field. Chico's was paced with the strong pitching of Krovich, clutch hitting of Antonini, and flawless outfield play of Guiliani, Kelley, Porterfield, Wells, and McGinley.

Game Notes. Chico's youngest player, Ethan Wells, pulled his groin for the second straight game.

Upon examination of the injury, Chico catcher Jon Vehse was heard to exclaim, "Wow! What a groin!"

3B Meatball transported Wells to the nearest brothel rehabilitation center at an undisclosed location on the Mileground for an evening of deep tissue massage and tactile stimulation for the injured appendage—JA

JUNE 9–CHICO'S (1–5) VS LANDSCAPE PLUS Bonders wilt in the heat, falling 8–7 in a BOPARC classic. Landscape Plus roared back from 6 runs down in record summer high temperatures and humidity with a walk-off, game winning double in the last inning, breaking the Bondsmen hearts. With a patchwork line-up, Chico's jumped out to an early 7–1 lead in the 2nd inning but couldn't sustain the offensive output as they were held scoreless in the last five innings. Landscape Plus last inning rally began with the Bondsmen missing an outfielder. 3B Meatball noticed that no one was playing right field and immediately called a timeout. After a brief stoppage in play, right fielder Porterfield was discovered sitting in the shade in foul territory, snuggled up to a cooler of icy cold Pabst Blue Ribbon beers.

Team Captain Krovich asked, "When are you going back to right field, Brian?" Porterfield responded, "When I sober up." He then paused for a moment, not budging from his shady spot before proclaiming, "and that could be years."—JA

JUNE–23 CHICOS' (1–6) VS HONEST ABE'S & CHICO'S (1–7) VS NORTHERN ELECTRICAL Losing streak continues as Chico's drop both games of a twin bill at sold out Liberatore Stadium.

In the 1st game, the Bondsmen played their hearts out, keeping pace with 1st place Honest Abes until falling late, losing 8–5. Chico's were led by the pitching of Krovich, the hitting of McGinley, and the fielding of 1B Leatherman who has discovered a fountain of youth. Nimble as a cat but bold as an ox, Leatherman dazzled the crowd with two diving catches, one ranging far to his right, the other, deep down the 1st base line to his left. Team management is contemplating finding another position for the suddenly invig-

orated Leatherman who spent the offseason drinking a murky concoction of one part fruit nectar, one part West Virginia pond water, and one part rye whiskey. Looking for a spark in the nightcap against Northern Electrical, Chico management turned to Jeff "Nolan" Ryan to give Krovich a breather on the mound.

Doubting teammates laughed at the move causing Ryan to respond, "I think I can pitch. I'm pretty good at horseshoes."

Ryan spun a gem, scattering just five hits over seven innings. Walks proved Ryan's downfall as two Northern Electrical runners who reached base on free passes scored in the top half of the last inning, leading them to the 5–3 victory. The Bonders were paced by the hitting of Nelms and Manilla and the creative baserunning of Clayton Neal and Porterfield.

Despite the disappointment, Chico team members reconvened at the 123 bar for a post-doubleheader celebration of epic proportions. Team management was so moved by the effort of the team's play, they changed curfew from 10 PM to 10 AM, allowing the Bondsmen a free evening to blow off a little steam. Unrestrained, Chico players lost themselves in a dizzying haze of

Jameson shots, cigarettes, stout beers, marginal women[1], and the jukebox sounds of Marty Robbins and Peggy Lee.

By morning curfew, twelve Chicos were accounted for, two were missing (Vehse, Porterfield), one had been arrested (Meatball), one was in the hospital (Neal), and one had been traded (McGinley) to Northern Electric for a 60-ft extension cord, a box of fuses, and a roll of silver metallic tape.

UPDATE – June 25: Catcher Vehse was located. He was found at Blue Moose Cafe, sipping a latte with three extra shots of espresso. His entire body had been wrapped in metallic tape, mumbling something about the new extension cord having a short and worrying about who was going to play right centerfield for the rest of the season—JA

JUNE 28–CHICO'S (1–9) VS CLASSIC'S BAR & GRILL
Bondsmen fall flat in softball laugher as losing streak reaches seven games. Overwhelmed and overmatched, the Bonders stumbled 17–4 in BOPARC late night action. Short-handed due to suspension, injury, and house arrest, Chico's fielded a team of ten eager and willing but doomed souls. The Bondsmen kept the game close early until Classic's exploded for 12 runs in a marathon 3rd inning that seemingly never ended.

Left centerfielder Pintus summed up the nightmare inning best, "I'd play back, and they'd drop the ball in front of me. I'd play up, and they'd knock it over my head."

Obviously frustrated with the night's result, Chico right centerfielder Wells disappeared over the center field fence into the darkness, while chasing down a ball that flew over his head.

Right fielder Porterfield responding to reporters after the game, "Wells got to the ball, but instead of picking it up, he just hopped over the fence and kept on running, as if something spooked him. It looked like he was headed towards the Grafton Road."

After the game, a somber Chico team retreated to the 123 bar to lick their wounds. With the Sex Pistols blaring on the jukebox and high on Irish whiskey, catcher Vehse exclaimed, "This is bullshit! I'm tired of losing! I'm tired of licking my own wounds!" God Save the Chico—JA

---

1 The Chico players would align themselves with many marginal women through the years. It must be noted that most of the significant women in the lives of the Bonders, however, were much more than marginal—they were exceptional.

June 30–Chico's (1–11) vs Master Debaters & Chico's (1–12) vs Colasante's Pizza

The misery continues; Chico's on life support. Chico's Bail Bonds dropped both ends of a doubleheader in late night softball action—the first a lackluster snoozer, the second an epic BOPARC classic that both thrilled and exhausted the boisterous Chico team members as well as the standing-room only Liberatore crowd.

In the opener, the Bonders delivered a lackluster performance, squandering several run-scoring opportunities early in the game. Jeff 'Nolan' Ryan pitched effectively in his 2nd outing on the mound, but it wasn't enough as Chico's got walloped 13–3.

With their season on the brink, the Bondsmen responded in game 2 with their best performance in years. Playing against the younger and more athletic Colasante's Pizza team, Chico's battled like they were playing in the last game of their lives. The aggressive tone was set early by Krovich who scored on a mad wild sprint from third after tagging up on a short pop-up caught in foul territory. For over sixty minutes, Chico's bashed out hit after hit and ran the bases like a team possessed. The Bonders banged out a season high 28 hits, highlighted by Neal's bases-clearing triple, Meatball's shots down the third base line, Bonner's well-placed

41

singles to right and left fields, Wells' beautiful deep drives to center, Porterfield's slices to right, and Batchelor's line drives over short. Guiliani and McGinley anchored a busy outfield. Meatball played third base like a hockey goalie, repeatedly taking line shots off his chest, arms, and face, not letting anything get by him. Shortstop Antonini found some new hops, contorting his body and going high in the air to stab liners out of the air over his head.

But all that STILL was not enough to stop Chico's 9-game slide. As the clock struck midnight and down 19−18 in the last inning with two outs and two Bonders on, hot-hitting Ethan Wells hit a deep, majestic drive to center field, bringing the roaring Chico followers to their feet. To the Bonders' dismay, the Colasante left centerfielder dashed out the darkness and fog of the thick, hazy summer night and made a diving, tumbling catch, that ripped the hearts out of the chests of the Chico followers and team members. In disbelief, 1B Leatherman retreated to his car and wept, not about the loss but about the pride and love he felt for his fellow Bondsmen. On this night, Chico's were everything they had not been during this forgettable season—daring, hustling, bold, youthful.

Not wanting to go home, six or seven Chico's milled aimlessly around the closing 123 bar at 3:00 AM. An exhausted and worn down, Vehse stood over the darkened jukebox, its plug pulled and the power long shut off after last call. He still tried to make selections, just wanting to hear Peggy Lee sing '*Is That All There Is*' one last time—JA

JULY 19–CHICO PREGAME BENEDICTION To end the longest losing streak in Chico's Bail Bonds history, the Bondsmen gathered at the 123 bar for an hour before the game to ease pre-game tensions by engaging in a series of stretching exercises, listening to jukebox music, and knocking down Jameson shots. Before leaving for the game, Chico's shaman and naturalist Tim Nelms jumped up on the pool table and delivered a prayer. It went as follows:

> "*May Chico's rise from the ashes and the anguish who echo one hears in the 2nd verse of Genesis, the anguish inscribed in every one of the last lost tribes of a deserted and empty universe crushed under the spirit of God but from which the spirit of man not only is absent but not yet born or is it already extinguished –Ramen*"

A booming cheer, not like any other that has been heard before at the bar, rang out (and many great bands have played there over the years—Red Hot Chili Peppers, Dead Kennedys, Firehose, 63 Eyes, Bo Diddly, Dinosaur Jr, Fugazi, and on and on and on). Chico players, as serious as ever, calmly finished their beers, stubbed out their cigarettes, and pulled on their sacred orange jerseys. It was time to go to work. Chico's would not be denied—JA

July 19–Chico's (2–14) vs Sticks and Bricks

Chico's Bail Bonds ends long losing streak; Morgantown Mayor Manilla[2] proclaims July 20th as "Chico Appreciation Day!" An inspired Chico team, embarrassed by recent lackluster performances, took care of business in a workman-like manner, disposing of Sticks and Bricks 9–0 in BOPARC softball action. The game was highlighted by the return of Chico Hall-of-Fame pitcher Dave Foreman who hurled five masterful innings, limiting the opponent to only four hits and not allowing a runner past 2nd base. The Chico infield of Leatherman, Batchelor, Antonini, and Meatball was flawless. Kelley, Guiliani, McGinley, and Krovich anchored an error-free outfield. Jeff "Nolan" Ryan came on in the 6th in relief of Foreman to notch the save and keep the shutout intact.

The highlight of the game, and maybe in the history of Chico's Bail Bonds, was turned in by catcher Vehse. At a crucial point early in the game, 3B Meatball snagged a hot grounder down the third base line. Off balance, Meatball hurled a desperation toss to first base. 1B Leatherman lunged for the throw that was just out of his reach towards the home plate side of first base. In a flash out of nowhere as the batter sped towards first base, a hustling Vehse, backing up the play, dove for the errant throw, and all in one motion, snatched the ball out of the air and tagged the fleet-footed batter just before he reached first base. The overflow Liberatore Stadium crowd roared in applause. BOPARC umpires were stunned.

Rubbing his eyes, not sure what he had just witnessed, home plate umpire Tim Beery exclaimed, "Wow! I've been umping for 25 years and have never seen a play as good as that one! I've never seen a catcher who could run like that! He beat the batter down the line! Who is that man?"

From that point on, it was going to be a good night for the Bonders, and everyone knew it. After the game, the proud mayor of

2 Mayor Manilla. Chico reserve 3B Jim Manilla was indeed Mayor of Morgantown during this time. There are doubts, however, as to whether he had access to an actual key to the city.

00

JON VEHSE

CATCHER, FUTILITY FIELDER

BATS: RIGHT   THROWS: RIGHT   SEASONS PLAYED: 20
HOBBIES: CIGARETTES, CROWN ROYAL, COFFEE, CIGARETTES, ROTTWEILERS, CIGARETTES
WALK-UP SONG: "WORRIED ABOUT YOU" BY THE ROLLING STONES

Jon has his own personal CD on the 123 Pleasant Street jukebox with some of his favorite songs; played the entire 2004 and 2005 season without eating solid foods; sometimes after games would sleep under the South High Street bridge in Meatball's car.

Morgantown (and Chico team member) Jim Manilla presented the team with the key to the city and proclaimed July 20th to be a city holiday from that day forward. Catcher Vehse accepted the key for the team.

As the Bondsmen celebrated the victory late into the night at the 123 bar, a sweaty free-range Vehse was observed roaming the downtown streets with the key around his neck and using it to try to open the front door of the many closed liquor bars that lined High Street—JA

JULY 21–CHICO'S (2–15) VS MORGANTOWN SURGICAL Derailed by heat, women, and a photo shoot, Chico's Bail Bonds falls; Morgantown Surgical sweats out a 11–5 victory over the Bondsmen in BOPARC tussle. With a heat index hovering around 105 degrees, a resilient Chico's team battled back to close an early deficit. Down by five runs, Chico's tied game in the third inning with a vintage two-out lightning rally. Chico's youngest team members jumpstarted the offense. DH Koury slashed a line drive single over the third baseman's head and OF Wells kept the inning alive with a hot shot hit to right field. With the bases loaded, team captain Krovich delivered the big blow, a bases-clearing double to deep right center field that scored the speedy Bonner from the first base to tie the game. The delirious, partisan Chico crowd roared their approval.

Appreciative of their fans' support, Chico's team members mingled between innings with their sultry Chica supporters, wanting to steal them away to a cool bar with cold adult drinks, far away from the dust, sweat, and sun of Liberatore Stadium. A fashion photographer snapped pictures of the sweaty and brawny team members as they milled about the dugout during the game. A strong pitching performance by Ryan and a beautiful, running acrobatic catch by McGinley in deep right centerfield kept the Bonders close. But like most nights, their hearts and desires were elsewhere.

Playing to the vanity of the Chico's players, the photographer suggested a photo shoot, a calendar pictorial, after the game at the 123 bar. Upon hearing the suggestion, Chico's failed to score another run. Later in the evening, several shirtless Bondsmen were seen prancing about the bar, primping and preening for the camera and fighting each other for the attention of their lady fans. The photo shoot came to an abrupt halt when back-up catcher Nelms, who was to be Mr. Chico September, proudly appeared

for his shoot completely bottomless—no shorts, no underwear, no shame, full frontal male nudity. The photographer quickly put his camera away.

"I said topless only!" he shouted at Nelms. "I wanted to keep this classy!"

As the photographer stormed out of the bar, Nelms, who is hitting a devilish .666 for the season, remarked, "He doesn't know what class is."

Still without pants, Nelms hopped on a barstool and joined his tipsy teammates as sweat poured from places below his waist rarely seen in public—JA

JULY 26–CHICO'S (21–6) VS ALLIANCE REALTY Bonders embarrassed 20–5 in an empty Liberatore Stadium as losing season continues; Are the good times really gone?

Pitcher Ryan was ejected from the game by the home plate umpire[3] and suspended for the remainder of the season by Chico management. The evening started out in fine fashion as several Chico team members gathered at the 123 bar for a supposedly quiet pre-game team meeting. Reserve catcher and team spiritual leader Nelms showed up wearing a pearl necklace and holding a freshly written benediction that he had prepared to read before the game. After several cans of Pabst Blue Ribbon beer, a few shots of Irish whiskey, a toke here and there, an hour of loud jukebox music, and Nelms' inspiring words, the pregame meeting quickly escalated into a full-blown party.

The before game batting practice was replaced with a smoke-out and make-out session with random softball groupies in the batting cage behind Ogden Field. Pregame warm-ups and stretching exercises were ignored. Game faces disappeared; focus was lost. The game began badly.

> **"I CAN'T EVEN LOOK AT THE COLOR ORANGE RIGHT NOW. I'M DEVASTATED."**
> **—JEFF RYAN**

A high and inebriated Ryan couldn't find the strike zone, walking several of the game's first batters. As the 1st inning dragged on, a visibly frustrated, Ryan heaved an overhand fastball towards home plate, nearly beaning the shocked and stunned umpire in the head. The ejected and dejected Ryan was quickly escorted off the field by Chico team officials.

Pintus came on in relief and pitched effectively, but by the time the 1st inning ended, the Bondsmen were down 12–0. Plagued all evening by shoddy outfield play and a lack of clutch hitting, the Bonders were unable to recover. Highlights for Chico's included a bases-clearing triple by 1B Leatherman and some fine glove work by Meatball at 3B.

As the game neared the end, a remorseful Ryan asked team managers, "When do I get to go back in?"

No one said a word as the last Chico batter of the night grounded into a game-ending double play.

UPDATE – July 28: Chico management has suspended upstart pitcher Jeff 'Nolan' Ryan from all team activities for the rest of the 2011 season. The suspension involves: no active game participation, no use of Chico team training facilities, no participation in any Chico social activity, and revocation of Chico discounts at all 123 bar events (he must pay full price for all events until 2012).

Ryan commented after learning of the suspension, "I can't even look at the color orange right now. I'm devastated."—JA

---

3 Umpires. The relationship between Chico's and the umpires was initially icy. The early Chico teams were a feral and unruly bunch. Through the years, the relationship warmed a bit, likely because of the pathetic on-field performance of the more recent Chico teams.

2012 THE GREAT RACE

Chico's 2012: (standing) Jon Vehse, Jim Manilla, Greg Leatherman, Clayton Neal, Al Bonner, Jeff Ryan, Tom Batchelor, Chad Koury, Eric Ramón, (kneeling) LJ Guiliani, Jim Antonini, Raj Chandran, Ethan Wells, Dave Krovich, Mack McGinley, Meatball, Tim Nelms

APRIL 25–CHICO'S (0–1) VS STATE FARM Chico's Bail Bonds drops opener 9–3 in bizarre game in BOPARC softball action. Despite the loss, the Bondsmen felt good about themselves. There were too many positives to take away from the game to be disappointed, such as flawless infield play (Ravi at 3rd, Antonini at short, and Batchelor at 2nd were in midseason form), an encouraging display of power hitting (Leatherman, Koury, and McGinley all blasted balls to the fence for extra base hits), and solid pitching (Meatball and Krovich).

But the game turned strange in the 3rd inning. Trying to gain an advantage while the distracted BOPARC umpires played with their cell phones and the opponent's fielders were taking their positions in the field, Chico outfielder Koury jumped into the batter's box and mischievously swatted a warm-up pitch by the State Farm hurler between short and third and wildly dashed for 1st base—a Chico first in their long and illustrious history.

The State Farm pitcher hollered, "What are you doing?! I'm still warming up!"

Koury responded, "I was in the batter's box. You pitched it. I hit it. I'm working here!"

BOPARC umps made Koury return to the batter's box, "We didn't call 'batter up', no play".

A determined Koury didn't bat an eye, returning to the box before smacking the next 'legal' pitch to deep left centerfield for a double. A couple of batters later Chico star player, Ravi Shibley, smashed the first pitch he has saw to deep left centerfield. The pummeled ball quickly disappeared high into the cool spring night air. It might have been the farthest ball ever hit in BOPARC history.

Chico leftfielder Clayton Neal exclaimed, "Wow! I didn't know a softball could go that far!"

Chico relief pitcher, Jeff Ryan, wondered, "Is that ball ever going to come down?"

With jaws dropped, nobody at Whiston Field saw the ball land as it cleared the fence, the parked cars, and the road, most likely landing in the parking lot of South Middle school, at least 500 feet away.

Unfortunately, due to a bizarre BOPARC softball rule, the majestic blast was nothing more than an out, and an out on that occasion and every other time Shibley was to bat thereafter in the game—for home runs were illegal in Single-A ball that year.[1] Confused,

Ravi was halted in his home run trot by the laughter of the State Farm infielders as he rounded 1st base, and confessed, "I didn't know. I didn't know the rule."

Losing momentum and unable to mount a rally in the final innings, the Bonders dropped the first game of the season and retreated dejectedly but encouraged to the comforts of their beloved 123 bar.

"We're going to beat a lot of teams this year!" catcher Vehse proclaimed.

A rousing cheer rang out among the sweaty, weary players. After several shots of whiskey, outfielder Wells led a small expedition of Chico players on a journey back to Whiston field.

"We're going to find that ball Ravi hit," he promised. "It'll be a symbol for all the big things that Chico's will accomplish this year. Maybe we'll make the playoffs."

With flashlights, a case of red stripe beer, a bottle of Jägermeister, and a Rottweiler named Rudy, the Chico players searched for hours. The ball was never found. Giving up the search as morning neared, the suddenly dizzy Chico players lounged in the lush, misty left field grass of Whiston Field, feeling good about themselves and the prospects for the new season. Staring to the clear sky above, they wondered if the ball Ravi hit had joined the blinking stars that smeared the sky above.—JA

---

1 Home runs. In some years, balls hit over the outfield fence in the A division were ruled outs. This was to prevent teams from stacking their lineups with ringers in the lower divisions of the BOPARC league.

APRIL 27–CHICO'S (1–1) VS BUSTER'S AUTO SALVAGE Chico's Bail Bonds dominate with impressive 15–9 win in early BOPARC softball action. On the slow, sloppy, and muddy track of Whiston Field, an invigorated and confident Chico team led from start to finish, playing inspired and flawless ball in all phases—pitching (Krovich hurled a gem), fielding (Shibley was spectacular with both his arm and glove in the outfield), and most importantly hitting (Leatherman knocked three doubles, Shibley delivered four hits, McGinley was now 6 for 7 for this season), banging out an impressive 24 hits for the game. At the end of the night, the few Chico players who remained in the bar grooved and grinded with each other to the jukebox music—except for Vehse who packed up his catchers' gear.

Utility player Neal asked, "What's wrong Vehse?"

"I want to make the playoffs. I'm tired of losing year after year," he snapped. "I'm heading back to Whiston Field."

"At this hour?" Neal asked.

"I'm going to work on my base running."

The bar went silent until Porterfield spoke up, "I'll go with you, Vehse."

"Me, too," said Krovich.

"I'll go," Leatherman agreed.

Soon, most of the Chico starting lineup (except for Shibley who went back to Dairy Mart for more chicken tenders) followed Vehse out of the bar into the cool, frosty night for some late-night practice. After the players had loaded the team bus, Meatball started the engine. But before he could pull away, outfielder Wells pounded on the side of the bus. Meatball opened the door and Wells boarded, carrying an unopened bottle of Irish whiskey. Wells took a seat and cracked open the bottle. He took a big swig before passing the bottle around to the other Chico players.

Meatball pulled the bus onto Pleasant Street, turned onto High, and passed Whiston Field without slowing down. A cheer rang out from the back of the bus as Meatball eased the bus onto Interstate-79 and headed south.

"I really do need to work on my base running." Vehse mumbled, wiping his mouth as whiskey dripped down his chin onto his sweaty orange Chico shirt.

During the bus trip south, Jim March was unanimously elected as the Head of the Chico Bloody Mary and Sunday Morning Batting Practice Committee.—JA

MAY 16–CHICO'S (2–3) VS COLASANTE'S PIZZA A gritty Chico's Bail Bonds team loses heartbreaker to Colasante's Pizza on the synthetic turf of Mylan Park[2]. Depleted by injury [OF Shibley (shoulder), P Krovich (neck)] and obligation [OF McGinley (beauty pageant)] to key team members, a short-handed Chico team battled until the end, stranding the bases full in the final inning. The Bonders were paced by the hitting of 1B Porterfield (a bases loaded double in the 1st inning), LF Kelley (three-line

---

2 Mylan Park. Chico's played for the first time on the spongy, synthetic turf of Mylan Park. It was not a favorable surface for the aging Bonders. The surface was fast and bouncy. Chico's managed only one win out of seven games there.

drive singles) and 3B Meatball (two line drives down the 3B line). Pitcher Jeff Ryan hurled a gem, striking out three and holding the doughboys scoreless in the final three innings. LCF Neal anchored the outfield with several fine catches. SS Antonini turned a double play at second, and 2B Batchelor showed off his range, picking multiple bloop hits out of the air in short right and center fields. But the effort wasn't enough. The team took the loss hard, knowing this was one game they could have, and should have, won. As the disappointed and silent Chico faithful filed out of Mylan Park, LCF Neal and C Vehse sat behind home plate on the plastic painted turf, sucking on a flask of 15-year-old Scotch that they had hope to share with the team in victory. A hallucinating OF Ethan Wells flew over the centerfield fence and disappeared into the high grass of the sprawling cow pastures that surround the park. A distraught Meatball peeled off in his car and sped towards the seedy side streets of Sabraton, the one part of town his probation officer forbade him to go. The early promising season was turning sour. The team could sense it. The aging Bonders' flaws, warts, and addictions had been exposed by a younger, more energetic opponent. The Bondsmen return to action in two short days. Injuries need to heal quickly; and hangovers must subside. For Thursday's game may be the biggest in Chico's Bail Bonds softball history. A season, and more importantly a legacy, is on the line.—JA

MAY 23–CHICO'S (2–5) VS HONEST ABE'S Chico's Bail Bonds shit the bed in sloppy 10–8 loss to archrival Honest Abe's, and third baseman Meatball changes his name. The Bonders fell behind early and never recovered. The night quickly turned ugly as the Chico outfield misplayed a line shot to deep left centerfield. Backing up the play, hustling RCF Wells retrieved the ball and flipped it to LCF Neal who heaved it towards home plate just after the Honest Abe batter scored, turning the error into a bases-clearing, game-changing, 3-run Chico blunder. The momentum behind Wells' aggressive play caused him to violently slide under the outfield chain-link fence.

Entrapped, Wells struggled to free himself. The game was delayed for over thirty minutes as BOPARC officials worked to extract the agitated Wells from the fence. Impatient and wanting to keep the night's full slate of games on schedule, the BOPARC umpires resumed the game with Wells stuck and Chico's left to play the next several innings minus one outfielder.

As Honest Abe's dinked base hit after base hit while building a 6-run lead, all means were used to free Wells. Nothing worked until Vic's Towing showed up with the "jaws of life" and a reciprocating saw. Wells was eventually freed, but the

Bonders had fallen to a nearly unsurmountable 10–2 deficit. Chico's attempted to make a comeback, rallying for six runs in the sixth to cut the deficit to two.

With the bases full and two outs and the winning run on base in the Bonder's final at-bat, 3B Meatball took warm-up swings in the on-deck circle of Liberatore Field. His flock of floozy female fans chanted his name over and over again, "Meatball! Meatball! Meatball!"

> **"WHO THE HELL IS GARY? MEATBALL IS A 'GARY'? HE DOESN'T LOOK LIKE A 'GARY'."**

As he stepped into the batter's box, Meatball's main squeeze at the time, shouted out, "Let's go, Gary!"

Puzzled, Chico team members looked at each other and wondered out loud, "Who the hell is Gary? Meatball is a 'Gary'? He doesn't look like a 'Gary'."

Meatball turned towards his lady friends, blew them a kiss, and ripped off his sweaty, sleevelss, and faded #12 orange jersey, exposing a new, brighter and fresher Bail Bonds' orange shirt underneath with the number "45" outlined in gold and silver sequins.

"Don't call me Gary anymore," he sneered, before looking to his teammates, "and don't you assholes call me, Meatball. I've been called Meatball all my life. I hate that name!"

He paused as the packed Liberatore Field went silent, "From now on, I am Colt Cuatro Cinco!"

The partisan Chico crowd roared as Colt Cuatro Cinco dug into the batter's box and stared down the pitcher. As the game's final pitch easily floated towards home plate, the Colt took one last mighty swing. Chico team members held their breaths as the bat contacted the ball. And in typical Chico fashion, the batted ball was not mashed into pieces. Instead, it fluttered harmlessly and weakly into the mitt of Honest Abe's third baseman who caught it for the game's final out. The Bonders lost again for the fourth time in a row.

Chico catcher Vehse yelled out, "We need to stop drinking and start hitting!"

The distraught Bonders looked at relief pitcher Jeff Ryan who pulled the team's orange painted flask from his lips, shrugged, and wiped at the Yukon Jack that hung on his lips.—JA

JUNE 8–CHICO'S (2–6) VS SHAFT DRILLERS Playoff hopes fade as Chico's Bail Bonds lose their 6th straight 12–2 as trade deadline nears. Many words have been used to describe the Bonders through the years, but 'anemic' has never been one until tonight's debacle. Chico's managed only five hits in a lackluster effort that was only highlighted by the efficient pitching of Koury, the spectacular tumbling catch by Wells in deep right field, and the spectacular play by Meatball at third base. The sad Chico box score told the sad story of the night that started with promise but ended in missed opportunities, disappointment, and misery.

As the night drifted away and the alcohol flowed, the players quietly worried to themselves as the trade deadline loomed. No player was safe from losing his position on the roster, and every Chico knew it.[3]

"I was traded for a stale, untoasted bagel and six pack of Stoney's beer once," OF/DH/1B Porterfield piped up, breaking the silence. "Worst summer of my life."

As 3B Meatball ordered his sixth Long Island Iced Tea of the night, his phone, sitting on the bar, began to ring. The Chico players

---

3 Trade deadline. Four Chico's have been traded to other teams through the years—Brian Porterfield, Mac McGinley, Meatball, and Chris Evans.

glanced at one another and drank hard on their beers. The phone continued to ring. Meatball checked the number but didn't answer it. Instead, he hurled the phone out the front door and onto Pleasant Street.

The players sat in silence for a moment until OF McGinley spoke up, "I can play third base." Chico C Vehse flashed him a dirty look. "I'm jus' sayin," McGinley mumbled. "I'm jus' sayin." —JA

JUNE 13—CHICO'S (3–6) VS LANDSCAPE PLUS
Kelley delivers dramatic walk off single in final at-bat as Chico's Bail Bonds outlast Landscape Plus 4–3 in BOPARC thriller. In typical Chico fashion, the Bonders dug themselves in an early 3–0 hole with play described by Liberatore Field spectators as "a laughable comedy of errors and a hilarious highlight film of softball blunders and bloopers." "The Bondsmen suck! I've never seen softball play this awful."

For five innings, Chico's could do nothing right, botching routine plays in the field and providing absolutely no punch on offense. But everything started to change as the game neared its finish. The gray overhead skies that had threatened to storm all evening started to lighten, turning to a bright and brilliant creamsicle orange color as the sun began to set on Landscape Plus.

Suddenly, the difficult plays became routine—catcher McGinley backing up an errant throw from the outfield and gunning a runner down at third base, shortstop Antonini ranging far to his left, diving and catching a ball behind second base to end a rally, pitcher Koury hurling several strong innings late in the game to keep Chico's within striking distance, and outfielder Wells making a tremendous catch in shallow right center field to end the Landscape Plus' last at-bat.

Oft-injured Chico legend and slugger Ravi Shibley led off the bottom of the seventh and final inning for Chico's with a smash single to right field. In a brilliant tactical move by Chico management, an ineffective Porterfield, who has been mired in a four-game slump, was replaced by pinch hitter Raj 'the Bombay-bino' Chandran who rapped a solid base hit to centerfield, sending Shibley, the game's tying run, to third base. Next up, 3B Meatball banged a hard single between third and shortstop, plating Shibley to tie the game as a speedy Raj hustled all the way from first to third, sliding into the base in a cloud of dust just before the throw. The stage was set. Chico's would not lose. They knew it. Landscape Plus knew it. And the Liberatore Field crowd knew it. On the first pitch, leftfielder Sean Kelley smacked a line drive single over the shortstop's head, easily scoring Raj from third base.

"Chico's wins! Chico's wins! I don't believe it! Chico's wins!" The field's public address announcer bellowed over the roar of the dozens of loud and screaming Bonder fans who now believed in a season that wasn't ending but just getting started.—JA

JUNE 20—CHICO'S (3–7) VS MYLAN CRUSH & CHICO'S (3–8) VS CITY NEON
A depleted Chico's squad drops both games of a doubleheader in BOPARC softball action, succumbing to Mylan Crush 9–6 in the opener and falling to City Neon 16–6 in the nightcap.

As the dejected and exhausted Chico team players retreated to the dugout, team spiritual leader and left centerfielder Clayton Neal spoke up, "Chico's has lost a lot of games these past several seasons, but boys, that there was two 'hard-earned' losses. We earned those."

The Chico players took little comfort in Neal's encouraging but somewhat confusing message as they knew the toughest stretch of the long season was upon them—four games in three days in the upcoming week. Concerned about the team's endurance and stamina, Chico management herded the players on a bus and took them to 123 Pleasant Street for their nightly vitamin B-12 injections and linseed oil massages. As the players sipped on the murky concoction of one part fruit nectar, one part West Virginia pond water, and one part rye whiskey, a recipe believed to rejuvenate the soul, team doctors applied ice and DMSO to the players' aching joints and muscles. Rest up Chico, rest up.—JA

JUNE 27–CHICO'S (3–9) VS MORGANTOWN SURGICAL & CHICO'S (3–10) VS SUSTAIN U

Chico's Bail Bonds wait for miracle as they lose both games of a doubleheader for the second week in a row. In typical Chico fashion, the Bonders fell behind early in game 1 with a listless performance, swinging at bad pitches and struggling to toss strikes to a patient Morgantown Surgical team. The Bonders were held to two hits in the 11–1 opener and did not score their lone run until the last inning when SS Antonini drove in LCF Neal from first base with a two-out double.

During the break between games, injured OF Porterfield told of a story of a statue of the Mother Mary that resided in a tiny Italian town. The residents of the town swore that real tears would flow from the eyes of the statue on special occasions—a forecast for a miracle to occur somewhere in the world (e.g., the crippled would walk, the blind would see, a once slow-footed Chico would suddenly turn fast, etc…). As Porterfield told the story of the crying statue to the Chico players, 1B Leatherman discovered an old 2002 Tim Nelms Chico baseball card in the equipment bag and studied the eyes of Nelms' odd and distant gaze in the photo. (Note. Nelms was not present at the game as he was in the middle of a nude bicycle ride across central Europe.)

Searching for inspiration in game 2, the Chico's players taped Nelms' card to the team bench. A more relaxed and confident Chico squad got out to an early lead in the second game that they maintained until the last inning over a much younger Sustain U team. The Bonders were more selective at the plate, banging out base hit after base hit in the first several innings. The defense also improved in the nightcap. 2B Batchelor covered the entire area behind the infield from the first base line to left center field, making a diving, rolling spectacular catch in short right field in the first inning—maybe the catch of the year. Leading 7–5 late in the game, relief pitcher Jeff Ryan checked the Tim Nelms baseball card. It was moist.

"I think this card's been crying!" Ryan exclaimed. "It's a miracle! No way we lose this one!"

RCF Wells bravely confessed, "No, no, sorry, guys. I spilled my beer on it."

The team players looked to Wells who sheepishly shrugged and drained what was left of his can of Black Label. In the top half of the last inning, Sustain U busted the game wide open, plating nine runs and breaking the spirit of the revived Chico players. There would be no miracle for the Bondsmen as they were quietly retired in order in the bottom half of the final inning.

As Leatherman returned the Tim Nelms card to the equipment bag, he noticed something odd—the eyes on the card were glistening. There are ten games left. Chico's could still finish with a winning record. All they needed was a miracle. Leatherman swears, but can't prove it, that he saw a lone tear roll from Nelms' eye before putting the card away. Don't give up Chico's.—JA

JUNE 28–CHICO'S (3–11) VS WESTOVER VFD

Bonders stunned in BOPARC classic by arch rival. A walk-off single by Westover VFD scored the winning run in the bottom half of the last inning to defeat Chico's 17–16 in a thriller. Despite a patch work line-up depleted by injury, incarceration, and mental illness, the Bonders played their best game of the year, banging out 25 hits and scoring 16 runs. It was a back-and-forth affair with multiple lead changes. Both teams knew the game would be decided in the final inning.

Every Chico contributed—from the return of road weary team veteran Nelms who manned first base to the dashing and daring outfield play of Vehse to the hitting and base running of Raj (who has found his hitting stroke) to solid pitching of Koury to the base-running exploits of a banged-up and injured Krovich (who looked like he had scored what would have been the winning run in the top half of the last inning to put the Bondsmen up by three).

As has been the case all season, the Bonders couldn't hold the lead and came up short. A tired Chico team has little time to lick their wounds as they return to action at Mylan Park with another late-night game the next evening—their fourth in three nights. Maybe Chico's bats have finally come alive.—JA

AUGUST 1—CHICO'S (4–17) VS BLUE HORIZON Chico's inspire BOPARC League doormat but can't inspire self in disappointing 13–5 loss in softball action. The color orange brought out the best in the slumping last place Blue Horizon (2–18) team that won for only the 2nd time on the season. Blue Horizon played wall ball, battering the wounded Bonders with multiple deep shots to the fences of Liberatore Field. Chico's, unable to sustain rallies early in the game, had no offensive answers, falling out of contention by the 5th inning. It was a bitter pill to swallow for a confident Chico squad, juiced on vodka and hope.

The game was delayed briefly in the 4th as inactive relief pitcher Jeff Ryan called timeout while coaching 1st base. Confused BOPARC umpires shrugged as Ryan, who was nursing a sprained back, dashed form the field to the parking lot. The distant sound of an ice cream truck had caught Ryan's attention. After the short delay, Ryan returned to the coaching box at 1st, holding a cherry-lime Italian ice.

Ryan was quick to point out, "This is good but not nearly as good as what I get at Rita's in Mount Morris."—JA

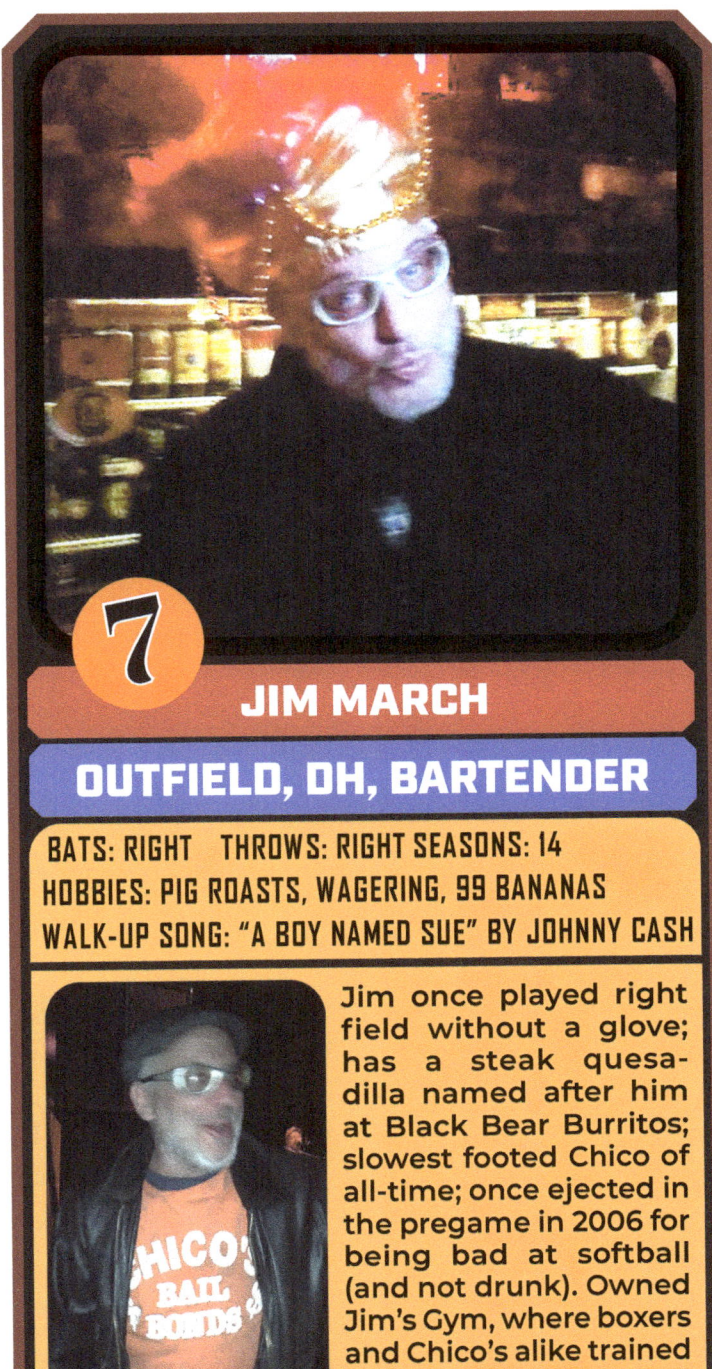

7

JIM MARCH

OUTFIELD, DH, BARTENDER

BATS: RIGHT   THROWS: RIGHT SEASONS: 14
HOBBIES: PIG ROASTS, WAGERING, 99 BANANAS
WALK-UP SONG: "A BOY NAMED SUE" BY JOHNNY CASH

Jim once played right field without a glove; has a steak quesadilla named after him at Black Bear Burritos; slowest footed Chico of all-time; once ejected in the pregame in 2006 for being bad at softball (and not drunk). Owned Jim's Gym, where boxers and Chico's alike trained for glory.

Slowdown Showdown in Motown, April–July 2012

Before Jim March joined Chico's Bail Bonds softball team, he was a part-time bartender at 123 Pleasant Street. He owned a boxing gym that was located behind Black Bear Burritos across from 123. Several members of Chico's regularly worked out at his boxing gym, including Chad Koury, Mac McGinley, Tim Nelms, Tom Batchelor, Jim Manilla, among others. Jim started tending the lower bar at 123 on Tuesdays and would show the most famous matches throughout the history of boxing that he had recorded on VCR tapes. Tuesday nights in the lower bar were dubbed Boxing Nights with Jim. Later, Jim would start working on Fridays, opening the 123 lower bar at 6 PM. This weekly event (and it was certainly an event) would become what was called Supper Club. There was only one rule at Supper Club—no food. Jim would dispense so many Jameson whiskey shots during the three hours of Supper Club each Friday that management starting hiding the bottles from him. Many of us regular attendees of Supper Club are lucky to still be alive.

Chico outfielder Raj Chandran was a regular at Supper Club, and for many months every time he walked through the door, Jim would point at him and loudly proclaim, "Hey, it's the slowest Chico! I'm faster than that guy!" No one was sure where Jim got the idea of why he though Raj was slowest Chico at that time. Did you ever see Brian Porterfield run the bases? How about Jeff Ryan? And what about Jim March? Did you ever see him run the bases?

In the batter's box after hitting the ball, Jim looked like a Looney Tunes cartoon character trying to run. For a short moment, his legs would be furiously moving like a blur, windmilling; his arms wildly flailing in desperate determination, but the rest of his body would fail to react or even move from its spot as if anchored in the deep dust of the batter's box, like quicksand. Finally, released from this imaginary grip, his body would lurch forward, he'd violently pump his arms; his legs and feet, seemingly heavy as if wearing cement boots, would struggle to lift off the ground with each step—his stride, unsteady, as he awkwardly plodded towards first base.

Finally, one Supper Club Friday, after a few shots of whiskey and being called the slowest Chico one too many times, Raj challenged Jim to a foot race, "Any place, any time, Jim! You pick the location, the day and time. I don't care where or when! I will show up, and I beat you!"

Jim chose the steady incline of Moreland Street, situated behind Jim Gym's, as the location. He picked 7 PM on Friday, July 1 during Supper Club. He showed up in his Chico softball jersey and sneakers. No one had ever seen him wear sneakers before. Raj showed up wearing a cape. The back of cape read The Bombay-bino. The rest, as they say, is history. Because on that night, Jim March proved, without a doubt, that he could outrun no one.—JA

Jim March, Raj Chandran post-race at 123

"THAT was epic! I don't know who else could draw that crowd into that alley in 100-degree heat at 7 PM! I want to thank my opponent for REMOVING HIS SKIRT before trouncing me! But I am compelled to point out that he is the ONLY person EVER that I've challenged to a race! If you see the film, you can tell why I had to learn to fight. I can't out-run ANY-BODY! That being said, and this covers a LOT of ground, THAT was hands-down THE BEST SUPPER CLUB EVER! CHICO! CHICO! CHICO!"

—Jim March, post-race interview

2013 CHICO'S HAS HOPE

2013 Chico's: (standing) Eric Ramón, Tom Batchelor, Jeff Wiles, Jon Vehse, Aaron Hawley, Brian Porterfield, Chad Koury, (kneeling) Colt Cuatro Cinco, Raj Chandran, Dave Krovich, Jim Antonini, Sean Kelley.

MAY 10–CHICO'S (1–3) VS GST Bats go limp as a spent Chico team drops both ends of twilight doubleheader. Three games in 24 hours proved too much as a worn-down Bonders' team choked away the opener 13–5 and then fell 17–2 in an ugly nightcap to a resurgent GST Softball squad. Not even the return of two Chico veteran stalwarts, pitcher Jeff "Nolan" Ryan and catcher Jon Vehse, could help maintain the positive momentum of the first two weeks of the early season. Other than the stellar defensive play of 3B Meatball and LF Kelley, the continued perfect hitting of Krovich, and the backward running of the bases by utility player Neal, there were not many positives to report on the beautiful spring night in front of hundreds of Chico fans at Liberatore Stadium. Several team members loudly voiced the need for more practice after the disappointing night. However, team management had already given the players the weekend off to celebrate Mother's Day. Yes, as hard as it is to believe, Chico's have mothers too.—JA

MAY 23—CHICO'S (1–5) VS J&J ELECTRIC Bonders buried alive in mud and left for dead, falling 30–6 (yes 30–6) to young opponent. In a steady downpour under an unforgiving midnight sky filled with whip cracks of thunder and blinding flashes of lightning, the Bondsmen drown in the muck of an unplayable Whiston Field. Chico's played no defense whatsoever, getting lambasted by a fresher and more cock-sure opponent. As advised by team management, all videotapes of an ugly 1st inning were tossed in the Monongahela River. The game was called after only 3 innings—the shortest game in Chico history. By the final inning, several Chico defenders were missing lost in a quicksand infield and swamp-like outfield. Only two Chico players made it to the 123 bar after the game–manager Krovich and catcher Neal.

"Maybe we should go look for them," mumbled Neal, sipping on his whiskey.

"No, they'll be fine," a showered Krovich answered with Chico groupies draped over each of his arms.

While still back at Whiston Field, LF Vehse spoke up, struggling in mud up to his chest, "This is how the Donner party met their fate. No one could find them. They had to eat each other to stay alive."

As starving and emaciated 1B Porterfield moaned in agony, 2B Batchelor spoke up, "I don't care how desperate I get, I ain't eatin' Porterfield!"

Game Notes: Chico reserve player Nelms did not show up for the game. He has since been reported missing, possibly drugged—last seen in the back of a beat-up flatbed truck registered to a group of Georgia pig farmers, wearing nothing but sandals, a faceless leather mask, and Viking helmet with horns on his head. The truck was headed south; Nelms's inviting bare ass was pointed north. Unsettling pig moans were heard coming from the back of the truck as it disappeared onto a nearby dirt road.—JA

JUNE 6—CHICO'S (1–8) VS BUSTER'S AUTO SALVAGE

"Hey Chico's come out for your whuppin,'" Buster's called out.

"We'll be right there," Chico's eagerly responded.

Chico's Bail Bonds shit bed and roll around in it, embarrassing themselves in 20–0 debacle while losing their 7th game in a row. The vital stats tell the whole gory story—the game lasted a brief 15 minutes, Buster's only needed 2 innings to score 20 runs and invoke the mercy rule, and, pitifully, Chico's recorded only 6 outs and sent only 12 men to the plate. And sadly, they couldn't find one soul to lick their wounds at the 123 bar after the game. At this point, a rain out would be a victory.—JA

JUNE 7–CHICO'S (1–9) VS WV NATIONAL GUARD Flawless defense and outstanding pitching were not enough as Chico's drop heartbreaker by the score of 9–5 on a cold, wet, and sloppy night to their talented and athletic opponent. Despite a continual heavy downpour, nearly unplayable field conditions, an agonizing and dispiriting 7-game losing streak, a fragile team psyche, below average male genitalia (except for Meatball), and numerous bumps, bruises, strawberries, and pulled and strained muscles, sixteen (count 'em sixteen!) eager, ready, and earnest Bondsmen showed up hungry, hoping to right a train wreck of a disappointing season that was quickly fading away. Every single Chico contributed in a positive manner from the spectacular outfield play of Kelley, Krovich, and Tuck to the steady infield contributions of Meatball, Antonini, and Batchelor to the dynamic pitcher-catcher battery of Vehse and Koury. Game highlights included a daring and dashing pop fly snag by Koury at the fence in foul territory and the 'greatest play that never happened' by 1B Porterfield—who must have hypnotized both umpires into calling an out as he neither caught the ball at first nor had his foot on the bag.

Even though the game will appear as a loss in the annals of Chico history, the Bonders walked off a sloppy and unrecognizable Liberatore Field on the gloomiest of gloomy nights with their heads held high, proud and privileged to be a Chico, in love with their teammates and numerous adoring female fans, but most importantly feeling like world champions.—JA

JUNE 20–CHICO'S (1–10) VS HARTZELL'S EXXON Chico's Bail Bonds softball team shellacked 13–1 in disappointing loss to perennial cellar dweller. There were few bright spots to report as the reeling Bonders stumble into the 2-week All-Star break, not having won a game since April. Hartzell's outhit and out fielded the Bondsmen, running them right off the Whiston Field diamond in front of a throng of disappointed (but loyal) Chico fans. Young Chico outfielders provided the only sparks of the game as RF Wiles and RCF Raj both made fine inning-ending catches. The highlight of the game was turned in by LCF Hawley who made a spectacular over-the-shoulder, leaping stab of a sharply hit liner to deep centerfield. Not only did he come down with ball, he had time to celebrate his catch with a brief dance and high five with fellow outfielder Raj while not allowing the runners on 1st and 2nd bases to advance.

As the disappointed Chico squad milled about the 123 bar after the game, a nasty odor filled the downtown Morgantown air.

"What's that awful smell?" wondered 1B Porterfield.

"That's the stench of the Chico softball's team carcass rotting on Whiston Field," a stranger wisecracked.

Before anyone could respond, 3B g threw a hard overhand right that caught the stranger between the eyes. As the stranger writhed in pain, laid out flat on the Pleasant Street sidewalk, each Chico team member stepped over him, entered the bar, and had a glorious time, drinking beers and sipping whiskey until the sun came up.

Game Notes: For the second season in a row, no Chico team member made the BOPARC Single-A League All-Star team.—JA

JULY 10–CHICO'S (1–12) VS WVU HOSPITAL

Shorthanded, Chico's Bail Bonds drop heartbreaker 4–0 to 1st place WVU Hospital in softball classic. With a patchwork line-up of only 9 players, Chico's turned in their finest defensive and pitching performances of the year, only to come up short against a stacked, but overconfident and undeserving WVU Hospital squad. Several Chico team members were asked to step out of their comfort zones and assume positions virgin to them—Hawley played first, Wiles manned second, relief pitcher Ryan caught, and Ramón anchored the spacious right field of Liberatore Stadium without the aid of a right centerfielder. Each and every Chico on hand stepped up to challenge. Pitcher Koury tossed the game of his career, only allowing 7 hits and fanning 6 WVU Hospital sluggers over 7 innings. LF Kelley and CF Tuck ran down gap shot after gap shot, killing multiple WVU Hospital rallies. 3B Meatball, SS Antonini, 2B Wiles, and 1B Hawley turned in error-free performances in the infield, highlighted by a beautiful 4–6–3 double play to end the 3rd inning. But as good as the Chico defense played, the Bonders offense was exponentially worse. Words like weak, feeble, inept, and limp are much too kind in describing the Bonders offensive output. Down to their last out as an angry, black summer sky rolled over Liberatore Field, the Chico squad had accepted their fate. Victory would not come on this night. But there is another game in less than 24 hours. And because of that, Chico has hope.—JA

JULY 17–CHICO'S (1–13) VS PIRATES A beleaguered Chico softball squad drops heartbreaker; BOPARC Director Schilling weeps; Sports media giant ESPN exploits the Bonder's misery. Chico's Bail Bonds does everything right but comes up inches short, losing their 11th game in a row as they fall to a young, energetic but spoiled and pouty Pirates teams 5–4 in softball thriller in front of a national ESPN televised audience.

The Bonders turned in their 2nd great defensive and pitching performance in a row. Pitcher Koury hurled another gem, scattering just 6 hits and keeping the opposing batters off balance all night. Emotional leader and 2B Batchelor was brilliant, making rally-killing plays in the field every single inning and running the bases like a possessed, but focused demon. Infielders Porterfield 1B, Antonini SS, and Meatball 3B played flawlessly turning two 'ESPN web gem quality' double plays early in the game. Catcher Vehse put up a barricade around home plate that dwarfed both the Berlin Wall and the Great Wall of China combined. Chico offensive production was provided by outfielders Wiles, Kelley, Krovich, and Hawley. RF Ramón and Raj extended the game with dramatic clutch hits in the last inning to pull the Bonders within 1 run of the Pirates. But the game ended with the bases full of orange, two outs, two strikes, and no fouls to give, Krovich smashed a line drive down the 1st base line. The ball kicked up dirt. The Bondsmen saw white chalk fly, rushing onto to the field and hoisting Krovich onto their shoulders.

> **"THIS MIGHT HAVE BEEN THE GREATEST SOFTBALL GAME I HAVE EVER WITNESSED IN THE 75 YEARS OF BOPARC SOFTBALL...YOU GUYS SHOULD BE PROUD OF YOURSELVES"**

The near-sighted and surely hungover home plate umpire saw only brown dust, no white, "Foul! The Batter's out!"

As The Pirates team celebrated, BOPARC Director Gordon Schilling rushed over to the dejected Bonders' team bench.

"This might have been the greatest softball game I have ever witnessed in the 75 years of BOPARC softball," he proclaimed, wiping tears from his eyes. "You guys should be proud of yourselves."[1]

Unfortunately, the director's kind words did nothing to soothe the wounds of another Chico loss in a long and disappointing season—for pride alone does not win softball games. There are no are no moral victories. Of little consolation, ESPN dubbed the contest 'an instant classic' and showed a replay of the game on their ESPN Classic channel continually for 24 hours.

As the night turned to morning, Chico team members, as guest of Meatball (now calling himself Balle de Carne), gathered around a 16" black and white TV at the Capri Massage and Health Spa located in a nondescript motel on the Mileground next to the Blue Parrot Steak and Cabaret joint. Despite watching the replay of the entire game over and over, the result was always the same— 'foul ball' and another Chico loss.

Game Notes: An 'official Chad Koury fan club' made their 1st appearance of the year. The beautiful young ladies of the fan club greatly aided pitcher Koury as they dusted off his skinny jeans and held and protected his 'man purse' during the game. They also answered all his incoming calls from each of the four mobile phones that he always carried.—JA

JULY 18–CHICO'S (1–14) VS CARTOONS Bondsmen bravely battle top flight teams but wilt in the heat and humidity in softball doubleheader action. It was the same disappointing story of a season that just gets longer and longer- see Chico's pitch well;

---

1 This is untrue. This quote was never uttered by BOPARC League Director Shilling.

see Chico's play flawless defense; see Chico's fail with the bats in key situations. The Bonders came up short both games, falling to a bunch of unoriginal, macho pricks. Despite the 13-game losing streak, Chico team members celebrated late into the night as if they had won both games. Because in the end, the final score of each game and the team record at the end of the season doesn't really matter. I would rather be a Chico on a last place team than a Cartoon on a 1st place team. As their opponent gloated and celebrated with their cans of Bud Light and Sprite, their girlfriends, wives, and significant others eyes blazed with excitement, knowing that their oversized vaginas would be later filled that night with sweaty penises the size of Rice Crispies

Game Notes: The results of an MRI on 1B Porterfield's throwing arm after the game revealed significant ligament damage. Unable to foot the bill for Tommy John surgery, Chico team management has offered to pay for Elton John surgery (don't ask) or Olivia Newton-John surgery. Porterfield opted for Olivia Newton-John surgery[2] which amounted to the purchase of an old trunk of aerobics VCR tapes, several soiled unitards, headbands, and wool leggings for $199.—JA

JULY 25–CHICO'S (1–15) VS ALPHA DAWGZ
Bonders dominate pre-game festivities but lose when it mattered (for the 14th time in a row), falling 15–7. An eager, enthusiastic, extremely drunk, mostly ineffective, somewhat inefficient, erratic, and maybe psychotic Bonders team arrived at Liberatore Stadium in high spirits—very high spirits, only to underachieve on defense and squander several early offensive chances with runners in scoring position. Not one single Chico player stood out.

BOPARC umpire Casteel observed, "the drunk ones played a little better than the sober ones, but not that much better."

Game MVP honors were unanimous, going to Chico bartender Donnie Duppee at the 123 bar.

---

2 What is the relationship between the Chico Bail Bonds softball team and the infamous Olivia Newton-John?

Chico's Bail Bonds is a raggedy collection of middle-aged men from all walks of life whose love for softball is only eclipsed by their thirst for cheap beer, shots of Irish whiskey, and jukebox music.

Brian Porterfield is the long time but fragile Chico outfielder and first baseman who was often hurt.

Olivia Newton-John was an Australian singer who had numerous number one hit songs, including "Let's Get Physical" and "You're the One That I Want". She skyrocketed to fame after playing opposite to John Travolta in the movie adaption of the musical, *Grease*.

Elton John is a British singer, pianist, and composer. The flamboyant performer and glam rock legend has sold over 300 million records worldwide. His hit songs have included "Rocket Man", "Goodbye Yellow Brick Road", "Daniel", and "Candle in the Wind".

Tommy John was a Major League baseball pitcher for 26 seasons for several teams, including the New York Yankees and Los Angeles Dodgers. He was a four-time All-Star and won an incredible 288 games which ranks 7th all-time among left-handed pitchers. He was often referred to as The Bionic Man. He is most known for a surgery that was performed on his arm to prolong his career, now called Tommy John Surgery. He won 164 games after the surgery was performed.

Tommy John Surgery is a surgical graft procedure where a damaged ligament in the elbow of a pitcher's arm is replaced with either a lightly used tendon from elsewhere in the body or from a deceased organ donor. It was first performed by Los Angeles surgeon, Frank Jobe. One in seven pitchers in the Major Leagues have received the surgery since 2012.

Game Notes: The plans for Wiles to bring Preston County moonshine for next week's games have been finalized.—JA

JULY 30–CHICO'S (1–16) VS COOMBS FARM

Bonders knocked out and loaded as they fall in dismal softball laugher 12–3 to a stacked opponent. In a front of a capacity crowd on the synthetic orange pasture of Mylan Park, the Bonders limp bats stayed limp, losing for an unprecedented and unheard-of 15th time in a row. Chico sympathizers continue to talk only about the positive aspects of the Bondsmen play—the great infield defense, the solid pitching, and good team chemistry. They optimistically point out that the 'glass is half full' and not 'half empty' as Chico's play has vastly improved as the season has progressed. But as the dejected team members retreated to the 123 bar after the game and bunkered down for a long, somber evening of beer and whiskey in the company of friends and supporters, the players knew that the 'glass was not half full' or even 'half empty'. It was completely empty as the nightmare of a season dragged on. With a makeshift line-up decimated by injuries and vacations, the Bonders needed to regroup and regroup fast as they return to Mylan Park in less than 24 hours. Starving for a victory and searching for their dignity as the season faded away, the Bonders have only three more chances to end a losing streak that started in late April.

Game Notes: Chico's 1B Porterfield's Olivia Newton-John surgery on his throwing arm was a great success. He was able to throw a ball all the way from first base to third base with only two bounces.—JA

JULY 31–CHICO'S (2–16) VS TIRE LADY

Drought ends as Vehse drives in Batchelor with dramatic walk-off single in the last inning to win by score of 7–6. The unprecedented 15-game losing streak is OVER! Under a drizzly overcast sky on the slick synthetic turf of Mylan Park, Chico's Bail Bonds would not be denied, clawing for every out on defense and busting their asses run-

ning the bases even on the most routine ground balls. The Bonders held an early five-run lead only to see Tire Lady fight back and tie the game in the fifth. With the game still tied at 6 with one out in the bottom half of the last inning with 2B Batchelor on second, catcher Vehse lined a hard shot to center. Batchelor easily scampered home like a wolfman, howling and growling the whole way from second to home. As Batchelor scored, all hell broke out at Mylan Park as ecstatic team members piled on top of each other and doused themselves with cheap beer. Chico fans, significant others, and sympathizers dropped to their knees and wept uncontrollably. BOPARC umpires canceled the remaining three games that were to be played that night on Mylan Field.

The heroes for the game were many. Chad 'Skinny Jeans' Koury pitched a gem, striking out five opponents and walking none as well as delivering a key two-out run scoring triple in the 3rd. Newcomer Terry Ferret played a flawless left center field, snagging three game-saving deep fly balls at the fence late in the game. 1B Hawley stabbed an errant throw to first while tagging the runner at the same time to end an inning and save a run. 2B Batchelor wowed the Mylan Park crowd with his crazy, aggressive base-running exploits.

Game Notes: Breaking out a new pair of Versace skinny jeans for the game, fashion-plate Koury tried to stop at 2nd on his big hit, but his jeans (thankfully) kept on running, dragging his ass all the way to 3rd base. 1B Porterfield sat out the game, suffering from complications of his recent Olivia Newton-John surgery. Chico team doctors reported significant chaffing in his thigh and groin area caused by an orange unitard that the surgeon requires him wear for workouts and games. And finally, it has been nearly five hours since the game ended and nobody has seen Meatball.—JA

AUGUST 1–CHICO'S (2–17) VS THE JESTERS On moonshine night, Bonders fail to leave the celebration of the previous night's victory at the 123 bar. Chico's started slow and fell 13–5 in a dismal performance against the world's fattest, slowest, and ugliest softball team of all time. A hungover and despondent Bonders team had nothing, nothing at all—offensively or defensively for the first four innings. By the time the Bondsmen gloves and bats awoke, it was too late. The hole was too deep as the Bonders scratched to keep the game alive for the full seven innings. With the season over and a long offseason looming with likely hard

personnel decisions to be made, the Chico players retreated to the 123 bar, disappointed in themselves and not too optimistic about the future of the team. With a spot in the BOPARC playoffs out of the question, the few Chico players (Porterfield, Krovich, Antonini, Hawley, Ryan, and Hindal) who remained at the bar at last call had over-medicated themselves with whiskey, cheap beer, and shots of Yukon Jack (Ryan), desperately looking for hope—anything. But nothing could soothe the pain of another Chico loss and another long season of missed opportunities and unfilled dreams. And the hangover was worse. It lasted months.—JA

2014 Chico's : (standing) Brieve Morrison (Hooligan), Chad Koury, Walt Sarkees, Terry Ferrett, Ethan Wells, Aaron Hawley, Tyler Grady, Brian Porterfield, Jeff Wiles, Jeff Ryan, Andy Tuck, Tom Batchelor, Jeff Goodwin, Dave Becker, Monkey Clifton (Hooligan), (kneeling) Tom Moore, Dave Krovich, Mack McGinley, Eric Ramón, Meatball, LJ Guiliani, Jim Antonini, Jon Vehse, Candice McLaughlin (Hooligan)

MAY 8 CHICO'S (0-2) VS HARTSELL'S EXXON Opening night spells heartbreak as Chico's Bail Bonds drops both ends of a doubleheader in the final inning of each game. Despite scoring 38 runs and banging out a Chico doubleheader record of 64 hits in the two games, the Bonders start the season with two gut-wrenching losses. Chico's roared out of the gate in the opener against an overrated and overweight Hartsell's Exxon on the most beautiful of spring nights with bats a-blazing. Everybody hit—top, middle, and bottom of the order, staking the Bondsmen to an early 7–0 lead. But it wasn't enough as Chico's failed to hold the lead and dropped the first game 22–21 with the tying and winning runs on base in the last inning.

The 2nd game was equally heartbreaking as Chico's clung to a 3-run lead in the bottom of the final inning, but couldn't hold on, giving up a walk-off single with two outs and falling 18–17. There were so many great plays from the night—OF Tuck's two majestic long fly balls off the short Liberatore right field fence for a triple and an inside-the-park home run, several diving catches by Kelley in left, Becker's scoops at first in game 2, Meatball's leaping stabs of liners at third, a beautiful relay from Kelley to Antonini to Neal at home to prevent a run in the second game, a crucial game-ending acrobatic catch by Ramón in right center, the aggressive and productive base running of Batchelor, Wiles, and McGinley, the clutch hitting of Porterfield, Koury, Wiles, Hawley... The Bonders begins the season, like most seasons, 0–2, but this 0–2 FEELS different. Unlike previous softball summers of futility and an inescapable and inglorious past, this Chico team IS different—this Chico team will hit; this Chico team will run; this Chico team will pitch; this Chico team will not give up; but most importantly, this Chico team is going to win...a lot of games this season.

Game Notes: 18 different Chico's participated in tonight's opener—SS Antonini, 3B Meatball, 2B Batchelor, 1B Porterfield, LF Kelley, LCF Tuck, RCF-1B Becker, RF Hawley, RCF Wiles, RCF-AH Ramón, RF Ryan, C Vehse, C Neal, P Koury, AH Moore, AH McGinley, and LJ Guiliani.

Chico's welcomed two new players to the 2014 squad, Dave "the Tactical Beard" Becker and Tom Moore who all made positive contributions in tonight's games.—JA

MAY 15 CHICO'S (0-3) VS MORGANTOWN SURGICAL

Early lead not enough for the Bonders as they fall 20–10 at Whiston Field. Spirits were high as a confident and tipsy

Chico team stormed to an early 7-run 2nd inning lead on a beautiful spring night under a brilliant orange full moon. As the game sped along, it became apparent to the scores of vocal Chico supporters in attendance that the Bondsmen were no match for their more talented and physically imposing opponent. Despite a nearly flawless defense performance in the field by the Bonders, Morgantown Surgical bashed multiple line-drives and moonshots deep into the gaps of the Chico outfield and used their superior speed to run away to an easy victory. Second year Chico's, Hawley and Wiles, as well as Koury and Ramón, continued to swing hot bats. New acquisition Becker has provided a much-needed spark on the bases and at the plate for the aging Chico squad. The Bonders were not helped by the careless and boozy base running of Porterfield that killed a rally early in the game.

Manager Krovich yelled out to the red-faced first baseman who had just been picked off 2nd base, "What were you doing?!"

Porterfield replied, "That's what happens when you drink for six straight hours before the game."

The losing continues as the Bonders have now dropped an unbelievable 45 out of their last 49 games dating back over 2 years to the 2012 season. It won't be an easy trend to reverse as the BOPARC A league teams are getting younger, faster, and bolder.

Game Notes: After pulling his groin in the 1st inning, C Vehse was faced with a decision—go on the 60-day disabled list and miss the 1st two months of the season or take a ride with 3B Meatball to an undisclosed location in Point Marion to visit a "friend." Vehse took the ride. He will be available to play next week—another Chico miracle.—JA

MAY 22 CHICO'S (1-12) VS HONEST ABE'S Battered, bruised, and busted, Chico's battle to split doubleheader. Before an overflow partisan Chico crowd, the Bondsmen picked up their 1st win of the season in the night cap in dramatic fashion. In the opener, the Bonders battled for 7 hard fought innings. But it wasn't enough as they fell 9–2 in an uneven performance, punctuated by weak bats, pitches out of the strike zone, no energy, and poor base running (sponsored by the 'Brian Porterfield Institute of Base Running and Hopeful Decisions').

> **"I'M NOT A HERO. FIREMEN AND POLICEMEN ARE HEROES. I'M JUST A SOFTBALL PLAYER."**
> **—DAVE BECKER**

Chico players regrouped for game 2 against their dreaded rival. With a make-shift, line-up, the Bonders stayed even with Abe until the last inning. With their backs against the wall and down to their last out and losing by one run, Chico veteran 3B Meatball tied the game with a hard line drive between short and third, bringing home RF-Ramón from 2nd base. New acquisition and fan favorite, Becker then turned hero, winning it with a walk-off deep drive that disappeared in the heavy dampness of the spring night air and plating speedster Terry Ferrett from 2nd.

A post-game reporter asked Becker, "How does it feel to be a hero?"

The modest Becker responded, "I'm not a hero. Firemen and policemen are heroes. I'm just a softball player."

Game Notes: The Bondsmen are not aging well as injuries mount. Multiple Chico players (Antonini: broken finger, McGinley: pulled hamstring and gimpy arm, Vehse- flu-like symptoms, Jeff Ryan- unusual curiosities, Porterfield- high blood alcohol level, Neal: armpit surgery) were faced with a decision—go on the disabled list and miss the next two crucial weeks of the young season or take a ride with Meatball to an undisclosed location in Point Marion to visit a "friend." All injured/disabled Chico's took a ride with Meatball and all will be available for the next game except for Ryan—he has moved in with Meatball's "friend" at the undisclosed location in Point Marion.—JA

JULY 3 CHICO'S (2-6) VS CHEAT LAKE ROYALS Fisticuffs mar inspired Chico performance (and Krovich's birthday celebration) as the Bonders tussle with Cheat Lake Royals in game shortened by protested umpire decision. Playing like the world would end tomorrow, Chico's battled their asses off in the field, at the plate, and on the bases against their 1st place prima-donna opponent. In front of a raucous, vocal, and highly partisan Chico fan following at an overflowing Liberatore Field, the Bonders took an 11–9 nail biter into the bottom of the 6th when all hell broke loose. After a close play at 2nd base, Chico 2B Batchelor got tangled up with a cocky and

overly aggressive Royal base runner. Tempers flared, pushes were exchanged, punches flew, and benches cleared. In a knee jerk reaction, Batchelor and the base runner were ejected and the game was prematurely called and awarded to the Royals.

Stunned Chico players pleaded with the umps to continue but to no avail, leading to an official protest of the game's shortened result with BOPARC officials. As the Royals gloated and celebrated with their cans of Pepsi and boxes of Juicy Juice, their young girlfriends' eyes blazed with excitement, knowing that their oversized and rotting vaginas would soon be filled with sweaty, dusty victory penises. But in reality (overheard from the Royals parking lot post-game):

"I thought it'd be bigger."

"But baby, I had three triples tonight."

"I was REALLY hoping it would be bigger."

"Didn't you see me stretch that single into a triple?"

"What's a triple?"

"I'm the best player in BOPARC Single A softball EVER, see my baseball pants and eye black?"

"I thought that Chico 1B was kind of cute. I hear he plays guitar."

In the meantime with vuvuzelas blaring, Chico players and Hooligans[1] celebrated the night away—puffing cigars, dancing on rooftops, swimming with the sharks in the Mon River, and pissing on walls of faceless downtown establishments that nobody ever goes to—all before setting the whole damn town on fire. Happy Birthday, Krovich! I'd rather be a Chico on a last place team than to be a Cheat Lake Royal. CHICO!—JA

BREAKING NEWS: July 6. After 72 hours of witness testimonies, artist renderings, and actor reenactments of the Chico–Cheat Lake Royal softball incident, it is now official- Chico's Bail Bonds has been declared the WINNER by BOPARC officials in their protested contest against the Royals.—JA

---

1 Hooligans. The unofficial fan club of Chico's Bail Bonds was started by Brieve Morrison, Candice McLaughlin, and Monkey Clifton (who would later play one season for Chico's). They wore bright orange jerseys and relentlessly blew orange vuvuzelas from the first pitch to the last pitch of a game. They may be most responsible for the bench-clearing brawl that occurred between Chico's and the Cheat Lake Royals on July 3, 2014 with their constant heckling of the overly sensitive young Royal players.

JULY 9 CHICO'S (2-10) VS CHEAT MOUNTAIN BANK Leading the whole game, Chico's fall 9–7 in last inning of softball thriller. Seven innings were one too many for a spirited but spent Chico squad that battled the gentlemanly and stellar unit from Cheat Mountain Bank. Holding the lead for the first six innings of the game, the Bonders squandered a 2-run advantage in the last frame as the Bankers brought out the lumber, delivering multiple deep, majestic moon shots over the heads and just out of reach of the Chico outfielders to seize control of the nail biter. The Bondsmen welcomed back pitcher Koury who hurled a gem, keeping the Cheat Mountain batters off balance all night. Also, it was good to see Chico hall-of-famer and fan favorite Guiliani admirably fill in at second base. The Bondsmen outfield was superb: LF Kelley, LCF Tuck, RCF Becker, and RF Wiles played flawlessly in defense. Despite the loss, Chico team members can hold their heads high. Sometimes defeat can be just as satisfying as victory. Every single Chico team member delivered a hit.

Game Notes: Chico's thank all their fans, especially the Hooligans, for their support. No other team in BOPARC softball history has such a rabid and loyal fan following.—JA

STATS, July 9, 2014 CHICO'S vs. CHEAT MOUNTAIN BANK				
CHICO	**AB**	**Runs**	**Hits**	**RBI**
Koury-P	3	1	2	0
Kelley-LF	4	1	2	1
Becker-RCF	4	1	1	1
Tuck-LCF	3	1	1	1
McGinley-C	3	2	2	2
Antonini-SS	3	1	3	1
Hawley-1B	3	0	2	1
Meatball-3B	3	0	1	0
Guiliani-2B	3	0	1	0
Vehse-DH	3	0	2	0
Ramon-DH	2	0	1	0
Ferrett-DH	1	0	1	0
Wiles-RF	3	0	1	0

JULY 10 CHICO'S (3-10) VS WESTOVER VFD Becker's walk-off home run blast blows out Westover VFD's fire in BOPARC laugher. Like a machine, the Bondsmen unmercifully rolled over their inadequate and inept cross-town firemen rivals 18–8 in convincing fashion. Chico's dominated the game from start to finish with a mix of stellar defense, timely hitting, and dashing base running. The Chico infield played their best game of the year in the field, led by the 3B Meatball, SS Antonini[2], and the spectacular return of 2B Batchelor. RCF Ferrett delivered three key line drive singles to right field to start multiple rallies. LCF Becker put VFD out of their misery with a rocket shot off the left field fence, plating an orange carousel of Chico base runners and giving the Bonders the 10-run win. An epic celebration followed as jubilant Chico team members marched down Pleasant Street lined on each side with adoring fans behind a parade led by blaring trumpets and exploding fireworks. AN ORANGE PHOENIX RISES…—JA

2 SS Antonini and 3B Meatball. Jim and Meatball first met in 1972 when they were eight years old while playing for the Kiwanis little league team in Suncrest. They would play together as SS and 3B for five years in baseball and later would play the same exact positions for another twenty years on the Chico's softball team. During their first game together as little leaguers, Meatball hustled for a misplayed batted ball from his position at third base all the way to the right field fence. He relayed the ball to Antonini in the infield who then threw the batter out at home plate attempting an inside-the-park home run for the final out of the game. Amazed by Meatball's hustle, the Kiwanis coach, Snake Fragale, loudly proclaimed, "If I had nine Meatballs on this team, we would never lose a game!"

JULY 17 CHICO'S (3-11) VS GST Bonders ambushed by underrated opponent, falling 18–7 in softball action. After winning two of their last three games, an optimistic but ill-prepared Bonders team crashed to earth, embarrassed by a hungrier and more desperate last place GST team. All of the positive energy that the Chico team had built up in the last two weeks flew out the window as the Bondsmen dug themselves an early grave that was too deep to crawl out from. Multiple, overconfident Chico team members had to reel in their week-long victory penises, knowing they wouldn't be adored or paraded down Pleasant Street on this night.

Game Notes: A Whiston Field attendance record was set: 474 people (mostly Chico supporters) officially attended the game.—JA

JULY 24 CHICO'S (4-11) VS MOUNTAINEER YOUNG LIFE Bonders mathematically eliminated from playoffs after disappointing 13–4 loss. A damaged Chico squad, so optimistic just a few short weeks ago, will fail to make the BOPARC softball postseason for the 5th straight year. On the most beautiful of summer nights, the Bonders started strong but faded fast, like a bloated, sinking luxury liner full of pasty white New England tourists. Too slow, too tired, and too gray. Chico's wilted under the fast-paced pressure of their younger and more energetic foe.

Bondsmen catcher Vehse piped up in the somber, but hardly sober, post-game Chico gathering, "I have bad habits that lasted longer than those guys have been alive!"

Armed with an orchestra of orange vuvuzelas, the faithful Chico Hooligans blew out their lungs over seven hard fought innings, trying to spur their beloved softball team to glory. In the end, the somber and monotone blasts from the plastic horns were not the sounds of victory but, unfortunately, the sad and painful drone of a long, slow Chico death.—JA

2015 NIGHTMARE AT WHITE PARK

APRIL 30—CHICO'S (0–1) VS KEGLER'S & CHICO'S (0–2) VS TANNER'S TAVERN Hope and optimism turn reality as Chico's Bail Bonds can't shake offseason rust, dropping both ends of an opening night doubleheader. Looking slow, tired, and old in the 1st game, the Bonders couldn't keep pace with the younger, fitter outfit from Kegler's, getting embarrassed 17–2 in five quick innings. Chico 1st game highlights were minimal—Hawley looked sharp at 3B filling in for incarcerated Bonder veteran Meatball, 1B Porterfield (who now wants to be called POWERFIELD) was a perfect 3 for 3 at the plate, and SS Antonini knocked a ball off the left field fence (helped by the fifty pounds added over the winter) but he was thrown out at third trying to stretch the hit into a triple (not helped by the fifty pounds added over the winter).

To commemorate the winless season, Chico outfielder Dave Becker constructed a trophy after the last game that he dubbed the Olivia Newton-John Trophy. Since August 2015, the trophy has been showcased on a shelf behind the bar at 123 Pleasant Street as a constant reminder of that forgettable season.—JA

However, a different Chico team showed up for game 2. The Bonders gallantly battled a hearty, well-fed Tanner's Tavern team, falling in the last inning 15–13 with the winning run on base. The raging bull, 2B Tom Batchelor, was in mid-season form, creating havoc on the base paths. Newcomer Monkey Clifton flashed speed not seen from a Chico in years, wearing his patented, specially fitted 'fast pants' and beating out three infield singles. OF Andy Tuck made the catch of the young season, running over 60 yards to track down a deep shot to left centerfield and killing a Tanner's rally. Multiple Chico players, including RF Wiles, 3B Sarkees, P Koury, C Vehse, and LF Goodwin, contributed key hits in the late inning rallies to keep the Bondsmen close.

Instead of reconvening at the 123 bar for post-game beers and shots, several team players hung around the field and took batting practice late into the night. Chico's are hungry this year—hungry for a playoff spot they haven't experienced in years.

Game Notes: RCF Becker slept in his uniform the night before the game. Interestingly, April 29th, is National Zipper Day. To celebrate, relief pitcher Jeff Ryan played the entire 2nd game of the doubleheader with his zipper down.

Ryan stated, "I gave my zipper the night off. I wanted my junk to be free, to be breath the fresh crisp air of spring."

It worked as Ryan delivered a crucial game-tying 2-run double late in the game. Attempts to fluff Ryan with assorted whiskey shots after the game reportedly failed.—JA

2015 Chico's: (standing) Chad Koury, Jim Manilla, Tom Batchelor, Tyler Grady, Brian Porterfield, Jeff Goodwin, Jeff Wiles, Walt Sarkees, Aaron Hawley, Terry Ferrett, Eric Ramón, (kneeling) Monkey Clifton, Jon Vehse, Ethan Wells, Sean Kelley, Meatball, Jim Antonini

MAY 14–CHICO'S (0–4) VS WESTOVER VFD Chico's Bail Bonds gag away lead to inferior Westover VFD team in most epic softball collapse. What was supposed to be 'the Summer of Chico' is quickly turning into 'the nightmare at White Park' as the Bonders drop their 4th straight game to start the young season, falling for the 1st time in 10 years to their rival 16–6. It all went wrong in the 5th inning of a tied game, partially due to an incompetent umpire's flawed interpretation of the rule book regarding a VFD runner leaving 2nd base too soon after a fly out. What should have been the final out of the inning turned into a 2-out, 9-run, game-clinching VFD rally. It also didn't help that the umpire's strike zone was squeezed smaller than Tom Brady's one deflated testicle, leaving Chico's pitcher Koury no room for error. Walk after walk was exactly what the doctor ordered for an unfit VFD team full of players who were

			CHICO'S BAIL BONDS W:0 L:0 T:0	
Wed	4/29/2015	8:00pm	at KEGLERS A	LIBRATORE
Wed	4/29/2015	9:00pm	TANNERS TAVERN	LIBRATORE
Thu	5/7/2015	6:00pm	at SMITH CPA	LIBRATORE
Wed	5/13/2015	6:00pm	WESTOVER VFD	OGDEN
Thu	5/14/2015	6:00pm	at WVU HEALTHCARE A	LIBRATORE
Wed	5/20/2015	6:00pm	MYLAN A	LIBRATORE
Wed	5/20/2015	7:00pm	PICKLED NIMRODS	LIBRATORE
Wed	5/27/2015	6:00pm	at GST	OGDEN
Thu	5/28/2015	6:00pm	BUSTERS	LIBRATORE
Thu	6/4/2015	6:00pm	at C&J WELDING	LIBRATORE
Wed	6/10/2015	6:00pm	at ATOMIC GRILL	OGDEN
Thu	6/11/2015	9:00pm	GEICO GEKOS	WHISTON
Wed	6/17/2015	7:00pm	at WOLF PACK	OGDEN
Thu	6/18/2015	9:00pm	VAN BUREN BOY'S	WHISTON
Thu	6/25/2015	6:00pm	at SUMMITT SLUGGERS	LIBRATORE
Wed	7/1/2015	8:00pm	at PICKLED NIMRODS	LIBRATORE
Wed	7/1/2015	9:00pm	WEBSTER INS.	LIBRATORE
Thu	7/2/2015	9:00pm	SMITH CPA	WHISTON
Wed	7/8/2015	6:00pm	at MGT SOBER LIVING	OGDEN
Wed	7/8/2015	7:00pm	MILEGROUND MARLINS	OGDEN
Wed	7/22/2015	8:00pm	RACER TV	LIBRATORE
Thu	7/23/2015	7:00pm	at IDK	OGDEN
Wed	7/29/2015	6:00pm	KEGLERS A	OGDEN

challenged to run the bases. But what does that say about an underachieving Chico team who entered the season with such high hopes—not very much. There were bright spots for the Bonders—Sean Kelley returned from injury and was stellar at 3B in the field, 1B Hawley drove a ball to the fence to plate two early runs to give Chico's the lead, 2B Batchelor dazzled the crowd with his patented high-flying style of base running, and RCF Wiles made two very nice catches to end VFD rallies.—JA

MAY 15—CHICO'S (0–5) VS WVU HEALTHCARE Chico's Bail Bonds fail to show up in uninspired performance to remain winless. The losing continued as the Bonders were over-matched against the more superior and vital WVU Healthcare team, dropping their 5th straight game by the score of 14–2. The numbers for Chico's spelled defeat: 10 players, 4 hits, 2 runs, 6 errors, 1 sprained ankle, 3 sore arms, 2 pulled groins, 5 cans of warm beer, 1 pack of cigarettes, and a very long and lonely walk home.

Game Notes: Come to Supper Club this Friday and watch Antonini punch himself in the face because of the string of losses.—JA

MAY 27—CHICO'S (0–8) VS GST The 'imperfect' season drags on (and on and on and on). Chico's Bail Bonds drop their eight straight game to remain winless, falling 13–3 to long-time rival GST softball. The Bonders have no answers to the many questions that dogged the team before the season. Are the Chico's too old, tired, weak, unmotivated, un-athletic, or just bored? It's easy to answer a resounding 'yes' to all the questions and concerns regarding this version of the Chico's Bail Bonds. As the losses mount, the pain of losing should ease. But it doesn't. And it won't. Ever. Each loss feels much worse that the one before it. The Bondsmen

valiantly will try again tomorrow at 6:00 PM on the lush green lawn of Liberatore Field against another overrated opponent full of obvious unoriginal cocksure energy. If you see your favorite Chico wandering the streets of Morgantown tonight, please give him a hug. He needs it.—JA

MAY 28–CHICO'S (0–9) VS BUSTER'S SALVAGE & GARAGE

Chico's Bail Bonds can't finish, already mathematically eliminated from the playoffs after 9th straight loss to start season (and it's not even June yet), falling 14–3 to Busters Salvage & Garage. There are no more adjectives left to describe the losing—

"Chico's wet the bed…",

"Chico bats go limp…",

"Chico's blow wad too soon…",

"Chico's dig an early grave…",

"Chico has no answers…",

"Chico's shits the bed and rolls around in it…"

Game notes: Chico legend McGinley returned and was immediately thrown into the fire, playing a solid right centerfield. Catcher Vehse missed the game—because he was literally put under the ether by his periodontist or the periodontist's chesty assistant. Right fielder Ferrett showed up to the game on time and proudly sporting a hickey on his neck- at least one Chico is winning.—JA

JUNE 10–CHICO'S (0–11) VS ATOMIC GRILL

One day. ONE DAY! A fiery orange sky will break apart and a real rain will fall and clean the scum off the sidewalk, but until then the imperfect season goes on.

The hapless, and still winless, Chico's Bail Bonds team was embarrassed in all phases of the game by Atomic Grill 17–2 in BOPARC softball action. On a hot, humid evening before a disappointed and dwindling fan base, the damaged Bondsmen couldn't keep pace with a collection of ugly, unsanitary, foul-mouthed, revolting, but quite athletic and even a little charming collection of goons hired to represent the Atomic Grill. The contest quickly spun out of hand as the Bonders fell behind 8–1 in the 1st inning

before completely fading out of sight by the 5th inning, when the game was halted due to the pity rule. RF Vehse and LF Goodwin shined in the field, LCF Wiles gracefully slid into 2nd while legging out an early game double, and lead-off hitter and P Koury scored the two lone Chico runs.

Ironically, the Atomic Grill showed the Bondsmen no pity off the field as well, cooking up and charging the Chico players at the 123 bar at the post-game meal FULL price for their appropriately named specialty—the CHICO BURGER[1]. Uggh! But don't pity this team, Chico fans. There are 12 games left and still hope for victory.—JA

JUNE 12—CHICO'S (0–12) VS GEICO GECKOS Not since the fall of the Roman empire has a collapse been so complete. The Bonders were humiliated 20–6 by Geico Geckos in late night softball action, falling for the 12th straight game to stay winless.

Game Notes: LF Goodwin paced the Chico offense with a triple and double, C Eric Ramón blasted a late game 2-run double down the left field line, and Chico reserve Tyler 'cleats' Grady made his season debut in spectacular fashion diving for line drives in right field and terrorizing the base paths. It has been reported on Chico internet fan boards that SS Antonini punched himself so hard in the face after the team's 9th loss that he detached his retina. His status is questionable for the rest of the season.—JA

JUNE 26—CHICO'S (0–14) VS SUMMIT SLUGGERS On the stormiest of summer Thursday nights, Chico's buries themselves in mud and wait to die with no one left to dig them out. The Bonders drop their unprecedented 14th straight, bitter and 'oh so' agonizing loss to the lowest bunch of creeps that BOPARC has allowed into the softball league EVER. Still winless, Chico's embarrassed themselves 18–3 in three short innings to an overrated, overweight, and most unoriginal Summit Slugger team who didn't even soil their perfectly starched and pressed matching baseball pants in the sloppiest of playing conditions. The stench of the Chico loss lingered in the downtown air for hours after the game, reeking of rotting corpse, sulfur, defeat, and disappointment. The imperfect season drags

---

1 Chico Burger. During the infamous winless season of 2015, the Chico players were forced to spend the postgame in the upstairs bar at 123 due to an open and functioning kitchen (operated by Atomic Grill) that offered barbecue sandwiches, hamburgers, and variety of side dishes. The lower bar at 123 where all the previous postgame parties were held would not open until later in the evening that season. The best-selling menu item in the upper bar was appropriately named the Chico Burger- a ½ pound beef patty cooked on the old but perfectly seasoned grill acquired from the closed Falstaff's. It was dressed with caramelized onions, cheddar cheese, and bacon. Catcher Jon Vehse blamed the winless season on two things: (1) Chico team players were spoiled and soft due to the readily available food during the postgame; (2) teetotaling pitcher Chad Koury didn't have enough vices. Neither of these had anything to do with the fact that the 2015 version of Chico's was terrible at softball.

on—fourteen straight losses with little hope left for victory and a sad season that has mostly faded away.

A casual spectator asked longtime Chico SS Antonini post-game, "What's the problem with Chico's?"

Antonini bluntly and unapologetically replied, "We got too many guitar players in the outfield."[2]—JA

July 2–Chico's (0–16) vs Webster Insurance

The misery continues. Under a fire orange summer moon, Chico's give great effort but drop hard-fought game 14–9 to remain winless on the season. The Bondsmen were at a disadvantage having to play a group of 10 sexless and emotionless identical but physically greater automatons—same trimmed haircuts, same pressed baseball pants, perfect in every way but sadly no ability to love. The Bonders were no match on the field but superior in the game of life. In the post-game the dismay of their fanatical fan base, Chico's helped their hated rivals by hiring a team of scientists who used a 3-D printer to successfully clone 10 copies of Chico legend Timothy Nelms' penis and transplant the artificial (but fully functional) penises to the crotch areas of the asexual opposing players. It was another Chico softball miracle!

Game Notes: Chico's welcomed back Chico legend 1B-Brian Porterfield who's surgically repaired knee was held together by rubber bands and also team favorite OF-Tom Moore.

OF-Walt Sarkees delivered a big 3-run, 2-out double. Despite car trouble, Chico favorite Ethan Wells drove 36 hours in a Chico orange car just to play softball.

As the full moon disappeared and a new day dawned, SS-Jim Antonini looked to C-Vehse and traded a bottle of Jameson. They each took the biggest drinks ever, as Antonini said, "There's worse things than losing."—JA

---

2 Guitar players who have played outfield for Chico's include Jeff Wiles, Jeff Goodwin, Greg Leatherman, Brian Porterfield, Tom Batchelor, Dave Brown, Aaron Hawley, Andy Tuck, Walt Sarkees, Chad Koury, Tyler Grady, Jon Vehse, Dave Krovich, Robert Raese, Bob Butler, Jeff Shilling, Jay Demco, Tom Moore, Tyler Grady—we're sure there were others.

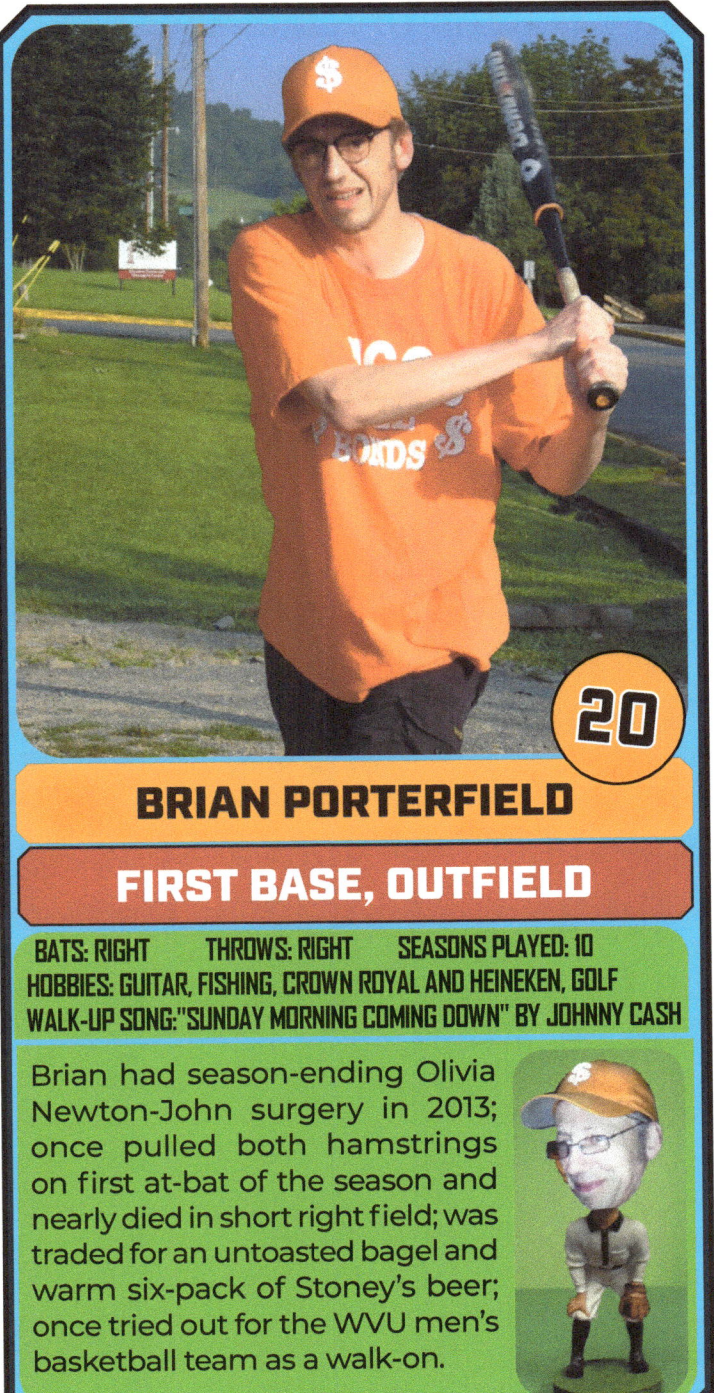

BRIAN PORTERFIELD

20

FIRST BASE, OUTFIELD

BATS: RIGHT   THROWS: RIGHT   SEASONS PLAYED: 10
HOBBIES: GUITAR, FISHING, CROWN ROYAL AND HEINEKEN, GOLF
WALK-UP SONG: "SUNDAY MORNING COMING DOWN" BY JOHNNY CASH

Brian had season-ending Olivia Newton-John surgery in 2013; once pulled both hamstrings on first at-bat of the season and nearly died in short right field; was traded for an untoasted bagel and warm six-pack of Stoney's beer; once tried out for the WVU men's basketball team as a walk-on.

JULY 3–CHICO'S (0–17) VS SMITH CPA I got nothing. Chico's Bail Bonds, the world's greatest softball team, got nothing. The whiskey bottle is empty. The 30-pack is gone. The winless season remains intact. The Bondsmen drop their 17th straight in spectacular fashion, losing 19–6 to Smith CPA (13–2). Chico OF Ferrett showed up without his game jersey.

Vehse: "Where's your jersey?"

Ferrett: "I lost track of time."

Vehse: "Doing what?"

Ferrett: "Having sex?"

Vehse: "With a woman?"

Ferrett: "Yes, with woman."

Vehse: "I guess that would explain the hard-on.

Ferrett: "I didn't want to be late."—JA

Ferrett in a blue shirt, Becker raising the broken arm.

JULY 23–CHICO'S (0–19) VS RACER TV Chico's Bail Bonds battle to the end but fall 11–9 and remain winless after 1st annual Futility Bowl against hapless Racer TV (2–16). Nobody loses like Chico's. Nobody. The Bonders were down 9–2 late in the game and rallied behind the incredible and unbelievable bases clearing inside-the-park home run by Chico rookie Tyler Grady (in 'skinny' jeans and all) to cut the lead to 9–6 with one inning to go. The miracle finish and dream for the season's 1st win died as Walt Sarkees long

majestic drive to left field was snagged with bases full of Chico's and two outs in the final inning.

Chico 1B Brian Porterfield put it best, "It was our best loss of the season."

Despite another devastating setback to a nightmare of a season, the Chico players celebrated as if they had won the World Series. Winning can be overrated, and there are indeed much worse things than losing. Game Notes. Chico's defense was stellar turning two beautiful double plays started by SS Antonini in the 6th and 7th innings to keep the game close. Chico legend Jim Manilla returned and delivered a key single late in the game but was thrown out in a dramatic rundown behind 3rd and home plate after his "old" momentum carried him off 3rd base. RF Sarkees delivered a clutch double down the left field line to plate two runs late.—JA

JULY 24–CHICO'S (0–20) VS IDK The losing streak remains intact. Chico's Bail Bonds drops their 20th game in a row without a win. The Bonders were over-matched and out-manned as IDK softball (12–7) pummeled Chico's 21–3 in a laugher. Chico's welcomed the return of LCF Andrew Tuck who hit two home runs and drove in all three Chico runs. Other than that—nothing. As the despondent Chico players and their ever-loyal fans filed out of Ogden Stadium, RCF Jeff Wiles asked 1B Brian Porterfield what he was doing after the game.

Porterfield replied (and pretty much summed up the feeling of Chico nation), "I'm going to the liquor store for dinner."—JA

JULY 29–CHICO'S (0–21) VS WOLFPACK Chico's embarrassed 20–5 by methodical but understanding Wolfpack squad and drop their unprecedented 21st straight game. A review of the season's top headlines tells the Bonders' pitiful story:

-Like a stuck pig, Chico's bleed out in five…

-Chico's shit the bed and rolls around in it…

-Chico's gag away lead in most epic softball collapse…

-Chico's bury themselves in mud and wait to die with no one left to dig them out…

-The steep price of too many years of low living (whiskey, cigarettes, marginal women, etc.) has caught up with the Bonders…

-Chico's blow wad then shit pants in BOPARC laugher…

Oh, make it stop. Chico's have only 2 more games to get that first win.—JA

AUGUST 10–CHICO'S (0–23) VS KEGLER'S A softball mistake. In a steady downpour on the unforgiving and muddy track of Whiston Field, Chico's drop final game of the season to finish an ungodly (0–23) for the season. It looked like the losing streak was over as the Bonders took a 4-run lead into the last inning. But a nervous Koury couldn't find the strike zone in the final frame as he walked in the winning run. An appropriate way to close out the painful season.—JA

Painting by Melissa Baker, commemorating the 2015 season.

2016 WINNING ON THE FIELD

2006 Chico's: (standing) Jeff Wiles, Aaron Hawley, Terry Ferrett, Walt Sarkees, Tom Batchelor, Eric Ramón, Dave Becker, Jeff Goodwin, Dusty Hays, (kneeling) Jon Vehse, Chad Koury, Jim Antonini, Sean Kelly, Meatball, Mack McGinley, Dave Krovich

MAY 12–CHICO'S (0-1) VS C&J WELDING A rain out would have been a better result. An ugly tradition of losing continued as Chico's Bail Bonds softball team was humiliated in four quick innings 22–0 by a more seasoned and veteran C&J Welding squad (2–0).

Catcher Jon Vehse summed up the night, "We jus' gave those guys the best twenty minutes they've had in years."

It's back to the drawing board for the struggling Bonders. They have not won a BOPARC League softball game since June 2014—a pitiful steak of 35 straight losses. But the season is young, so there still is hope—hope that Chico's can recover past glories that once made them the 'world's greatest softball team'...—JA

MAY 20–CHICO'S (0-2) VS RIVERSIDE ROCKIES As the Spring rainy season ends, the losing goes on. Chico's Bail Bonds dropped their record-setting 36th straight game in BOPARC softball action on the mudflats otherwise known as Whiston Field[1]. Like a bloated holiday pig stuck in mud, the Bonders slopped, slipped, and bumbled their way on defense to an embarrassing 27–7 loss to their hated and overrated rivals, Riverside Rockies. Taking advantage of a nearly unplayable, swampy outfield, the Rockies jumped out early to a big 12–0 lead in the 1st inning, challenging the over-matched Chico outfielders with several line drives to the gaps and deep high fly balls to the fence. The Bondsmen tried to keep the game close in the bottom of the inning by answering

---

1 Whiston Field. The Chico softball team has a losing record on Whiston, Ogden, and Liberatore Fields. They had the most success on Ogden. They have had the least success on Whiston, losing over 60% of the games there by 10 or more runs.

123 — JEFF GOODWIN

OUTFIELD

BATS; LEFT   THROWS: LEFT   SEASONS PLAYED: 10
HOBBIES: TATTOOS, PUNK ROCK GUITAR, 1970S TV, TAP DANCING
WALK-UP SONG: "DAYDREAM BELIEVER" BY THE MONKEES

Jeff leads the BOPARC softball league in the number of bands t-shirts owned; can explain the difference between metal core, hard core, speed core, death core, post-hardcore, heavy metal, punk rock, etc....

with seven runs of their own. But it wouldn't be enough. It's back to the drawing board, as the Bonders try to regroup. It's too early to give up on the season. But the losing must stop.

Game Notes: Chico's Aaron Hawley, Dusty Hays, Chad Koury, and Dave Becker paced the offense with two hits apiece and a beautiful line drive double to right field by Terry Ferrett. LF Sean Kelley did his best Tom Batchelor impersonation as he tried to stretch a single into a triple. Unfortunately, it didn't work. Pitcher Koury's ERA after giving up 47 runs in the 1st two games currently stands at 52.08. Game attendance: 1.—JA

MAY 25—CHICO'S (0-3) VS TBD In the summer of the cicada, Chico's didn't play like an insect that had been resurrected after 17 long lonely years in the cold ground. They were not loud, free, horny, or vital—they were none of those things. Instead, they aimlessly staggered around the dusty diamond, disoriented, seemingly blind, and listless, falling in embarrassing fashion 14–2 to the fattest, foulest softball team ever assembled, TBD. TBD is so lame they couldn't even come up with a name for their team. And what does that say about Chico's? Not very much. The Bondsmen's bats again were limp and the defense feeble. With no apparent relief in sight, the losing streak stands at 37 games. When will it end? Will it end? There were highlights—Jeffrey Goodwin's fantastic running acrobatic catch in left, Terry Ferrett's solid play in left center, the line drive hitting of Chad Koury and Meatball. But it wasn't enough, and it hasn't been enough for more than one year now.

Game Notes: Catcher Vehse stripped down to his jock strap and tattoos after the game just before climbing a tall maple tree at White Park. At press time, he was still in the tree, chain-smoking cigarettes and muttering nonsense.—JA

JUNE 9—CHICO'S (1-6) VS WESTOVER VFD Bondsmen brilliant as long losing streak ends! FINALLY! Tonight, for the first time after 39-straight losses, dating all the way back to July 2014, Chico's could celebrate! And celebrate they did! There were no burned couches or overturned cars, but the post-game beers were colder; the late-night whiskey was smoother; and the cool, crisp summer night air smelled fresher. Chico's were winners again! A determined Chico's squad took care of business, playing a clean, confident game and beating an over-matched Westover VFD team 10−6 in game 1 of a twilight BOPARC doubleheader. In front of a raucous and thrilled home-field crowd of hundreds on the hallowed grounds of Liberatore Stadium, Chico's would not be denied on this night, jumping out to an early 5−0 lead in the 1st inning and never falling behind. Chico bats were alive, lead by C-McGinley, OF-Becker, OF-Hays, and P-Koury. The star of the game was clean-up slugger 1B-Aaron Hawley who was perfect at the plate and lively on the base paths. Hawley ran more in two innings than he did in all 23 games last season combined, smashing a double to deep right center in the 3rd and later dashing home from second after a sharply hit single to right.—JA

> ## "WE JUS' GAVE THOSE GUYS THE BEST TWENTY MINUTES THEY'VE HAD IN YEARS."
> —JON VEHSE

JUNE 10–CHICO'S (1-8) VS BOAZ Victory celebration from previous night runs long; Chico's embarrassed, dropping both ends of doubleheader. Hungover, dehydrated, and uninspired, a depleted Bonders team was humiliated 21−1 in three short innings to a horned-up, sold-out Boaz squad in game 1 of late night BOPARC doubleheader. The one last whiskey, the one last Adderall, and the one last screwdriver during pre-game at the 123 bar couldn't revive a lifeless Chico squad, spent from a victory party that lasted 20 hours too long. Early signs weren't good—throws to bases with no runners, multiple whiffs at the plate with mighty swings of nothing but air, miscommunications on lazy fly balls in the outfield, busted fingers on bad infield hops, balky knees, and gimpy base running—it wasn't pretty, and Chico's never recovered from the early deficit. The Bondsmen did respond in game 2, battling Boaz for seven hard fought innings before falling late 13−3. The 2nd loss of the night brought Chico's record to an ugly 1−8 on the season and started a new three-game losing streak. The previous night's victory suddenly seemed like a long time ago.—JA

JULY 7–CHICO'S (1-11) VS SILS Not looking like a last place team, Chico's gives maximum effort but drops two; mathematically eliminated from playoffs again; Meatball goes crazy. Under a sweltering sun, an over-matched and short-handed Bonders team (1−11) battled their asses off for both ends of a doubleheader but fall short 19−9 in the opener and 18−12 in the nightcap on the hottest most humid night ever. For the first time all year, the bats came alive, but not enough to overcome some early shoddy defensive play. All ten Chico players contributed at the plate, in the field, and probably more at the bar post-game, but it wasn't enough—and it hasn't been enough for quite some time. For the 6th straight mother-fucking year, Chico's will not make the playoffs and will not have a winning season. So pissed about this, Chico 3B Meatball stole a backhoe, drove it upon the lush green turf of Liberatore Field, and bulldozed the entire outfield and infield down, making sure to bury all the Bonders equipment in the mud- bats, balls, caps, whiskey bottles, uniforms, and right fielder Tyler Grady.—JA

JULY 14–CHICO'S (1-13) VS VAN BUREN BOYS Overwhelmed and outmatched, Chico's Bail Bonds shutout 13−0 by the Van Buren Boys in late night BOPARC softball action. The Bonders fielded an inebriated, but still optimistic, squad that was

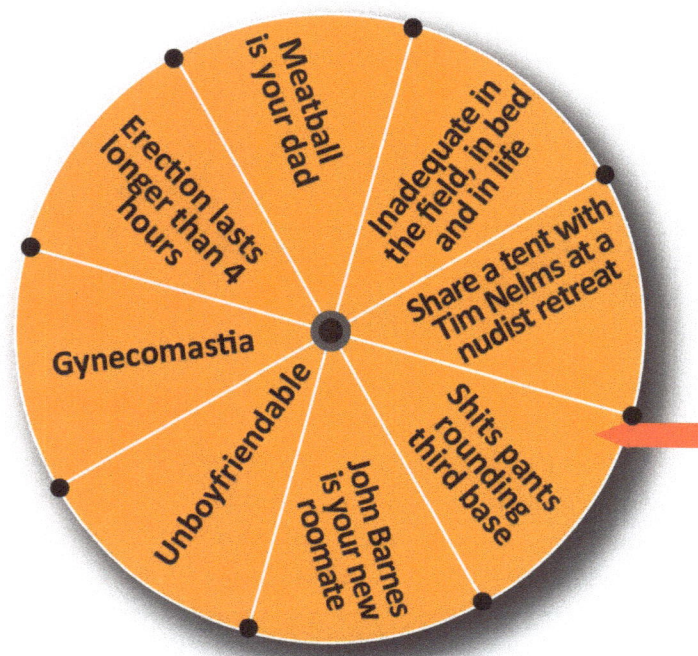

Chico's Bail Bonds Wheel of Misfortune 2016

(Wheel segments: Meatball is your dad · Inadequate in the field, in bed and in life · Share a tent with Tim Nelms at a nudist retreat · Shits pants rounding third base · John Barnes is your new roomate · Unboyfriendable · Gynecomastia · Erection lasts longer than 4 hours)

unfortunately depleted by sperm bank obligations, clinic treatments, and, sadly, a Pokemon Go infatuation. Because of this, the Bondsmen must spin the dreaded 'Chico Wheel of Misfortune'. Oh damn, the wheel lands on 'shits pants rounding third base'. This is an unfortunate and unrealistic result as no Chico reached third base on this night.—JA

JULY 28–CHICO'S (2-15) VS GEICO GECKOS Torrential rain, resulting mud bath, slows BOPARC's top-ranked softball team but just not slow enough. A gritty and energetic Chico's Bail Bonds squad fell in heartbreaking fashion 7–5 to first-place Geico Geckos (18–2) in the most epic of softball classics. The Bonders brought the leather, playing their strongest defensive game of the year. Chico veterans, Sean Kelley in left, Antonini at short, Jon Vehse at second, and Super Terry Ferrett Airways in right center, played like youngsters, making spectacular play after spectacular play. The Bonders turned two beautiful double plays in the middle of the diamond. LF Kelley made the standing-room-only Liberatore crowd almost forget Willie Mays with an over-the-shoulder acrobat catch on a deep drive to the fence. With the tying run on base in the bottom of the final inning and the partisan Chico crowd on their feet, the hot-hitting Tyler Grady came to the plate. Sadly, his long, lazy fly ball fell out of the haze of the late-night July sky, helplessly landing in the left fielder's glove for the final out. Never did a loss in the long, checkered history of Chico's softball feel like a win.

Later as the clock neared 3 AM, I sat alone at the computer in the dark. Soon, I'll need to be at work. Mud stained both my knees and splotched my face. My orange Chico jersey was soaked and heavy with sweat after a long, hard-fought battle on the muggy night. Whiskey flamed the fires in my mind. Chico's Bail Bonds came up short again. And I have run out of ways to describe how the Bonders lose softball games. But before I left the 123 bar after the game, I glanced back to my Chico teammates. The mood was upbeat, even jubilant. Sometimes winning can be overrated.—JA

AUGUST 11—CHICO'S (3-19) VS MORGANTOWN SOBER LIVING Sobriety wins. A fresh, rejuvenated Morgantown Sober Living (8–14) softball squad outlasts a spent, inebriated Chico's Bail Bonds in BOPARC thriller by the score of 12–10. The Bonders easily won the pre-game. As the Irish whiskey flowed through their blood and the jukebox roared, Chico players stormed out of the 123 bar, ready for victory—their confidence at an all-time high. But they wouldn't win another thing on this night. Morgantown Sober Living would beat them on the field, later at last call, and again at wake-up. Hurt by sloppy defensive play and some shoddy scorekeeping by BOPARC officials, a late Chico lead mysteriously disappeared.

A dejected Chico team retreated to 123 after the disappointment and tried their best to drink away the pain. Unexpectedly, Morgantown Sober Living team followed. As the night slipped away, the whiskey and cheap beer had clouded the Chico players' heads, wobbled their legs, and softened their manhood. High on victory and orange juice, the SOBER Sober Living players still at the bar won again—first for being good people by driving each of their drunk-ass opponents home, second, for being still fresh enough to pleasure (like they've never been pleasured before) the Bonders' now available and certainly unsatisfied groupies and significant others, and lastly, being free of hungover headaches in the morning unlike their Chico opponent.—JA

2017 ANOTHER CHANCE AT VICTORY

2017 Chico's: (standing) Jeff Wiles, Jeff Ryan, Dave Krovich, Tom Batchelor, Jon Vehse, Aaron Hawley, Dave Mistich, Walt Sarkees, Chad Koury, (kneeling) Jeff Goodwin, Jim Antonini, Tyler Grady, Eric Ramón

MAY 3–CHICO'S (0-2) VS WOLFPACK Wolfpack overwhelms Chico in BOPARC softball doubleheade-opener—and that is being very kind. Disappointingly, an aging and distracted Bondsmen team (0–2) was not prepared for the start of softball season despite rigid offseason workouts and practices. The Bonders dropped the first game 10–0 and got absolutely destroyed in game 2 by the ridiculous score of 27–2.

At some point in the middle of game 1, a Chico supporter innocently asked, "Is there a mercy rule?" Catcher Jon Vehse shot back, "Mercy rule! Did you say 'MERCY'? F*ck the mercy rule. The last thing Chico's needs is mercy."

Despite a lack of hitting, the Bonders played spectacular defense at times, highlighted by solid outfield play of Kelley in left and Goodwin in left center as well as Batchelor at second and Antonini at short. It was a sad start to season as Chico's easily defeated the Wolfpack last season in the teams' only encounter. It seems Wolfpack management greatly improved the team with important new acquisitions in the offseason. The same can't be said for Chico's at this point as the Bonders' management took a conservative approach to the upcoming season by adding only one new player Dave Mistich, who currently is still at extended spring training in Pikeville, KY getting ready for the season. But the season is young. And Chico's will win their share of games…—JA

JUNE 1–CHICO'S (1-5) VS MORGANTOWN SOBER LIVING

For the third year in a row, sobriety tops inebriation as Chico's drop both ends of a doubleheader[1] to Morgantown Sober Living (3–3) by the identical score of 17–7 in each game. After a long, three-week layoff due to rain-outs, a rested and eager Bonders squad returned to BOPARC's Whiston stadium, playing before their largest crowd of the young season. Two bad (and I mean really bad) 1st innings were all the gentlemanly MSL team needed to put both games out of reach. The sobriety boys started each game by putting up 8 and 13 runs in games 1 and 2, respectively. The deficits were too big of holes for the limited but gritty Chico team to dig out from. The Bonders battled back in both games with timely hitting

> **"MAYBE THERE'S SOMETHING TO THIS SOBER LIVING, BUT I DOUBT CHICO'S WILL EVER FIND OUT." —VEHSE**

and daring base running. P Chad Koury paced the Bonders with five hits in the twin bill. SS Jim Antonini legged out two triples. OF Tyler Grady delivered the big blow in game 2 with a base-clearing inside-the-park home run. But none of that was enough as Chico's couldn't keep pace with the relentless offensive output of MSL on the night.

"Maybe there's something to this sober living," C Jon Vehse mused, studying the jukebox selections while holding a quadruple Crown Royal as the spent Bondsmen retreated to the security of their safe house—the 123 bar. "But I doubt Chico's will ever find that out," he continued.

Game Notes: Chico newcomer Dave Mistich made a successful season debut with a couple of timely hits and steady defensive play at first base. The Bonders have already thrown out three runners at home plate this season via relays from the outfield to shortstop to catchers Vehse and Eric Ramón.—JA

A-MENS

Chico's Bail Bonds W:0 L:0 T:0

Day	Date	Time		Opponent	Field
Wed	5/3/2017	8:00pm	at	MVB - Wolfpack	whiston
Wed	5/3/2017	9:00pm		MVB - Wolfpack	whiston
Thu	5/4/2017	6:00pm		Westover VFD	liberatore
Thu	5/4/2017	7:00pm	at	Westover VFD	liberatore
Thu	5/11/2017	6:00pm	at	Master Batters	whiston
Thu	5/11/2017	7:00pm		Master Batters	whiston
Thu	5/25/2017	8:00pm		Classic's	liberatore
Thu	5/25/2017	9:00pm	at	Classic's	liberatore
Thu	6/1/2017	6:00pm	at	Morgantown sober Living	whiston
Thu	6/1/2017	7:00pm		Morgantown sober Living	whiston
Thu	6/15/2017	6:00pm		Morgantown Brewers	OGDEN
Thu	6/15/2017	7:00pm	at	Morgantown Brewers	OGDEN
Wed	6/21/2017	8:00pm	at	Kegler's -A	whiston
Wed	6/21/2017	9:00pm		Kegler's -A	whiston
Thu	6/22/2017	8:00pm		Martino	liberatore
Thu	6/22/2017	9:00pm	at	Martino	liberatore
Wed	6/28/2017	8:00pm		Stone Asphalt	liberatore
Wed	6/28/2017	9:00pm	at	Stone Asphalt	liberatore
Thu	7/13/2017	6:00pm	at	Pickled Nimrods	whiston
Thu	7/13/2017	7:00pm		Pickled Nimrods	whiston
Thu	7/20/2017	8:00pm		WCLG Rocks	liberatore
Thu	7/20/2017	9:00pm	at	WCLG Rocks	liberatore
Wed	7/26/2017	6:00pm	at	Rigid Fixation	liberatore
Wed	7/26/2017	7:00pm		Rigid Fixation	liberatore

JUNE 15–CHICO'S (1-7) VS MORGANTOWN BREWERS

Chico's Bail Bonds at the crossroads, drop both ends of doubleheader to pitiful Morgantown Brewers squad. Thirty minutes before the start of game 1, three eager Chico players (C-Vehse, SS-Antonini, 1B-Mistich) and the team's documentarian Jesse Wright stood in the rain sipping whiskey as a storm quickly passed over the hallowed grounds of Ogden Field.

Antonini predicted, "We're not going to have enough."

After a long and agonizing wait for first pitch and the arrival of only four more Chico's (Batchelor, Eric Ramón, Chad Koury, Meatball), the Bonders unexpectedly and unforgivably forfeited game 1 to the

---

1 Doubleheaders. For the 2017 season, it was decided by BOPARC that teams in the Single A division would only play doubleheaders. The schedule of doubleheaders has remained that way through the 2025 season.

weakling of the BOPARC softball league. There have been some low moments in the long and illustrious history of Chico softball, but this was by far the lowest—only the second time the Bonders have EVER forfeited a softball game.

As the seven dejected Chico players sat in the heat and humidity impatiently waiting for the arrival of two more players to field a legal team of nine for game 2, a concerned C-Vehse asked, "Are the good times really over? Will there be no more Olivia Newton-John surgeries? No more 'key to the city' ceremonies? Or swimming with the sharks in the Mon River? No more bobblehead nights? Or firework nights? No more 'Frankenchico's'? No more dancing on tables? Or jumping off rooftops? No more 'slowest Chico' foot races? AND NO MORE VICTORY PENISES?"

The wounded team retreated to the parking lot and broke into the cooler of beers that was being saved to celebrate later. As the players drowned their sorrows, OFs Jeffrey Goodwin and Sean Kelley suddenly appeared, lifting the team's spirit. An inspired and hungry Bonders team roared out to an early 7–0 lead after the first inning of game 2 and maintained a 9–3 lead through inning three. The defense and pitching were solid, the hitting even better. Then it all fell apart. Hamstrung with only three Chico outfielders, the shit hit the fan. The Brewers suddenly found the open outfield spaces and used their young fast legs to rally for nineteen fucking unanswered runs to close out the game with a convincing 22–9 victory, sending Chico's to the most painful of defeats.—JA

JUNE 21–CHICO'S (1-9) VS KEGLER'S The agony of defeat bests Chico glory and spells heartbreak. Despite maximum effort and supreme play, the Bonders deposit their soul in the forbidden dirt of Whiston Field and drop both ends of doubleheader to the more talented, more athletic, and much younger Kegler's squad. The Chico strategy of getting out to a big early lead and trying their hardest to hold on for victory has now failed in three straight games.

The Bondsmen raced out to a 10-run first inning lead in game 1 to fall in spectacular fashion 29–15 in a hard fought and physically draining affair. Every Bonder in the batting order had at least two base hits. Not to be discouraged by the disappointing loss, Chico's tightened up their defense and pitching and kept on hitting in game 2 to take a 4–0 lead early before falling behind 11–4 to only roar back to tie the hard-fought contest 11–11 in the last inning. With a two-out double to deep left centerfield, Kegler's would drive a stake into the heart of Chico's and pull out a 12–11 walk off win.

Game 2 was highlighted by the return and solid outing of veteran pitcher Jeff Ryan and back-to-back-to-back triples by Hawley, Antonini, and Batchelor—a first in the long history of Chico's. In softball, the bases are 75 feet apart, so that means Hawley ran 225 consecutive feet without stopping for either a sip of beer, a shot of whiskey, or a toke off his favorite vape pen. As the ball he hit rolled to the fence, he slowed coming to second, but spurred on by his cheering teammates, huffed and puffed his way to third and barely beat the throw. Peer pressure can be a bitch.

As always, the Bondsmen retreated to the 123 bar after the game in full celebration mode. No one at the bar would have ever guessed that they were losers of both games of a doubleheader. As veteran Chico players know, losing can be overrated. Chico's has lost over 300 games in 20 years of softball. But that didn't really matter to the team members on this night as they chugged beers and whiskey shots and shared cigarettes, excited to know they had another chance at victory come Thursday.—JA

JUNE 22–CHICO'S (1-11) VS MARTINO DENTISTRY

Chico's Bail Bonds at crossroads, drop two in hard fought doubleheader to first place Martino Dentistry. It's hard to beat the best team in league shorthanded with only nine players. It's time to recruit some new, more committed players. Game MVP was Terry Ferrett who showed up at first pitch and saved Chico's from forfeiting out of the league. He also delivered three hits, a triple, and drove in five runs.

Game Note: I have run out of ways to describe another Chico loss.—JA

JUNE 28–CHICO'S (1-13) VS STONE ASPHALT

Chico's Bail Bonds fail to rally in softball twin-bill until beers and whiskey are placed in front of them at the 123 bar. The Bondsmen sleepwalk through both ends of a doubleheader. Stone Asphalt played the games of their lives, constantly blooping weak hits in front or in gaps between Bonder outfielders. Taking advantage of shoddy and lazy Chico defense, they wildly ran the bases with daring abandon and great success easily outpacing the Bonders 23–5 in game 1 and 22–2 in game 2. Aaron Hawley twice scored Sean Kelley all the way from first base with doubles on the night. OF Dave Mistich chopped and hacked at every pitch that came his way, whether in the strike zone or not.

"What are you doing!" shouted OF Tyler Grady as Mistich recklessly swung at a pitch well over his head.

"You don't get out of the radio booth waiting for walks," Mistich barked back.

Game Notes: The highlight of the game, maybe the season, and

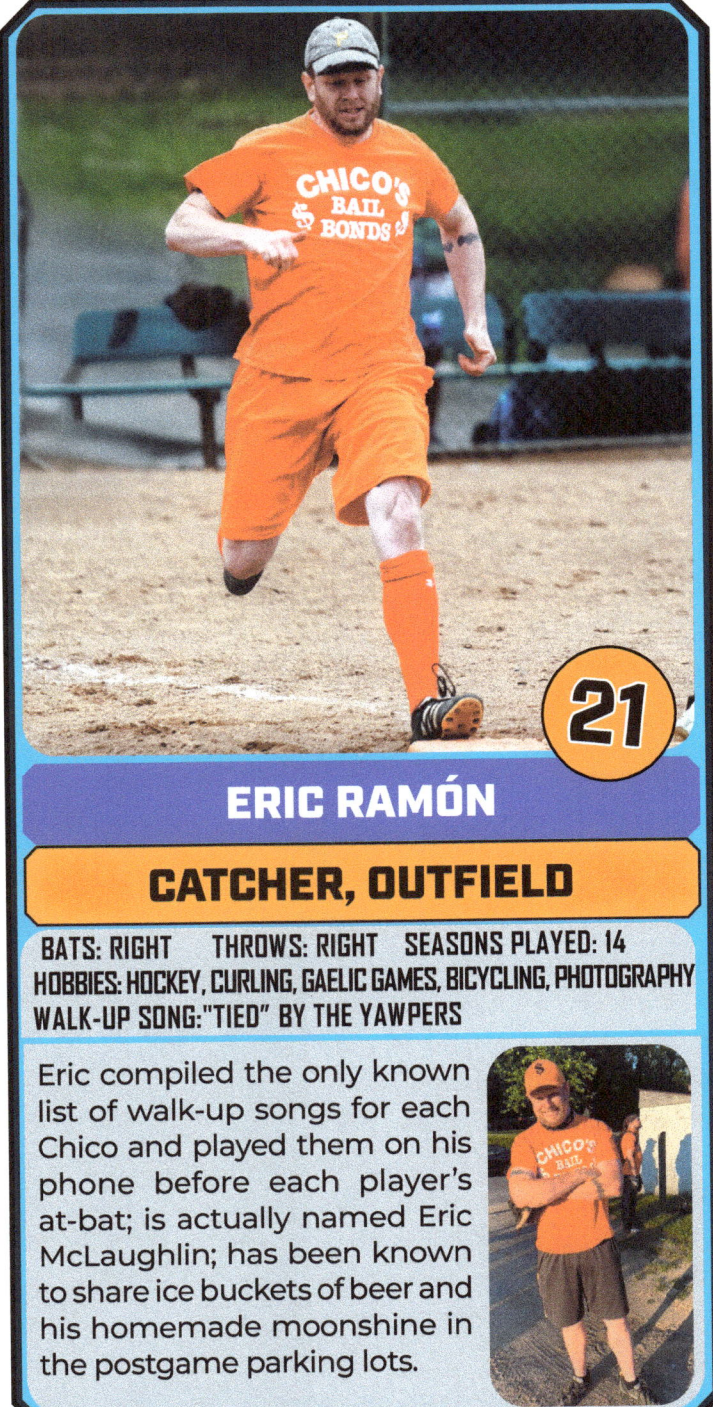

21

ERIC RAMÓN

CATCHER, OUTFIELD

BATS: RIGHT   THROWS: RIGHT   SEASONS PLAYED: 14
HOBBIES: HOCKEY, CURLING, GAELIC GAMES, BICYCLING, PHOTOGRAPHY
WALK-UP SONG: "TIED" BY THE YAWPERS

Eric compiled the only known list of walk-up songs for each Chico and played them on his phone before each player's at-bat; is actually named Eric McLaughlin; has been known to share ice buckets of beer and his homemade moonshine in the postgame parking lots.

perhaps Chico history was delivered by outfielders Jeffrey Goodwin and Jeff Wiles. Goodwin chased a hard shot hit to right centerfield and desperately stabbed at the ball. The ball tipped off the edge of his outstretched glove, bounced high into the air, and amazingly and divinely fell right into Wiles' glove fifteen yards away—'The Divine Deflection'. Chico has four games next week. If you we don't win three of them, I will hit myself in the face with a shovel….—JA

JULY 5—CHICO'S (1-15) VS CLASSIC'S LOUNGE
Under black stormy skies, Chico's Bail Bonds can't shake holiday hangover and drop both games of doubleheader against Classics Lounge in a dud of a performance. After days of joyous patriotic celebration, there would be no fireworks on this night for Chico's. The Bonders were outclassed in all phases to a more finely tuned Classics squad, losing 15–0 in the first game and 18–3 in the second. Game 1 Highlights. None. Game 2 Highlights. P-Chad Koury led off with an inside-the-park home run to give the Bonders their only lead of the night. OF- Tyler Grady added a two-run triple. Jon Vehse provided solid line drive hitting. Meatball was flawless defensively at third base. Injury Notes. 'Tadpole' Jeff Ryan required tape, bandages, and anti-septic solution to close his gaping score-keeping wounds caused by repeatedly stabbing himself with a pencil as he tried keep up with all the opponents nonstop scoring in an ugly game 1 performance. His availability is considered day-to-day. The banged-up Bondsmen need to regroup as they are scheduled to play the inept and winless Master Batters in the now named battle as the Impotence Bowl in less than sixteen hours.—JA

JULY 6.
Due to rain, tonight's Impotence Bowl between league doormats Chico's Bail Bonds (1–15) and Master Batters (0–16) has been postponed.—JA

JULY 20—CHICO'S (1-19) VS WCLG
Because C-Vehse and 1B-Mistich kept me out so late and I need an ice bath so bad, here are the quick take home points from the night's Chico hard fought doubleheader loss to WCLG:

1) With only ten players, 3B-Meatball pulled a calf muscle early in game 1, leaving the Bonders to play shorthanded with only nine players for most of two games on the hottest, muggiest night against a younger, more athletic opponent.

2) Chico's dropped the first game by the score of 17–11 and then fell in a heartbreaker 18–15 in the nightcap. Despite the two losses, it was arguably the best hitting and baserunning performances of the season for Chico's.

3) Bloated WCLG players arrived with a boom box blaring the station's redundant playlist of stale classic rock standards by the likes of Billy Squier, Bad Company, Journey, Styx, Boston, Eagles, blah, blah, blah, distracting an unsettled Chico's team already reeling from a disappointing season. Don't believe the slogan 'WCLG Rocks'—my ass…

4) Chico 1B Mistich got run over in the base-paths by the biggest

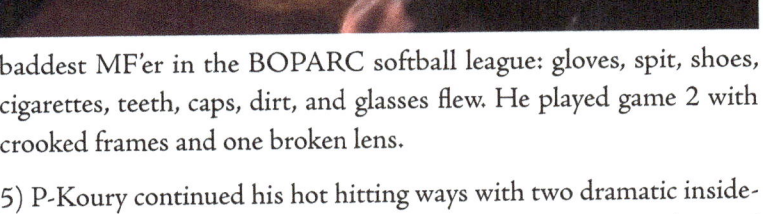

baddest MF'er in the BOPARC softball league: gloves, spit, shoes, cigarettes, teeth, caps, dirt, and glasses flew. He played game 2 with crooked frames and one broken lens.

5) P-Koury continued his hot hitting ways with two dramatic inside-the-park home runs and two more doubles, driving in eight total runs on the night. To celebrate, a hobbled Meatball took Koury after the game to an undisclosed location on the Point Marion Road for hours of deep tissue and muscle massages. Koury joined his other teammates later at the 123 bar with teeth marks and a hickey on the inside of both thighs.—JA

JULY 25. INJURY UPDATE: Breaking- Meatball is done for the season after blowing out his calf muscle in the last game. It's been a tough year for Chico's...—JA

JULY 26–CHICO'S (1-21) VS RIGID FIXATION On the most beautiful of summer nights, Chico's Bail Bonds shits bed, rolls around in it, and seemingly enjoys it. With the make-up of the 'Impotence Bowl'[2] looming against the winless Master Batters, Chico bats go limp as they squandered a golden opportunity to move up in the standings to improve their seeding for the upcoming BOPARC playoffs. Unable to generate any offense, the Bonders were embarrassed in both ends of a doubleheader by the soft

---

2 Impotence Bowl. Because of a rainout earlier in the season, the Impotence Bowl between Chico's (1–15) versus Master Batters (0–16) was rescheduled for the last day of the season. Appropriately (and fortunately for true softball fans), the game was never played. Master Batters forfeited due to a lack of players. Chico's were declared the victors without having to take the field.

and very much flaccid joke of a softball team Rigid Fixation. Chico's fell 12−1 in the first game despite the fact that their opponent played shorthanded with only nine players, one of which had claws instead of hands (and he could really pick it at third base). In game 2, the outcome was no different as Chico's got humiliated by the score of 15−4. Rigid Fixation could have fielded a team of jugglers, clowns, and banjo players and still would have easily won.

Game Notes: The regular season ends with the Impotence Bowl next week, pitting Chico's (1−21) vs. Master Batters (0−22). A first-round draft pick will be on the line. The defensive play of the Chico outfield of Tyler Grady, Sean Kelley, Jeffrey Goodwin, and Jeff Wiles was the only highlight on the night. CF Goodwin made the play of the year with a brilliant running, stabbing shoe-string catch in short center. 3B-Meatball's iron man streak of playing in 171 consecutive Chico games (not counting short periods of incarceration) came to an end as he sat out the game with a torn calf muscle. As already reported, he is done for the year.—JA

2018 CHICO'S TAKE THE FIELD

2018 Chico's: (standing) Eric Ramón, Jason Friggins, Mark Downs, Tyler Grady, Aaron Hawley, Jeff Ryan, Ken Price, Dave Lawson, Dave Becker, Chad Koury, (kneeling) Dave Mistich, Jeff Goodwin, Jim Antonini, Sean Kelley, Meatball, Jon Vehse.

MAY 10–CHICO'S (0–3) VS MOUNTAIN MOMMA'S Chico dragged himself out of bed. The sun had yet to rise. Naked, he lugged his heavy, damaged body into the kitchen. He pulled open the refrigerator. It was empty except for a half-filled bottle of cheap vodka.

"We don't eat much around here," she called from the bed.

He studied the vodka a moment, before reaching for it.

"I'll have some," she said.

He opened the cupboard and pulled out a couple of glasses. He checked the freezer. The plastic ice cube trays were empty. He poured two glasses full of vodka and joined her back in bed.

"I'm not mad," she said, swallowing the vodka in one gulp. "It happens."

He sampled the vodka and grimaced.

"What are you gonna do now?" she asked.

"I think I'll pray for rain." [1] —JA

---

1 Bullets for Silverware. This writeup would become an excerpt for a Jim Antonini novel (Chapter 3, pgs. 65–67) published in 2020 by Pump Fake Press.

MAY 11–CHICO'S (0–4) VS JOHN HOWARD MOTORS Car dealer bests shorthanded and gimpy Chico's Bail Bonds with dramatic last inning walk-off 12–11 in early season rematch. The heartbreak continued for the Bonders, depleted by injury, who led the entire game until the last John Howard Motors batter of the night. Despite the loss, it felt like a victory. It was by far the best Chico performance of the young season. The Bondsmen banged out 22 hits, highlighted by a dramatic 3-run inside-the-park home run by long-time Chico veteran Jon Vehse. He hit the ball so far he had time to hesitate between 2nd and 3rd base to light a cigarette.

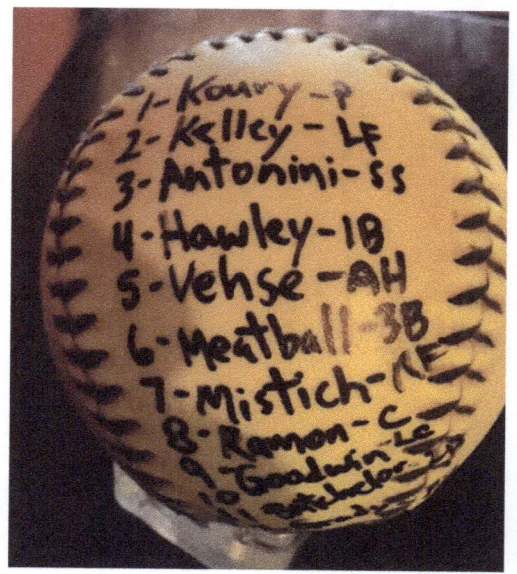

"That's the best hit I've had in 15 years since we beat the Morgantown cops," Vehse was heard to say, trying his best to catch his breath after crossing home plate and fumbling with a lighter and another cigarette.

The Chico defense also sparkled in defeat. Outfielders Sean Kelley and David Becker roamed the outfield as if teenagers, gliding deep into the power alleys of right and left center fields where hits, sure to be triples, found the palms of their gloves. —JA

MAY 17–CHICO'S (0–5) VS KEGLER'S Grady shows, Chico's humiliated 11–0 in laugher. As the clock ticked towards 6:00 PM and only seconds before the 3rd forfeit in the long, glorious Chico history, eight Bonder players looked in all directions, hoping for one more Chico to field a legal team.

"It's all right, guys," assistant manager and starting catcher Vehse reasoned. "We got a cooler of beer and a bottle of Crown in the van. It could be worse."

As the Bondsmen packed up their gear, OF Tyler Grady mysteriously appeared, like a ghost at midnight, in a speeding red Miata with David Lawson in the passenger seat. Lawson's beautiful long dreadlocks danced in the wind behind him. The Miata skidded to a stop, nearly ramming the Whiston field backstop.

"Play ball!" The umpire barked.

The partisan Chico crowd roared as the Bonders confidently took the field.

"Our hero, Tyler Grady!" An adoring Chico groupie squealed before passing out.

The Bondsmen battled for three hard innings, only to fall apart in the fourth. A limp Chico offense had no answers on the night, producing two weak singles and bouncing into three inning-killing double plays. The Bonders remain winless on the season and return to action the following Wednesday. Chico

Game highlights: none.—JA

photos by Jesse Wright

MAY 24—CHICO'S (0–6) VS MORGANTOWN SOBER LIVING Empty beer bottles and dirty ashtrays littered the cramped Liberatore Field locker room that smelled of menthol rub. A hot water pipe leaked. The ceiling was coming down. The team bats were at the pawn shop. No one said a word. The losing streak for the new season was at five. It was much longer if you counted last season. Tensions in the room ran high.

Chico players tried to distract themselves. SS Antonini repeatedly slammed a ball into his trusty mitt to keep it loose. Two Chico groupies quietly taped 3B Meatball's broken knees. 2B Batchelor sharpened his spikes. In the corner, OF Goodwin applied a fresh tattoo to his own neck. High on local IPAs, backup C Ramón oiled his red beard with one part diesel fuel and two parts beeswax. 1B Hawley, OF Grady, and OF Price sheepishly giggled in the corner. Utility-man Downs poured hydrogen peroxide on the open, festering infield wounds that dotted his legs. OF Kelley, C Vehse, and 1B Mistich rolled cigarettes and shared a bottle of Irish whiskey next to their locker. Staring into a cracked mirror, P Koury shaved his chest with a broken piece of a Nantucket Nectar juice bottle—orange-pineapple flavor. Relief pitcher Ryan was at a pay phone in the back ordering takeout steamed dumplings and teriyaki chicken on a stick.

But none of the Bonders could get the losing out of their heads. This night, they thought, would be different—they hoped. Suddenly, there was knock on the locker room door. It was the BOPARC umpire who was assigned to work the game.

"Chico's take the field!"

The Bonders poured out of the locker room with a roar (except for Hawley, Grady, and Price who still giggled in the corner).

"Victory is ours!"

But it wasn't to be... Despite an energized and inspiring performance, Chico's fell 7–2 to their rivals Morgantown Sober Living.

"Why were our bats at the pawn shop?" Vehse asked.

No one had a good answer for him. The lifeless offense that has plagued Chico all season was nowhere to be found.

Game Notes: Grady's beautiful diving, sliding catch in the swamp that was right centerfield and Goodwin's mad dash score from first to home on an errant throw.—JA

JUNE 1—CHICO'S (1–7) VS KEGLER'S Hours after Chico's Bail Bonds lost to a first place Kegler's (9–1) team for a second time this season 10–2 in seven hard fought innings, C Jon Vehse sat shirtless, lingering in the damp, musty locker room of Whiston Field. A 40-watt bulb from a lamp missing its shade lit the room. A lone janitor who knew little about softball swept up cigarette ashes and spent beer cups.

Vehse studied old, black and white photos that had yellowed with time of relatives that weren't around anymore. The Peggy Lee song, *Is That All There Is*, quietly played through the static of an old transistor radio. Its antenna aimed at the heavens. The younger Chico players had already retreated to the 123 bar for a night of juke box music, cheap whiskey, and marginal but fun women, not yet burdened with the prospects of another losing season.

Uncapping a bottle of Crown Royal, Vehse poured himself a tall one. Holding the whiskey, he stared at his worn reflection in the faded mirror through smoke from a long smoldering ash that clung to the end of a cigarette.

"Cheer up buddy," the janitor finally spoke, "there's always next year."

After a heavy sigh, Vehse raised his glass to the janitor and swallowed hard on the whiskey.

"This was supposed to be 'next year,'" he mumbled.

photos by Jesse Wright

Game highlights: With his long red locks flowing behind him in the heavy humid air, OF Sean Kelley made a brilliant running, diving catch in left center. OF Tyler Grady again dazzled the orange clad partisan Chico crowd with another diving, sprawling, sliding catch in swallow right center. But the play of the night belonged to 1B Dave Mistich who turned a slick unassisted double play at first on a wicked hot line drive down the first base line. Unfortunately, Mistich hurt his knee on the play and is questionable for the doubleheader the following week.—JA

JUNE 14—CHICO'S (2–9) VS 6-4-3 MAFIA; CHICO'S (2–10) VS LADDER BOYS The winning streak ends at one game. Chico's was slapped 10–2 by 6-4-3 Mafia (1–7) and 11–1 by The Ladder Boys (5–5) in the night cap. It'll be a long time before the Bonders get over this night.

Game highlights: OF Ken Price dominated the softball action for an entire 347-second period of time in game 1 with a defensive put-out in deep swampy right field that was quickly followed by a hot shot hit to center for a run-scoring single.—JA

JUNE 21—CHICO'S (2–11) VS WESTOVER VFD With blood alcohol levels higher than their batting averages, Chico's Bail Bonds, energized, fortified, confident, and hungry for victory, roared onto the muddy and soaked pasture of Liberatore Stadium to face Westover VFD during BOPARC rivalry week. Looser than they've been in years, the Bonders assumed a win was assured against the doormat of the league. A team they had beaten 8 out of the last 9 years. But it was not to be.

Chico's (2–11) was humiliated 14–6 by a fresh and more determined VFD squad. The Bonders tried their best to answer the VFDs best offensive performance in years by closing the gap to three runs, 9–6, to begin the last inning. Out of gas and obviously still hungover, the Bondsmen faltered in the field, allowing 5 runs in the top of the inning before throwing up the white flag of surrender. After the debacle, Chico's retreated to the 123 bar to lick their words and pour whiskey into the gaping hole where their souls use to be.

Chico futility player Jon Vehse noted, "Guys, we just got destroyed by Westover VFD. Westover VFD for god sakes…"

Before he could finish, he got 'sssssshhhed' for being too loud during the poetry reading that was taking place on the stage at the 123 bar. It doesn't get any lower than that for Chico's.

Game highlights: Fueled by local moonshine, C-Eric Ramón had the offensive game of his life, banging out three hard hit line drive singles to left and driving in three runs. As the night progressed, Chico team blood alcohol levels continued to rise as their batting averages remained below the Mendoza line.—JA

JUNE 21–CHICO'S (2–12) VS VAN BUREN BOYS Chico's season, and perhaps their existence, on the brink as the Bonders were overwhelmed and outmatched by first place Van Buren Boys 18–1. In a steady downpour under a black angry sky, Chico's were sucker-punched early and knocked out, face-first into the mud. Before the dazed Bonders could even look up, the dynamic, hard charging Van Buren Boys stomped on the backs of the vulnerable Chico heads every time they crossed home plate for five quick innings. Never had a Chico team look so deflated after a game. There are serious questions as to whether the Bonders will ever recover, not only this year but beyond. After the night's loss, the Bonders were guaranteed a losing season for the ninth year in a row.—JA

JULY 18–CHICO'S (3–13) VS LAKOTA More beers than runs. Chico's fall 15–3 in opener of twilight doubleheader against Lakota. Chico's found themselves down by seven early runs before they could shake off the rust of the midweek blues. It was a beautiful night, and there was plenty of beer…—JA

AUGUST 9–CHICO'S (3–16) VS GENE'S Multiple Choice Headlines: Bonders squeak out moral victory in a 33–12 loss or Chico's scores 12.

Another Chico loss. This time against an anonymous Genes squad (I guess Al Bonner will give money to anyone). Tonight, we saw Dave Lawson go 3 for 4 at the plate. Ken Price had a solid night in the field and was the RBI king. There was stellar base running by Meatball, and some solid hits by Jeff Goodwin. Eric Ramón had a good night behind the plate with a tag out at home, and pitcher Chad Koury had some quality plate appearances. Really everyone got into the act. Well not everyone—Aaron Hawley went 0 for 4 while mixing in a ground out with three weak fly outs. Game 2 saw a continuation of quality plate appearances by Lawson and Goodwin and the return of the Tactical Beard, Dave Becker. Down 8–4 in the bottom of the 3rd, God, in his infinite wisdom and mercy, decided enough was enough and sent the rain to wash out the nightcap. A quick turnaround awaits. The Bonders play two on the following night.—Vehse

August 16–Chico's (3–19) vs Good Times Lounge Multiple Choice Headlines: Chico's in it in seven or Chico's— Glimpse of the past; Glimpse of the future.

In a solid defensive game, Chico's goes down 7–2, playing a complete seven innings. Chico was up 2–0 till the fourth, thanks to a 2-RBI double by outfielder Jeff Goodwin. In a game that saw strike outs and double plays, Chico's battled, keeping it tied at two until the sixth. Then Chico's 'Chico-ed it', giving up five unearned runs. In an otherwise flawless outfield, Vehse missed the play in right field, giving up three, and the rest was history. It was enough to give one hope for the future or enough to call it quits. Only time will tell. The playoffs will start later with the 3rd to last place Chico's playing at 8:00. It is the time to be king makers.—Vehse

2018 Season Awards[2]:

Hustle Award – Mark Downs

Most Improved – Ken Price

Ironman Award – Jon Vehse

Spirit Award (puts team before self) – Eric Ramón

Most overrated – Jim Antonini

Most underrated – Sean Kelley

PBR Beer Drinker of the year Award – Aaron Hawley

Most likely to go shirtless after a game (tie) – Chad Koury, Meatball

Speed and Style Award – David Lawson

Best beard – David Becker (aka Tactical Beard)

Handyman Utility Player Award – Jeff Wiles

Gin & Tonic Award – Dave Mistich

The most Chico Chico Award – Jeffrey Goodwin

Yukon Jack Best Relief Pitcher Award – Jeff Ryan

Ravi Shibley Slugger Award – Jonathan Tyler Grady

Rookie of the year (tie) – Mark Downs, David Lawson

photos by Jesse Wright

---

2 Participation trophy. In the time period when every kid on a little league team got a trophy, we gave an award to every Chico on the team.

The 2018 Postseason Chico Epitaph by Tom Batchelor

The clubhouse should have been empty and even clean at this point in the offseason, but it was alive and raucous in the middle of winter. To say it was mayhem would be mild. The NPR story[3] about the team had changed everything. The boys found themselves suddenly hot. SS Antonini was telling 1B Hawley how the open flight league had come calling for him, and he would be playing/managing a group of finely tuned and highly conditioned athletes in the coming season. C Vehse and 1B Mistich screamed into cell phones, pacing in and out of the long dry shower room. The catcher was heard telling an unknown caller that the Pickled Nimrod group was over, and Vehse & Mistich were in. 3B Meatball strutted in front of his locker modeling a fur coat and diamond pinky rink bought with signing bonus money from Riverside Apostolic. He boasted that he had beat the drug test with goat piss and a powder procured from a witch he met at a 'spa' in Point Marion. He was playing for Jesus now, and how could that be wrong? 2B Batchelor lounged in the hot/cold tub filled with chocolate pudding and was loudly extolling the rejuvenating effects of pudding baths. Nobody had been ready for this, and while the scene was exhilarating, it had a somber undertone like the drone of the hurdy gurdy. Despite the five cases of PBR sent over from public radio, a congratulatory gift to the boys, few were really drinking. A mostly full bottle of Crown Royal sat lonely on a bench. Plans were being made. Schemes were being hatched. Besides, the boys were already drunk, drunk on something more powerful than alcohol. The outfield of Kelley, Goodwin, Grady, and Lawson were dressed in clean uniforms. Men's Health was on its way over for a photo session with the speedy group. Only pitchers Ryan and Koury were less than jubilant, they were pouring over statistics and probabilities.

Chad muttered, "Can you really destroy something that wasn't actually successful?"

The Bonders had seen a lot of horrible defeats over the years, so who could blame them for basking in the limelight. Sometimes orange is almost gold, other times not so much. —Batchelor

3 Tom wrote this piece in reference to the NPR-affiliate West Virginia Public Broadcasting's *Inside Appalachia* story "Morgantown's 'Bad News Bears': Chico's Bail Bonds More Social Club Than Softball Team" by reporter and Chico 1B Dave Mistich about the Chico softball team. The story aired on September 12, 2018. See the foreward of this book for excerpts or find the program on WVPB's website.

Tom Moore 1961–2018

December 5, 2018, Tom Moore passed away. When Tom was a Chico, he showed up for every game, he played when Chico's needed him, he shared his cigarettes, and he had fun—always.

I think of Tom almost daily. I learned a valuable lesson from him one night over beers at Gene's Beer Garden. As most people know, Tom was the dynamic leader and guitar player for the legendary local band, Velez Manifesto. In the early 90's, on the verge of catapulting into the spotlight of the national music scene, Tom and the band moved to Baltimore and soon were named the "Best Unsigned Band in America" by Rolling Stone magazine. I started to ask Tom about those early days of Velez Manifesto, but he immediately stopped me.

"Those days are over," he said. "I don't live in the past. I'm a better guitar player and songwriter now. If what I did long ago was any good, what I'm doing now and what I'm doing next will be better."

Ever since that night, I constantly remind myself to move forward, not backward, and don't dwell on something that's over and can't be changed or brought back. Your best days may be ahead of you. And with that, you will always have a chance.—JA

2019 GETTIN' IT, BITCH

2019 Chico's: (standing) Tyler Grady, Jeff Wiles, Eric Ramón, Aaron Hawley, LJ Guiliani, Mark Downs, Dave Lawson, Jeff Ryan, (kneeling) Meatball, Jon Vehse, Jim Antonini, Dave Mistich, Ken Price, Jeff Goodwin

APRIL 24–CHICO'S (0–1) VS VAN BUREN BOYS

Chico's Bail Bonds were toilet paper soft in opening night 12–1 loss to Van Buren Boys. The winter months were not kind to the Bonders as they surely would have lost even a pillow fight at a grade school sleepover. They looked slow, weak, and spent. Hell– they were slow, weak, and spent. Their stick arms and spindly legs were atrophied from little physical activity and too many heavy winter meals of nothing but Gene Supremes, beef gravies, pork bellies, double IPAs, Lefty's calzones, and gin & tonics. It was obvious that key Chico players spent far too many hours during the off-season on face time with their significant others, sipping cheap whiskey by the fireplace, and updating social media posts than on softball skill preparedness and conditioning.

All was not lost however— Chico's welcomed the return of all-star OF David Becker who provided the Bonders biggest hit on the night— a deep majestic high fly double to left centerfield. He also provided Chico's biggest blunder— a not so majestic attempt to score from second base on an infield hit to shortstop. Pitcher Chad Koury delivered a hot shot RBI single to center in the third inning for the Bondsmen only run. Despite the disappointing loss, there is hope. It was the most beautiful of April evenings, and the season was young. Late into the night, Chico team members retreated to the 123 bar. They didn't hang their heads in defeat. Instead, they celebrated with shots of whiskey and cheap beers—it was the start to a new softball season. Spring has returned, and summer was not far behind. And it doesn't get better than that. The Bonders have 19 more games ahead of them this season. I predict this current incarnation of Chico softball may surprise the local softball establishment and scores of Facebook doubters. The Bondsmen may not win the single A league championship, but they will disappoint some teams who think they can. And that's all that matters.—JA

MAY 9—CHICO'S (1-1) VS WV SOBER LIVING & CHICO'S (1-2) VS. CITY PLUMBING & HEATING

In game 1 of BOPARC doubleheader on a beautiful spring night, drunken bastards Chico's Bail Bonds put their cleats to the head of the overrated Sober Living squad and kicked them the fuck off the wagon in epic softball beat down. The boozy Bonders humiliated the tee-totalers 16-0 with 29 hits in four quick efficient and clean innings, sending their arch-rivals to the local Applebee's bar to

photos by Jesse Wright

DAVE LAWSON   23

OUTFIELD, DIVA

BATS: BOTH (ON THE FIELD AND OFF)   THROWS: RIGHT   SEASONS: 6
HOBBIES: LATE NIGHTS, DANCE PARTIES, BIG BOYS, BEING 'RIGHT' ON TIME
WALK-UP SONG: "BAD GIRLS" BY DONNA SUMMER

David was voted team MVP in 2019 and 2024; often the last Chico standing after games; always voted team's best dancer and most stylish; forever known to be 'gettin' it'.

search their souls and question their life's direction. As the Sober Living team members sipped their Shirley Temples and over-priced grapefruit-flavored seltzer water, they thanked God for the 15-run, 4-inning mercy rule because the relentless and determined Bonders would not be denied on this night.

Game 2 was an entirely different story for Chico's as they were overwhelmed 18–0 to perennial league favorites, City Plumbing & Heating. Obviously, the Chico opponent team members must not have received enough participation trophies when they were young as they showed up in oversized pick-up trucks with matching pressed polyester baseball slacks, batting gloves, ball caps, duffel bags, $200 cleats, and $1,000 plutonium bats. They looked much better than they actually were. But the Bondsmen only have so many hits in them, and at that point in the night, they were spent. They needed beer and whiskey as they quietly disappeared to the warmth, darkness, and comfort of the 123 bar, happy to have their first victory of the season under their belt. The Bonders return to the diamond the next night for another doubleheader on the glorious green pasture of Liberatore Field. Chico's is heavily favored in game 1 against laughingstocks Davis Cabinetry, but they are a decided underdog against the Pancake Batters in game 2.

Game Notes: Eric Ramón had his best night as a Chico in his long career, banging out 4 hits. Dave Becker set a BOPARC record with his first inning triple that was recorded at 102.3 mph exit velocity off the bat. Long-time legend 3B Meatball turned two double plays on the night.—JA

MAY 16–CHICO'S (2–4) VS WESTOVER VFD OF Tyler Grady's acrobatic catch ripped out the heart of arch-rival Westover VFD in the most dramatic Chico softball win. The surging Bonders (2–4) scored five runs in the top of the last inning to take an 11–8 lead that would be the difference. Every single Chico was a hero on this night— from David Lawson's bases-clearing, two-out triple that plated Hawley and Antonini with the go-ahead runs to Downs' head-first Charlie Hustle dive over the catcher for the tying run to Jeffrey Goodwin's dramatic base-clearing triple to keep the game close in the sixth inning. What a night

to be a Chico! With word of the victory– High Street was closed, and the 123 bar was emptied for a celebration that may last for days. When you've lost as many games as Chico's the past few years, you can't appreciate what a special win this was for Chico Nation.

Game Notes: Several Chico players are questionable for the next night's game with pulled shoulder and quad muscles after trying to carry the happy but hearty Grady on their shoulders into the 123 bar in celebration after the game.—JA

MAY 17–CHICO'S (2–5) VS LAKOTA In lackluster effort, Chico's Bail Bonds out-manned and overwhelmed in BOPARC softball laugher 10–0 to Lakota. Hungover and sick, the Bonders were everything they were not the night before—tired, sore, slow, heavy, and bandaged. It's unlikely Chico's will ever win two games in a row. They enjoy winning too much. And they enjoy celebrating winning even more. It's a long season, and the Bonders already look exhausted.

photos by Jesse Wright

Game Notes: After walking new teammate Bill Rittenour home after the post-game celebration, Chico heartthrob David Lawson was seen closing three bars late into the night, even washing dishes at the long closed McClafferty's Irish bar as the sun came up. Chico star David Becker returned to action after a short absence. Unfortunately, he delivered an uneven, rusty performance. His only highlight was he bought a new Jeff Ryan-designed Chico dollar-sign hat.—JA

MAY 22–CHICO'S (2–6) VS ANDERSON EXCAVATION & CHICO'S (2–7) VS. KEGLER'S Chico's drop two hard fought games in BOPARC doubleheader. In opening 10–4 loss to Anderson Excavation, it was a similar theme for the Bonders at the season's midpoint– good pitching by Chad Koury, great outfield play by David Lawson and Jeffrey Goodwin, but not enough hitting. In game 2, the Chico squad melted down, falling 17–4 in pathetic breakdown to perennial league favorites, Kegler's. But the night was not without heroes especially at 123 bar afterwards where the Chico's remain undefeated and unmatched after 21 long and hard softball seasons.

Game Notes: Star outfielder David Lawson made the catch of the season with a dramatic, long running stab of a hot shot line drive to right center to kill a rally in game 1. Unfortunately, Lawson would have to leave the game early with a sore shoulder. His status for the next game is questionable. OF/1B Dave Mistich won the weekly Little Head-Big Helmet Award. Of course, it's the fourth time he's won that award this season.—JA

photos by Jesse Wright

MAY 31–CHICO'S (3–10) VS BIG TIMES As the month of May winds to a close, the Chico softball team is tired, and the injury list grows. The Bonders have played 13 games in the past 3-1/2 weeks. On this night, the Bondsmen jumped out to a quick 3–0 lead against Big Times and held the advantage until the 4th inning. With a line-up depleted by injuries to 3B Meatball and OF Becker, Chico's eventually ran out of gas, giving up four runs in the fifth and seven more in the sixth as they dropped the rainy affair by a

final score of 11–4. The Bonders were led by the hitting of Koury, Lawson, and Tuck as well as solid outfield play by Jeff Goodwin. But the injuries continue to mount– LF Sean Kelley tweaked an ankle, and SS Antonini was drilled in the ribs by a hard errant throw to first base.

Game Notes: Chico rookie Bill Rittenour was inserted into right field late into the game. Not wanting to get burned by a hit over his head, he played a deep right field. So deep, he stood behind the fence on the adjacent little league field. Needless to say, Big Times batters dropped several hits into swallow right field that turned into several easy doubles.—JA

Standings

A

Team	Won	Lost	Tie	Win %	Streak	RF	RA	Diff
Lakota	11	1	0	.917	Won 2	157	42	115
City Plumbing and Heating	10	1	0	.909	Lost 1	184	68	116
TLC Dental	8	1	0	.889	Won 7	110	54	56
Kegler's Sports Bar	11	2	0	.846	Lost 1	161	69	92
The Frosted Mug Too	7	2	0	.778	Won 2	123	66	57
(Morgantown Surgical's) Pickled Nimrods	9	4	0	.692	Won 4	170	139	31
John Howard	6	3	0	.667	Won 4	113	84	29
Big Times	9	5	0	.643	Won 6	167	142	25
Pancake Batters	8	5	0	.615	Lost 1	123	131	-8
Komatsu Crushers	7	6	0	.538	Won 1	190	153	37
The Van Buren Boys	6	6	0	.500	Lost 2	114	83	31
Solvay	6	8	0	.429	Lost 1	107	173	-66
Extremity Pain	5	8	0	.385	Lost 1	109	92	17
Anderson Excavating LLC	4	7	0	.364	Lost 2	58	106	-48
The Ladder Boys	3	7	0	.300	Won 1	89	131	-42
Davis Cabinetry	4	10	0	.286	Lost 1	91	174	-83
Chico's Bail Bonds	3	11	0	.214	Lost 2	71	151	-80
Westover VFD	2	9	0	.182	Lost 5	51	129	-78
West Virginia Sober Living	1	11	0	.083	Lost 6	76	180	-104
Wade Auction Service LLC	1	14	0	.067	Lost 6	103	200	-97

JUNE 27–CHICO'S (4–11) VS PANCAKE BATTERS On the muggiest and most miserable night of the summer, Chico's Bail Bonds would not be denied, beating the Pancake Batters 12–9 in a comeback for the ages. The Bonders fell behind early 9–4, squandering numerous scoring opportunities and stranding the bases loaded three times in the first three innings. Everything changed in the fourth when Chico left fielder Sean Kelley made a game changing, and perhaps season defining, decision to become a roving, shallow outfielder. After the decision, the Pancake Batters never scored again as they lofted easy fly ball outs to a perfectly positioned Kelley in short left and right centerfield.

"Sean Kelley is a genius!" Shouted Bonder shortstop Antonini as their opponent's batted balls fluttered like wounded birds into the mitts of Chico outfielders Goodwin, Lawson, and Vehse for the easiest of outs in their feeble attempts to beat 'the Kelley shift'.

But still, the Chico offense needed to respond, and respond they did, scoring seven runs in the bottom of the sixth against their shell-shocked opponent, sealing one of the most improbable victories in the long and illustrious history of Chico softball. Every single member of the Chico team responded, from the daring base-running of Kelley and Jeff Ryan to the run-scoring hits of Meatball, Price, Goodwin, and Antonini to the descriptive clutch pitching of Koury. After a spirited and productive Sunday morning

batting practice, Chico's banged out a season high 26 hits for the game. To make the playoffs, Chico's need to win their final six games. They won their first one tonight. This is a different Chico team- no longer the doormats of the BOPARC softball league. It never felt so good to be a Chico.—JA

JULY 17–CHICO'S (4–12) VS KEGLER'S A rusty and outclassed Chico's Bail Bonds were pummeled 15–1 by first place Kegler's. With a playoff berth still in reach, Chico's assembled an A-team of 16 of the most rested and eager of eligible players from the official team roster. But star outfielder David Lawson was late.

Chico 1B Dave Mistich asked the tipsy and tardy OF David Lawson who showed up in the 2nd inning, "Where you've been?"

With bleary red eyes, an outstretched right arm, and a snap of his fingers, Lawson replied, "Gettin' it, bitch!"

With that, a woozy Bonders' team, high on tequila and PBRs, took the field with every intention of knocking off BOPARC's top-rated team, Kegler's Sports Bar. But sadly, it wouldn't be. It wasn't long before Chico's knew that this night belonged to their opponents, and their razor-thin hopes of making the playoffs were sadly fading. Having played only one game in four weeks, the rust showed as Kegler's jumped out to an early nine-run lead over Chico's in the first three innings, a hole much too big for the Bondsmen to climb out from.—JA

photos by Jesse Wright

107

JULY 3–CHICO'S (4–16) VS PICKLED NIMRODS Chico's Bail Bonds end season in disappointing fashion, turning in their worst performance of the summer against playoff-bound Pickled Nimrods, losing 22–2 in softball laugher. Right fielder Tyler Grady delivered the only big hit for the Bonders, a two-out triple. Catcher Jon Vehse hustled out an infield single and scored one of the two Chico runs, garnering the player of the game award. It will be a long off season for the Bonders as they look ahead to next year, knowing this was no way to end what had been a successful campaign.—JA

2019 Season Awards

Chico best batted ball launch angle award- Ken Price

Chico Ironman Award- Jon Vehse

Chico Speed Award- Jeffrey Goodwin

Chico MVP- David Lawson

Tiny Head Nice Helmet Award- Dave Mistich

Timothy Nelms Pants are Optional Award- Aaron Hawley

Yukon Jack 'Put Out the Fire' Relief Pitcher Award - Jeff Ryan

Chico Most Likely to be Straggled Award - Jeff Ryan

Chico Most Underrated Award- Eric Ramón

Most Soulful Chico Award- Andrew Tuck

Chico Infielder of the Year Award (tie)- Jim Antonini and Meatball

Chico Best Beard Award- David Becker

Best All-around Chico Award and Best Outfielder Award- Sean Kelley

Chico Defensive Play of the Year Award and the Ravi Shibley Slugger Award- Jonathan Tyler Grady

Chico Rookie of the Year Award and the Chico Spirit Award- Bill Rittenour

Battered and Bruised Chico Award and the Chico Hustle Award- Mark Downs

Most Improved Chico- Chad Koury

Chico Most Likely to go Topless after the Game- Jon Vehse

109

Ravi Shibley 1970–2020

Before the 2020 season started (delayed by the COVID pandemic), Ravi Shibley, the most prolific slugger in Chico softball history, sadly passed away on May 25. He was an elite athlete who was an All-Big East infielder for the West Virginia University baseball team in the 1990s and played in the famed wooden bat summer league in Cape Cod, MA. He also had opportunities to play professionally for the Chicago Cubs and St. Louis Cardinals. My favorite Ravi, and maybe favorite Chico, story was a few years prior when he crushed a ball deep over the left field fence at Whiston Field. The batted ball flew over the parking area, hit the street, and bounced into the boundary of weeds between the field and South Middle School. It was the furthest I've ever seen a softball hit. In our league, it's the batting team's responsibility to retrieve any ball that leaves the field of play. Chico reserve that game Brian Porterfield volunteered to get the ball. The game resumed and lasted another hour or so. Instead of searching for the ball, Brian secretly got into his car and left Whiston Field without informing his Chico teammates. After the game ended, many Chico players thought that Brian was still searching for the ball, but he had instead gone to the 123 bar. He already had consumed four Heinekens and three shots of Crown Royal and smoked a half pack of cigarettes by the time the other Chico players had gotten there.

"What took you guys so long?" Porterfield wisecracked as the Chico team members started to file into the bar.

Returning to the field several days later, a few Chico players went to the weeds where Ravi's ball had landed. They searched for over a half an hour. No one ever did find that ball. It seemed like an appropriate final resting place for it. Out of all the Chico players through the years, Ravi was perhaps the sweetest and gentlest. RIP, Ravi.—JA

2020 POSTGAME PARKING LOT

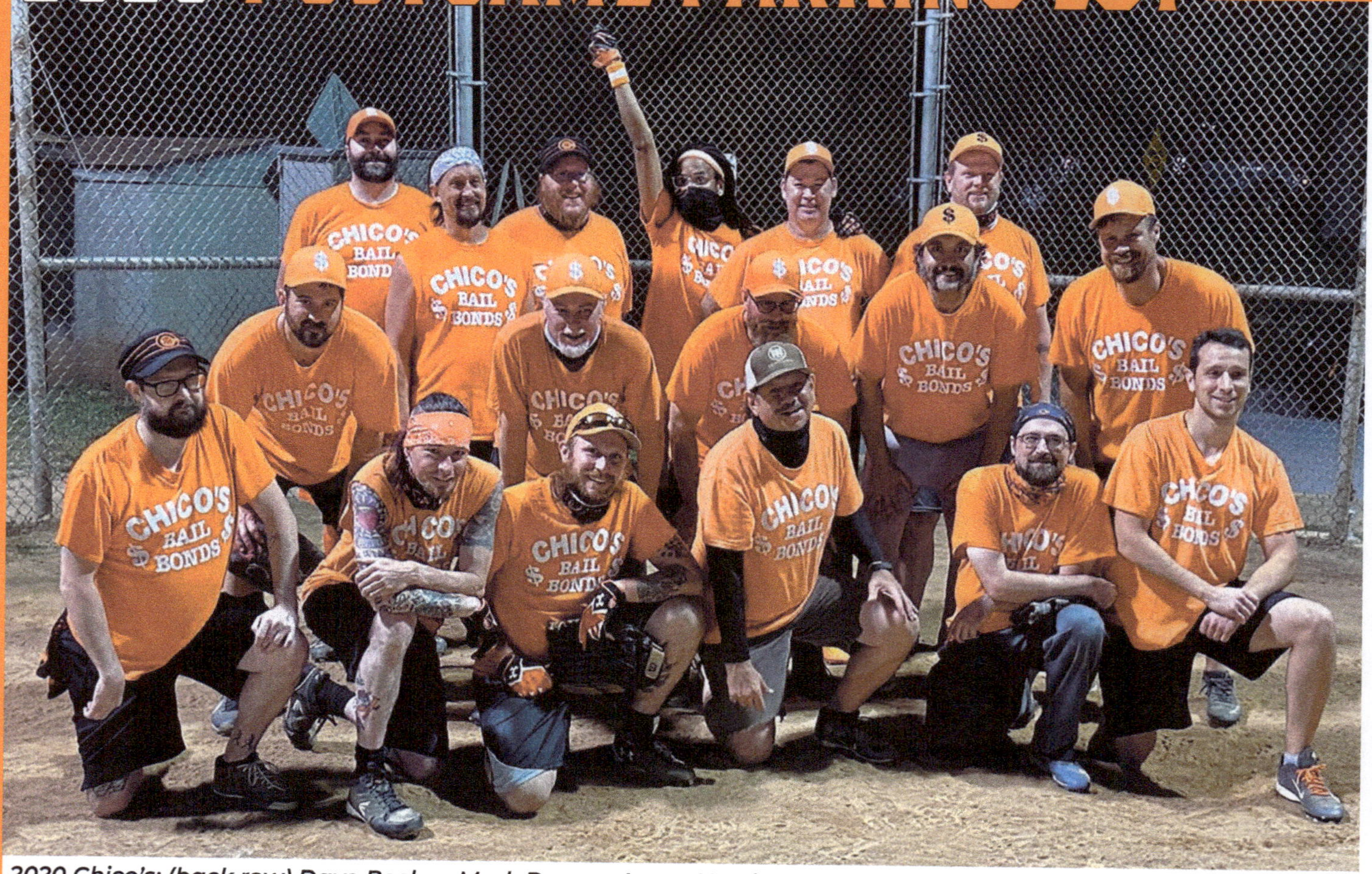

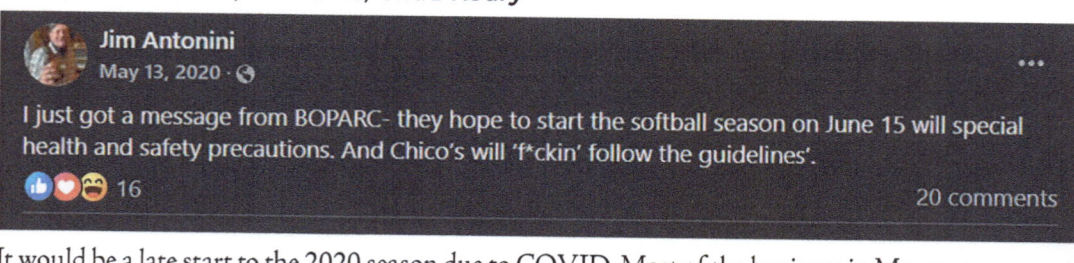

2020 Chico's: (back row) Dave Becker, Mark Downs, Aaron Hawley, Dave Lawson, Jeff Ryan, Eric Ramón, (second row) Chris Simons, Sean Kelley, Chris Evans, Bill Ritenour, Andy Tuck, (kneeling) Dave Mistich, Jeff Goodwin, Ethan Wells, Jim Antonini, Ken Price, Chad Koury

Jim Antonini
May 13, 2020 ·

I just got a message from BOPARC- they hope to start the softball season on June 15 will special health and safety precautions. And Chico's will 'f*ckin' follow the guidelines'.

16 20 comments

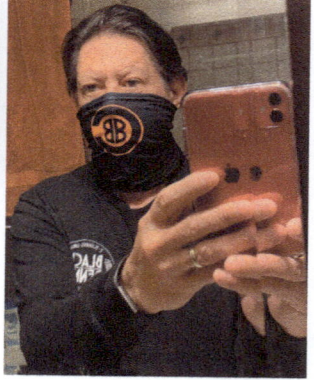

It would be a late start to the 2020 season due to COVID. Most of the business in Morgantown were shut down or had limited hours and access. Player face masks were encouraged on the field of play. Spitting and touching the other team's bats during a game were prohibited. The Chico team members needed an outlet that summer with a world placed on pause. BOPARC softball provided that outlet. Because all the bars and restaurants in town were closed, park officials allowed the softball

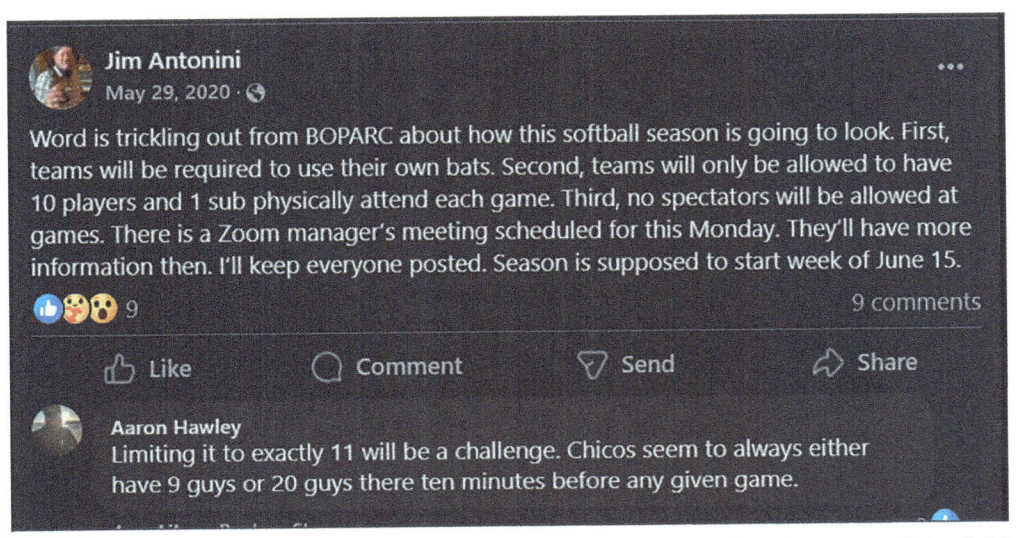

Jim Antonini
May 29, 2020 · 🌐

Word is trickling out from BOPARC about how this softball season is going to look. First, teams will be required to use their own bats. Second, teams will only be allowed to have 10 players and 1 sub physically attend each game. Third, no spectators will be allowed at games. There is a Zoom manager's meeting scheduled for this Monday. They'll have more information then. I'll keep everyone posted. Season is supposed to start week of June 15.

👍😮😆 9   9 comments

👍 Like   💬 Comment   ✈ Send   ↗ Share

Aaron Hawley
Limiting it to exactly 11 will be a challenge. Chicos seem to always either have 9 guys or 20 guys there ten minutes before any given game.

teams after the games to celebrate, responsibly of course, in the parking lots around the fields. The Chico postgame celebrations for the 2020 season didn't disappoint, oftentimes lasting late into the night. No one wanted to go home. Even Donnie D., the team's personal bartender from 123 Pleasant Street, attended the postgame parties equipped with bottles of Jameson and plastic shot cups. The epic postgame parking lot celebrations have continued since that year.—JA.

JUNE 25–CHICO'S (0–2) VS WV SOBER LIVING
It was the most anticipated opening night in the long, glorious history of Chico's Bail Bonds in their match up against arch-rival. Many expert softball prognosticators predicted the current Bonders team to be a dark horse to compete

for the BOPARC title that season. But in true Chico fashion, the Bondsmen fell flat, disappointing a large turnout of Chico fans on a most beautiful summer night.

The newly assembled power hitter-heavy lineup that featured prodigious sluggers Andy Tuck, Chris Simons, David Lawson, and David Becker stacked in the heart of the order proved impotent, falling to the teetotalers 7–2 in game 1 of a lackluster Chico performance. Highlights included the solid pitching of "Mad" Chad Koury and the stellar defensive play of a lighter and rejuvenated shortstop Jim Antonini. In game 2, the

113

Bonders roared to an early 4–0 lead in the first inning in hopes of taking the nightcap, punctuated by a 3-run inside-the-park home run by Chico MVP[1] Andy Tuck. But their opponents had other plans. Playing like a team possessed (or 'under the influence'), Sober Living exploded for 13 runs in the third and decisive inning on their way to a 18–6 humiliating rout of the beloved Chico's Bail Bonds.

Chico first baseman Dave Mistich commented, "They may claim to be sober, but I have my doubts."

And what has become a common pattern in recent seasons, the Bonders were undone in game 2 by shoddy defensive play in ONE BAD INNING. Late in the game outfielder David Lawson delivered a big blow with a triple, scoring pitcher Jeff Ryan from first base.

Lawson was heard to say postgame of the dramatic hit, "Next game, bat me behind Jeff Ryan. I Just love chasing him around the bases. He's my favorite Chico." —JA

JULY 2–CHICO'S (0–4) VS PICKLED NIMRODS In the strangest of times on the hottest of summer nights during a pandemic, a depleted and wounded Chico's Bail Bonds, down to only 11 compromised players, battled a far superior and stacked Pickled Nimrod squad in both ends of a losing twilight doubleheader. Unfortunately for Chico's, the score sheet was short but the injury list was long. Winless on the season, the Bonders (0–4) dropped a tightly contested game 1 by the score of 11–8 to the undefeated Nimrods (4–0) behind the solid defensive performance and the clutch hitting of outfielder Chris Simons, catcher Ken Price, and infielder Aaron Hawley. Outfielder David Lawson delivered the game's big blow with a bases clearing three-run triple late as the Bondsmen mounted a valiant last inning comeback. Game 1 marked the pitching debut of Chico's infielder Chris Evans who lasted only 1-1/2 innings due to spraining what appeared to be a muscle in the groin area. A muscle that Evans described as "being small, actually quite small, between each groin, but not a groin, a tiny piece a flesh." In game 2, a spent Chico's squad wilted in the heat, falling in what was a close contest for six innings 15–4 to the Nimrods. The Bonders again were victims of one bad inning, allowing 12 runs in a decisive fifth inning.

Injury Report: OF Jeffrey Goodwin (strained left bicep), OF Sean Kelley (leg muscle cramps), 3B Meatball (right collarbone strain), C Jon Vehse (drunk), 3B Christopher Simons (leg quad tightness), and UTL Chris Evans (pulled penis).—JA

most photos this page by Jesse Wright

JULY 16–CHICO'S (0–6) VS TIGER KINGS Chico's drops two to first place and undefeated Tiger Kings in hard fought doubleheader to remain winless for the season. Despite being outclassed and overmatched by their much younger opponent, the Bonders held their own in game 1, falling 19–14. The bats finally came alive in what looked to be a laugher at the start as Chico's fell behind big in the early going. Pitcher Jeff Ryan struggled with his command early before settling down and recording four strikeouts. Multiple Chico hitters delivered key run-scoring hits, including bases-clearing doubles by Dave Mistich, Chris Simons, and David Lawson. Game 2 was much the same for the first four innings before the wheels completely came off for the Bondsmen in the fifth giving up 15 runs (14 of them after 2 outs), eventually dropping

the nightcap 24–8. Pitcher Chris Evans delivered the big blow, driving in two runs with a majestic deep drive to left centerfield. His ERA however ballooned to an unsightly 51.2 on the young season.

Game notes: Chico legend Thomas Batchelor returned and displayed the aggressive base running that has been lacking in recent seasons. Injuries on the young season continued to mount – OF Lawson (sprained shoulder), 2B Mark Downs (concussion after a gruesome play at the second base bag), and Meatball (collarbone). Because of the recent rash of injuries, team physician Dilip Chandran was present to attend to the wounded. And because the 123 bar is closed due to the pandemic, the bar sent team bartender Donnie D. to pour postgame shots of medicated Irish whiskey. The MVP[2] for the night as voted by his teammates was 3B Chris Simons (unanimous). Last Chico Standing – Ken Price.—JA

---

2 County orange smoking jacket. Starting in the 2019 season, the game MVPs would wear the orange smoking jacket in the parking lot during the postgame. The jacket was designed by Mark Downs. It was stolen once by Chico pitcher Jeff Ryan. It was once worn by a shirtless Meatball. The jacket was never the same after and was soon retired.

JULY 17–CHICO'S (2–6) VS BASIC PITCHES Chico's complete first doubleheader sweep in more than a decade. The Bonders (2–6) pick up their first two wins of the young season, edging Basic Pitches 14–11 in game 1 before humiliating them in the nightcap 21–10. In the first game, pitcher Jeff Ryan struggled for the second night in a row with his control that allowed the Basic Pitches team to keep

it close, but key defensive plays, particularly by SS Jim Antonini, and clutch hitting by numerous Chico's late proved to be the difference.

In game 2, the Bondsmen fell behind early 8–2 before the skies opened and a storm of historical portions rolled through, bringing driving rain and gusty winds. By the time the storm ended, the midsummer sky transitioned from a dreary gray to a magnificent and jubilant orange color. Chico's had seized control of the game, banging out a season high 31 hits that led to 21 runs. Outfielder David Lawson hit a bases-clearing triple to deep center field; first baseman Aaron Hawley followed an inning later with a two-run double. Outfielder Ethan Wells continued his hot hitting banging out five hits on the night, including a clutch double in the decisive fifth inning of game 2. But the big blow came from slumping slugger Andy Tuck who put the game away with a dramatic three-run inside-the-park-home run. After the game, Chico team players celebrated long into the muggy night in the parking lot of Whiston Field, drinking beer and moonshine. It felt good again to be a Chico.

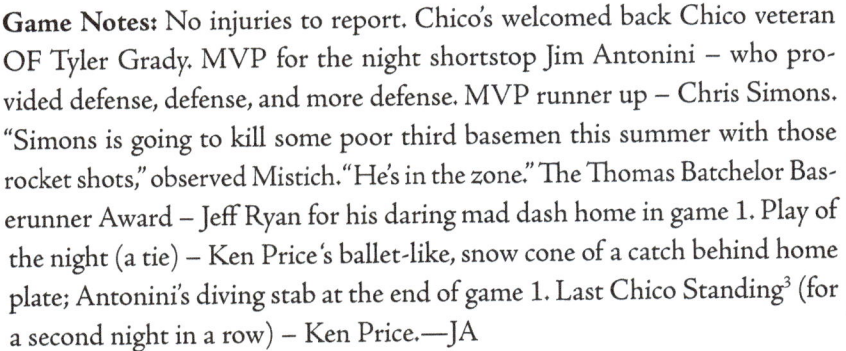

Game Notes: No injuries to report. Chico's welcomed back Chico veteran OF Tyler Grady. MVP for the night shortstop Jim Antonini – who provided defense, defense, and more defense. MVP runner up – Chris Simons. "Simons is going to kill some poor third basemen this summer with those rocket shots," observed Mistich. "He's in the zone." The Thomas Batchelor Baserunner Award – Jeff Ryan for his daring mad dash home in game 1. Play of the night (a tie) – Ken Price's ballet-like, snow cone of a catch behind home plate; Antonini's diving stab at the end of game 1. Last Chico Standing[3] (for a second night in a row) – Ken Price.—JA

---

3 Last Chico Standing Award. Because the world was mostly shut down due to COVID, including 123 Pleasant Street. Chico's (and all the other teams in the BOPARC softball leagues) took their postgame parties to the parking lots that surrounded the different softball fields of White Park. Some of the Chico parking lot parties would last deep into the morning when all of the other teams had long gone home. Even Donnie from 123 would show up for many games with a bottle of Jameson Irish Whiskey and a sleeve of plastic shot cups. There were a couple occasions when different team members would stay out so long, they would see the sun come up over the lush green hills of White Park. These late postgame night outs led to what is now referred to as the Last Chico Standing Award. Dave Lawson currently holds the all-time record- a record that likely will never be broken.

123 MVP Duppee

DONNIE DUPPEE

CLUBHOUSE MANAGER

SERVES: RIGHT   **POURS: LEFT**   **SEASONS: 27**
HOBBIES: GARDENING, CONCERT ROAD TRIPS, WOODS, MUSIC, DOGS
WALK-UP SONG: "DON'T STOP NOW" BY GUIDED BY VOICES

Donnie efficiently runs the team clubhouse; is the heartbeat of Chico Nation; directs traffic in the 123 bar during crowded Chico post-games; more than 12,000 Chico whiskey shots served; has attended one official team meeting during his tenure; discovers all the good new music first.

AUGUST 13–CHICO'S (2–12) VS LADDER BOYS

Chico bats come alive in late night doubleheader but drop both games to fall to a dismal 2–12 on the 2020 softball season of COVID. The Bonders roared out to a 5–0 early lead in game 1 against the younger and physically more gifted Ladder Boys team behind an early 2-run triple by OF Andy Tuck. But as usual Chico's couldn't hold the lead allowing 8 runs in a decisive 4th inning. Hitting stars for the Bonders in game 1 included Ken Price and Jeff Goodwin. In game 2, the wheels completely came off for the Bondsmen, giving up 12 runs in the 1st inning—sadly, all after two outs. Before Chico's bats could come back to life, they were already down 19–3. But the Bonders didn't quit. They never quit, cutting the lead to 8 runs in the 4th before finally falling 24–14.

Game notes: Game 1 MVP was Meatball who delivered a key bases-clearing bases-loaded double to put the Bonders ahead 10–8 late in the game. Game 2 MVP Chris Evans, who despite giving up 24 runs (most of which were earned runs) and wildly throwing two balls into the ground for errors, banged out three hits at the top of the order. Last Chico Standing – Sean Kelley—JA

AUGUST 14–CHICO'S (3–12) VS PLEASANT DAY-CARE

Chico's returned to the softball diamond to face Pleasant Day Care less than 18 hours after dropping two disappointing games to an overrated Ladder Boys squad on the previous night. The Bonders looked hungover in game 1, falling behind early 12–1 after a terrible 2nd inning before eventually folding without much of a fight 15–5 in the most lackluster of performances. Game 2 was a completely different story as the Bondsmen battled in a back-and-forth affair with stellar defense and solid hitting, leading 9 to 8 going into the last inning. It appeared as if Chico's were doomed after a bases-clearing three-run home run by the young and speedy Pleasant Day shortstop, putting his team ahead 11–8. But the Bondsmen responded in the bottom half of the inning, quickly scoring two runs starting with a single by gimpy OF Tyler Grady. In a brilliant tactical move, 2B Mark Downs was put in to pitch run for the injured Grady who kept the inning alive by beating a close throw to 2nd base that would have ended the game. Multiple clutch hits by Eric Ramón, Bill Rittenour, Ethan Wells, and Chris Simons followed that led to one of the most dramatic hits in Chico history—a bases-loaded walk off inside-the-park-home run by game MVP Andy Tuck to lead the Bonders to a thrilling 14–11 victory. It was glorious. The sixteen orange clad Chico players from the bench area poured onto the field (all wearing face masks and adhering to established social distancing measures, of course) and mobbed the hero Tuck. The game had been over for hours, but several Chico players were reported to be still celebrating in the darkened parking lot of Whiston Field. It may take the rising sun of dawn to break up that party. It was a great night to be a Chico.—JA

AUGUST 19–CHICO'S (4–14) VS FORD-LIN-COLN MORGANTOWN

On the hallowed (and Chico friendly) grounds of Ogden Field, the Bonders split a doubleheader against Ford-Lincoln Morgantown. In game 1, the Bonders won in dramatic fashion as shortstop Jim Antonini delivered an extra-inning single to score Andy Tuck from third for a 9–8 victory, the fourth Chico victory of the season. The game was not without fireworks as multiple base runners from Ford-Lincoln Morgantown tried to take out the knees of infielders Aaron Hawley and Antonini on different occasions. Tempers flared until the other team of twenty-somethings realized that they were playing a Chico team with an average age of 43.6 years old and were well over their heads in terms of class, skill, and fight.

Game Notes: Game 1 MVP catcher Eric Ramón delivered three hits in the opener. Also, 1B Hawley drove in 4 important runs. In game 2, Chico's were spent and lost 11–3 to their younger and overly enthusiastic opponents. Co-MVPs in game 2 included Tuck who hit two triples and OF Ethan Wells who led the game off with a dramatic inside-the-park-home run to deep right centerfield. The seventh place Bondsmen (4–14) get some much-needed rest with a week off to heal minor injuries to key players Ken Price, Jim Antonini, David Lawson, and Meatball.—JA

photos by Jesse Wright

all photos by Jesse Wright

all photos by Jesse Wright

Richard Lewis, Pickled Nimrod

SEPTEMBER 2–CHICO'S (4–16) VS PICKLED NIMRODS Chico's Bail Bonds, the world's greatest softball social experiment, not only lost two crucial late season games, but they were absolutely lambasted, embarrassed, humiliated, and battered by arch-rival Pickled Nimrods[4]. The Bonders got blanked in game 1 by the score 20–0. It was as if Chico's had never played the game of softball before. It was as low as a Bondsmen team has ever gone before, and that is really saying something in the long and illustrious history of Chico's. Game 2 was somewhat better as Chico's (4–16) kept the game close early until falling 14–4 to the superior Nimrod squad (12–8). If softball was a two out per inning game, the Bonders would be in first place in the BOPARC standings. All 34 runs given up by Chico's on the night were plated by the Nimrods after two outs. If there was any consolation, Chico's won the postgame parking lot, partying long into the night. With the world shut down and the bars in town closed, probably forever, the late-night Chico dance party was all they had left.

Game Notes: Chico pitcher Jeff Ryan and catcher Eric Ramón were out with injuries. OF Andrew Tuck was once again named MVP, driving in two runs with a triple in game 2. Last Chico Standing (a tie) –pitcher Chris Evans, catcher Ken Price, and OF Tyler Grady.—JA

SEPTEMBER 10–CHICO'S (4–18) VS WV SOBER LIVING The Bonders struggled in both ends of the doubleheader, falling 14–6 in the opener and 22–5 in the nightcap. Chico's had run out of steam after playing 22 games in seven short pandemic weeks in a row. The Bondsmen end the regular season 4–18.

Game MVPs – Ken Price, Aaron Hawley. Honorable mention – Jeffrey Goodwin. But the win-loss record was not indicative of the highly successful season that could not be measured in wins and losses. Because of the circumstances of a world placed on hold, this season felt good and especially needed. It may have been the best one ever. The postgame pandemic parking lot gatherings were epic. They had an end-of-the-world kind of vibe. All the team members and most of their followers liked that feeling.—JA

photo by Jesse Wright

---

4 Richard Lewis is the only player that Chico's has poached from the another team. It happened to be from their arch-rival, the Pickled Nimrods. In his short time as a Bonder, Richard has become the most popular player on the Chico squad. He is a significant contributor on the field (as a pitcher and hitter) and off (e.g., Team Meetings).

2020 Season Awards

Chico MVP – Andy Tuck

Chico Rookie of the Year – Chris Simons

Chico Most Likely to go Shirtless – Meatball

Pitcher of the Year Award (tie) – Jeff Ryan, Chris Evans

Most Improved Chico (2nd year in a row) – Ken Price

Thomas Batchelor Hustle Award – Mark Downs

Chico Comeback Player of the Year – Ethan Wells

Ravi Shibley Slugger Award (tie) – Andy Tuck, Chris Simons

Jon Vehse Tools of Ignorance Catcher Award – Eric Ramón, Ken Price

Chico Best Hair Award (tie) –David Lawson, Jeffrey Goodwin

Chico Outfielder of the Year – Andy Tuck

Chico Most Likely to be Seen with a Cocktail – David Mistich

Chico Who Looks Best in his Uniform (aka Style Award) – David Lawson

Too Many Guitar Players on Chico Award (tie) – Jeffrey Goodwin, Aaron Hawley, Andy Tuck, Tyler Grady

Chico Infielder of the Year – Jim Antonini

The Greg Leatherman/Brian Porterfield 1st Basemen Award (tie) – Aaron Hawley, David Mistich

Chico Ironman Award (tie) – Sean Kelley, Jim Antonini

Chico Spirit Award (tie) – Bill Rittenour, Jeffrey Goodwin, David Lawson

Last Chico Standing Award (tie) – Ken Price, Eric Ramón, Chris Evans

Chico Villain of the Year – Sheik O'Malley

Chico Speedster Award – Ethan Wells

Chico Pat Mears Utility Award – Chris Evans

There is still hope as Chico's earned a postseason berth with their four victories and return to the diamond next week with one last chance of glory.—JA

SEPTEMBER 16 PLAYOFFS   Bittersweet. The Chico (4–20) season ended. During the strangest of times, the Bonders had one of their most successful seasons. The season was not defined by wins and losses but by the love the Chicos had for each other and the unconditional fun of the pandemic parking lot gatherings after each game. It truly was magical.

The Bonders played a near perfect defensive game in the playoff opener against Ford-Lincoln, holding the game close before falling 15–9. Game MVP Jeff Goodwin banged out 3 hits and OF Andy Tuck drove in four runs. In game 2, the 9th seeded Bondsmen were overmatched against 3rd-seeded Solvay 24–9. Chico's briefly held the lead 7–4 in the second inning, before pulling up lame. OF Goodwin delivered a bases-clearing three-run triple. Game MVP Meatball turned in an immaculate unassisted double play at third base late in the game.

Game Notes. Being the special occasion that it was with the Bonders earning a playoff berth – the doubleheader was catered by Lefty's Place and the massive pizza order was delivered by one of our favorite local celebrities and bartenders, Steve Brady. Chico's thank Louis Giuliani and Lisa Marie Giuliani of 123 Pleasant Street for the support and sponsorship. The Bonders also would like to again acknowledge the passing of our friend and Chico legend Ravi Shibley – RIP Ravi...

It will be a long offseason, not because of the 4–20 record but for the fact the weekly Wednesday night doubleheaders are over. For many of the Chico players, these Wednesday get-togethers were all they had during this pandemic summer. As the clock struck midnight, several Bonders partied in the Liberatore Field parking lot in the cool autumn night, vying to be that one Last Chico Standing, not wanting the season to end. Catchers Ken Price and Eric Ramón we're still there, as were Pitchers Jeff Ryan and Chris Evans, OFs David Lawson and Tuck, and 1B Dave Mistich. It was highly likely that at least one of them would still be there when the sun came up.—JA

2021 Chico's: (standing) Dave Mistich, Chris Simons, Tyler Grady, Ken Price, Mark Downs, Aaron Hawley, Jeff Ryan, Eric Ramón, Andy Tuck, Chris Evans, (kneeling) Nic Crouso, Jeff Goodwin, Ken Price, Bill Ritenour, Jim Antonini, Meatball, Sean Kelley

MAY 13–CHICO'S (1-1) VS FOUR HORSEMEN COMICS Bonders split doubleheader and surprisingly but briefly occupy first place in the Blue Division on opening night of BOPARC softball. THIS IS NOT A TYPO BUT CHICO'S, WITH A LINEUP DEPLETED BY INJURY AND CIRCUMSTANCE, SCORED 12 RUNS AGAINST THEIR FLABBERGASTED AND MORE TALENTED OPPONENT IN THE 1ST INNING OF GAME 1. The Bondsmen built an almost insurmountable lead of 14–2 and only needing 2 outs in the 5th inning to close out a 10-run mercy victory. But in true Chico fashion, the Bondsmen left the door open with shoddy defense as the bats of the Four Horsemen exploded, roaring back to tie the game in the last inning. But the Bonders would not be denied, OF Jeffrey Goodwin drove in SS Jim Antonini with the game winning run in the last inning to cap a dramatic and most satisfying 19–18 victory, propelling Chico's into first place in the league. Stars of game 1 were plenty and I can't list them all because it's late, I've been over-served, and I don't remember well anymore – P Jeff Ryan fielded his

127

position flawlessly accounting for over 10 assists on comebackers to the mound. Lead-off hitter and second basemen Chris Evans was defensive player of the game with many fine plays in the field as well setting the tone in the 1st inning with two hits and two runs scored. SS Antonini was 5 for 6 with 2 doubles, 4 runs scored, and 5 RBIs. In game 2, the Bondsmen were far too tired, drunk, high, and wounded to challenge their superior opponent, falling 18–3 in a 5-inning laugher. Chico's enjoyed the rest of the night in the parking lot and finally at the 123 bar. There wasn't a sad face in the place at last call.

Game notes: Quote of the night: To Chico rookie, "Nic Crouso, you're in right field." His response, "Where's right field?" Chico 2B Evans, "You'll make a perfect, Chico." Second best quote: Early in game 1, P Jeff Ryan was struggling with his control. "We got guys who can replace you." He responded defiantly, "I pitched last season through a pandemic. Don't worry, I'll be all right." Last Chico Standing – 1B Dave Mistich.—JA

MAY 19–CHICO'S (1-3) VS RIDGELINE CROSSFIT

Chico's loses two tough games to fall to 1–3 on the young BOPARC softball season. The Bonders battled in the oppressive spring heat in game 1, dropping a mostly tight, contested contest for the first five innings, until the dreaded 'one bad inning" and losing to the much younger Ridgeline CrossFit squad 16–7. In game 2, the Bondsmen wilted in the heat like the prettiest ignored flower, humiliated in five quick innings 15–4.

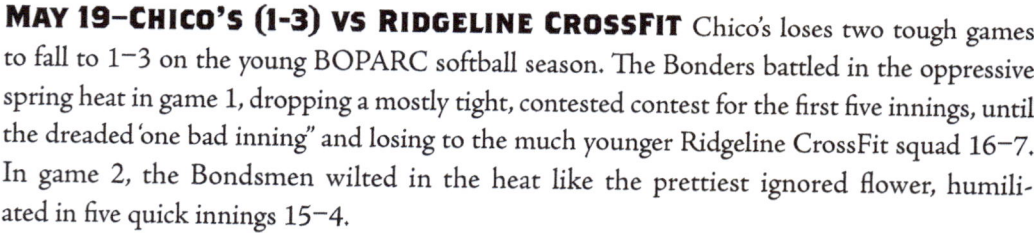

Game notes: The Bonders welcomed the return of longtime OF Tyler Grady who banged out 4 hits on the night, including a bases loaded, 2-out double in game 1. Other Chico stars included SS Antonini who knocked a bases-clearing double off the left field fence as well as made a dramatic over-the-shoulder-Willie-Mays-catch in shallow left field. Also, 3B Downs filled in admirably for the compromised and aging Chico veteran Meatball. Downs played a flawless third base in the field and led the team in runs scored with three. Rookie Nic Crouso picked up his first hit in a Chico uniform in the 2nd inning of game 1. Also, 2B Chris Evans almost made the greatest play in Chico history, a running, falling, tripping, diving, and time-stopping bare-hand stab of a bloop in shallow center field that innocently rolled out of his right hand when his body awkwardly slammed the ground. The damaged Bonders squad who are nursing multiple leg muscle injuries get a much-needed bye for next week. Chico's return to the diamond in the first week of June, heavy favorites to take the next two games against no-name losers The Foundry Church (0–4).—JA

JUNE 2—CHICO'S (1-5) VS THE FOUNDRY CHURCH

With God on their side (but most importantly, having younger legs and clearer lungs), The Foundry Church outlasted Chico's in two hard fought games on the most beautiful spring West Virginia nights that decided last place in BOPARC softball. Despite falling into last place, the Bonders got their money's worth playing a full 14 innings in a little over two hours. The more energetic and much quicker Foundry team ran the Bondsmen ragged with their dink and dunk style of play, winning game 1 by the score of 17–11 and then 18–10 in the nightcap. The night was not without stars for the pesky Chico team. Chris Simons was game 1 MVP hitting 3 doubles and driving in 7 runs. In game 2, LCF Andy Tuck took MVP honors, blasting a dramatic grand slam deep over the short fence in right field of Liberatore Stadium that pulled the Bonders close late in the game. It was the first over-the-fence home run for Chico's since 2015 when the late great Ravi Shibley sent the Chico faithful home happy with the longest home run ever hit at Whiston Field.

Game notes: A tired and worn-out Chico SS Jim Antonini was told postgame that he was 36 years older than the wonderful SS for The Foundry team. Catcher Ken Price revealed an extra but unknown running gear as he scored on a mad sprint, dusty play at home plate in game 1. The air around first base had to be poisoned. Both Chico 1Bs Dave Mistich and Aaron Hawley dropped routine pop-ups. Chico rookie Richard Lewis is now referred to as "Big Sexy". Last Chico Standing (a tie) –2B Chris Evans, OF Richard Lewis, and OF Andrew Tuck.—JA

JUNE 9—CHICO'S (1-7) VS SUNCREST PUB

The young cocky second baseman for Suncrest Pub said 20 minutes before the first pitch of the game, "Chico is but a ghost of those early teams 10–15 years ago."

Long time Chico veteran, Sean Kelley, loudly responded as he rolled four hours worth of cigarettes, "Bullshit! We're too young for ghosts!"

And the older, undermanned and physically brittle Chico squad

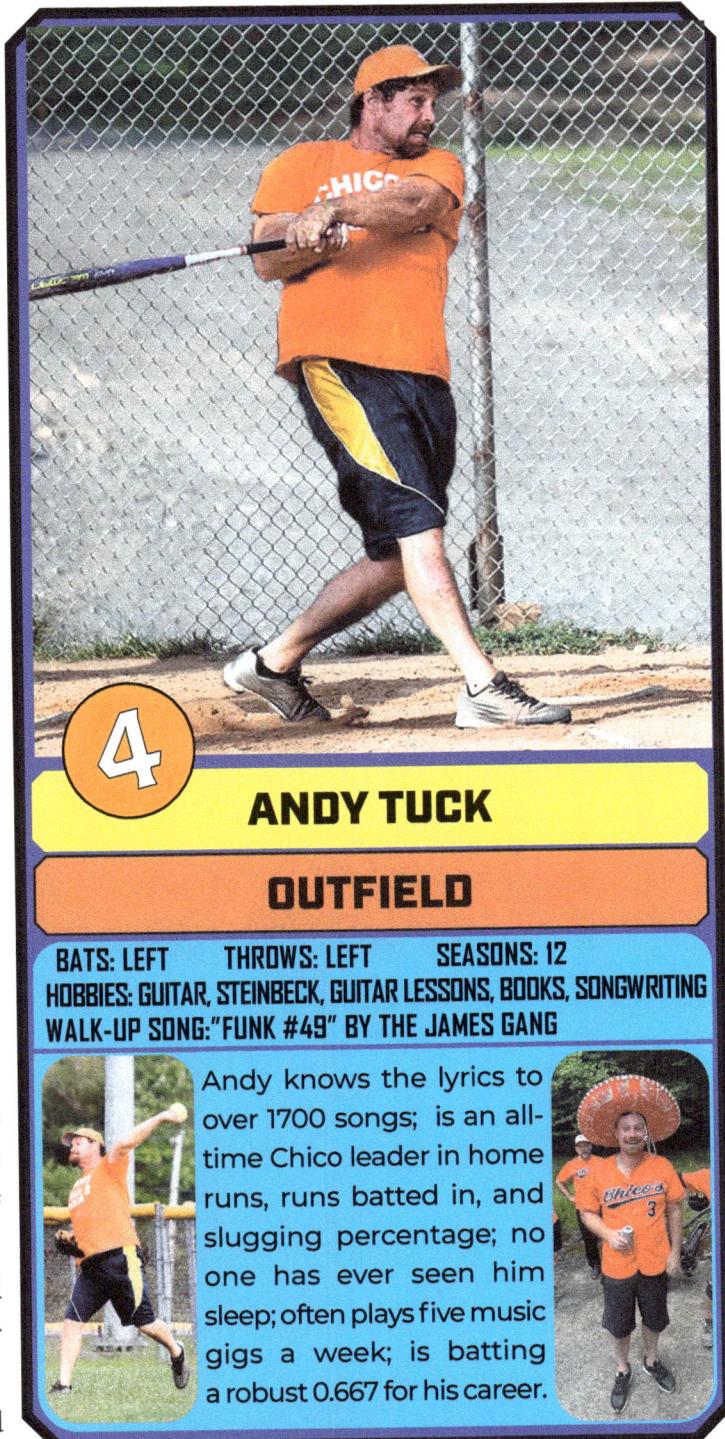

4

ANDY TUCK

OUTFIELD

BATS: LEFT   THROWS: LEFT   SEASONS: 12
HOBBIES: GUITAR, STEINBECK, GUITAR LESSONS, BOOKS, SONGWRITING
WALK-UP SONG: "FUNK #49" BY THE JAMES GANG

Andy knows the lyrics to over 1700 songs; is an all-time Chico leader in home runs, runs batted in, and slugging percentage; no one has ever seen him sleep; often plays five music gigs a week; is batting a robust 0.667 for his career.

battled those assholes on a hot humid night for two games, 14 innings, and over two hours before valiantly dropping both ends of the hard-fought doubleheader. Game 1 shouldn't have counted as the Bonders 1B Dave Mistich and OF- Richard Lewis were forced to chug and shotgun numerous exploding beers in the pregame coolers that were too tightly packed with ice. Chico's found themselves down by over 10 runs before they had even submitted their batting lineup for the opener, eventually losing 22−9. Game 2 was a different story. The Bonders scratched and clawed their way to a 12−11 lead late in the game before falling 19−16 in a heartbreaker.

Game notes: Chico MVP was pitcher Jeff Ryan, who despite giving up 41 runs on the night and surviving two line drives off his chest, provided 30 PBRs in the pregame parking lot. OFs Andy Tuck and Chris Simons continued to deliver the big deep hits. Despite dealing with a tightened back, SS Antonini reached base all ten times at the plate. Chico rookie Nic Crouso had his best night as a Bonder. Last Chico standing (a tie) – Richard Lewis, Ken Price, and Eric Ramón. After the game, a tipsy Bonders team retreated to a raucous 123 bar and drank shots of whiskey and listened to The Rolling Stones until near day break. Chico's have lost 7 out of 8 games this season, but it sure feels like they've won many more than that.—JA

JUNE 23–CHICO'S (1-11) VS KEGLER'S Groundhog Day at Liberatore Field. It was the most pleasant of summer nights. An eager and short-handed Chico squad showed up with their trusty bats, balls, mitts, coolers, and jerseys[1]. They battled hard early in both games before eventually failing in each to an elite Kegler's team, extending their losing streak to 11 games. The Bonders were

---

1   Baseball jerseys. Chico's debut the new baseball-style, button-up orange jersey with black lettering in 2021. As a going away gift to Jon Vehse who was leaving for New Orleans, Dave Mistich got Vehse and himself the jerseys in September 2020. The new jersey type was accepted by the team and first worn in the 2021 season. Later that season, a black version of the jersey with orange lettering would debut during a playoff game. The game was dubbed – "The Blackout". The change in jersey color didn't help the performance on the field as the Bonders were quickly and efficiently eliminated from the playoffs by their opponent that night.

sad and disappointed in themselves. They retreated to their coolers and swilled beer before going to the 123 bar to swallow lots of whiskey and listen to loud jukebox music for hours. They soon were happy again and proud to be Chico's.

Disclaimer: This recap was actually written the morning before the game. All events of the evening were predicted exactly as they occurred. Game MVPs were Nic Crouso (people's choice) who made a dramatic catch in deep right field and also reached base three times, and SS Antonini who doubled to deep left, driving in the Bonders only two runs on the night. Also, the stitches in OF Chris Simons' belly were removed on the 123 bar after the game. It is important to note that Jameson Irish whiskey was used as both an antiseptic and an analgesic—a win-win for all involved in the process.—JA

JUNE 30–CHICO'S VS PICKLED NIMRODS
Despite the rain-out against their arch nemesis Pickled Nimrods, eleven thirsty Chico's still showed up at the 123 bar to celebrate friendship, team, loyalty, and love. It was odd to go home at the end of the night tipsy without the sweat, dirt, and sore muscles. Chico's thank bartender and super fan Brieve Morrison for opening the bar early and playing a killer musical selection. The Bonders return to the diamond next Wednesday against the pushover and Adderall-addicted Pleasant Day Care squad. Last Chico standing (a tie) – Ken Price, Dave Mistich, and Richard Lewis.—JA

JULY 14–CHICO'S (1-15) VS BENCHWARMERS
Chico's was outmatched and bulldozed in two laughers against 1st place Benchwarmers (18–2) in BOPARC doubleheader softball action. Number one Chico pitcher Jeff Ryan hasn't been the same the past couple weeks as he's struggled to find the strike zone. Chico management can't decide whether it's due to his bad lifestyle choices of cheap cigars, Wild Turkey, a daily

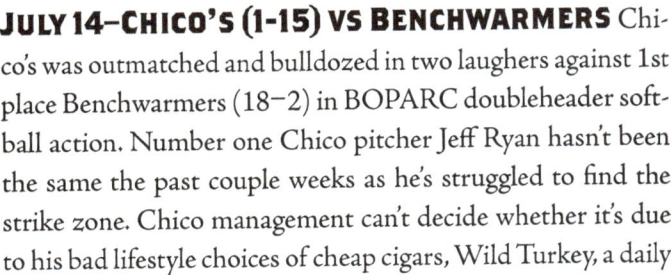

diet of fatty steak bombs, or all the recent tick bites he's received working his homestead on the old Pt. Marion Road. There were bright spots—OF Andy Tuck was the night's MVP, hitting two triples and driving in five runs. The Bonders celebrated the return of outfielder Tyler Grady who reached base in all three of his at-bats. Last Chico Standing – Time Share Cat, Jeff Ryan. Game Fan Favorite Chico – Richard Lewis.—JA

JULY 14–CHICO'S (1-17) VS MOUNTAIN MAMA

Chico's drops two hard fought games against a superior Mountain Mama team. But the Bonders made them sweat, taking each game to the limit. In game 1, Chico pitcher Jeff Ryan, high on cheap weed with a belly full of greasy cheesesteaks, struggled to find the strike zone that dug a hole early that was too big to overcome. Chico outfielder and game one MVP Chris Simons kept the Bondsmen close, by actually breaking the left field foul pole (see picture) with the most majestic 3-run home run since the days of the late great Ravi Shibley. Chico 2B and game one anti-MVP Chris Evans took the blame for the loss, pulling up lame in the first inning and admittedly getting Ryan too high to toss strikes.

In game 2, relief pitcher Richard Lewis stabilized the erratic pitching situation, keeping the Mountain Mama hitters off balance with his assortment of junk ball curves and never-ending trash talk. Game 2 saw the dramatic return of Meatball who had been shelved for an assortment of injuries and had yet to play a game this season. Defensive highlights included a beautiful third base rundown that resulted in a throw out at the plate from Shortstop Jim Antonini and catcher Ken Price. Like every week for the past couple summers, the Bondsmen retreated to the parking lot then 123 bar drinking beer and whiskey and feeling like winners. And anyone who saw them would think the same thing. Last Chico standing - a tie: Richard Lewis and Nic Crouso.—JA

JULY 14–CHICO'S (3-17) VS MORGANTOWN SOBER LIVING

The losing streak is over. Sober Living has forfeited[2] tonight's game. Do the Chico's want to meet at Ogden Field for batting practice at 6:00? There will be a cooler of beer.—JA

---

2 When a team forfeits, the opposing team is awarded a win, or two wins, in the case of a doubleheader.

Sean Kelley 1970–2021

Sadly, Sean passed away on August 15 during his 15th season as a Chico. Sean was the ideal Chico. He played drums in numerous local bands through the years. For over a decade, he was the regular bartender at 123 Pleasant Street on Mondays and Fridays. He rolled and smoked his own cigarettes. And he loved Irish whiskey and singing Irish folksongs. But most importantly, he was everyone's best friend. He was well-liked by all who knew him—a lot. There's no better legacy than that.—JA

2019 Best All-Around Chico Award and Best Outfielder Award

August 17. Jim March's Tribute to Sean Kelley

"...So, NOBODY has gone through more Chico gear than me. I must've worn every number that there IS (and 00 isn't a number, Vehse). I borrowed them, then left without returning them, or, and this happened OFTEN, the other Chico just didn't WANT it back. I thought that I would spruce up my style today with a little Chico Orange. I SCOURED this place. Nuttin'... Nuttin' at all... I DID though, during my scouring, notice a handle of Jameson. ALL IS NOT LOST! RIP, SEANDOG..."

In Sean's memory his jersey is displayed at 123 and team members wear his number 9 on their jerseys..

AUGUST 19–CHICO'S (4-18) VS PLEASANT DAY CARE Despite the muddy conditions, it was great to get on the field and finally play some softball after a month of rain-outs. The Bonders split the doubleheader against Pleasant Day Care, winning the first one by forfeit– 12 players to 8. Chico's dropped a hard fought full seven inning game by the score of 9–3 to their younger and quicker opponent in game 2. The night was not without stars—in the game 1 scrimmage Bill Bill Bill Rittenour slugged 4 base hits. Chico catcher Ken Price had multiple hits and a couple of beautiful pop up catches behind home plate. In Game 2, the Bonders turned a couple of nice double plays and played solidly in the field except for a disastrous 'one bad' fourth inning. Chico pitcher and game 2 MVP Jeff Ryan regained his pitching touch and batting stroke playing his best game in years. Word has it that he has successfully avoided second baseman and bad influence Chris Evans for over a month now. Speaking of Evans, he delivered the biggest blow in game 2– a deep majestic drive for a double to left centerfield. He also won muddy Chico award for the night for several dives in the infield and his daring slide at home plate in six inches of mud that unfortunately resulted in the game-ending out.

But tonight's games didn't feel right. Something was sadly missing. Future Chico games will never be the same. It was the first Chico game without beloved left fielder Sean Kelley. He will always be missed. He was everybody's favorite Chico. Please keep Sean. Erin Kelley, and their kids in your thoughts. Before the games, several Chico players lined up in his old spot in left field before the first pitch in honor of Sean.—JA

AUGUST 26–CHICO'S (4-20) VS CITY PLUMBING & HEATING Chico's Bail Bonds dropped two in a Thursday night doubleheader to City Plumbing & Heating (are these guys getting paid to play softball?) in a Bayou-like late summer swelter. Still yet, the Bonders displayed competence rarely seen during the 2021 campaign. Skipper and shortstop Antonini blew off the team —under the guise of helping aging in-laws—but instead blew his cover by documentation of him lounging on edge of the cool

and refreshing waters of Long Island Sound in Connecticut. By the time he reads this, though, he will likely smell of butter, lobster, and Narragansett Lagers.

In game 1, right centerfielder Jeff Goodwin showed Golden Glove-level play, snagging three consecutive outs in the same inning. Goodwin talked about it late into the night, saying multiple times "that felt good," referring to the final—and most acrobatic—of snags. Some Chico's took the "that felt good" out of context and wondered what the hell he meant. 3B Mark Downs would have made an incredible run-scoring trip from first base (no one had seen Downs move like that since a memorable mud-slide a couple weeks ago), but 3rd base coach Jeff Ryan literally shrugged his shoulders and made Downs eat shit in a rundown that could have —and should have—been avoided. So, it goes. Utility man Chris Evans ripped the seams off the ball for a bases-clearing, 3-RBI double. (This writer can tell he'll be talking about it for weeks.) It should have been a triple, but he admittedly would have torn a hamstring upon trying to leg it out to third.

In game 2, veteran Chico ace Ryan held a no-hitter through a full inning—the first inning. Of course it was, or else it wouldn't have been a no-hitter at all. The Bonders had never seen such grace on the mound. The 1B platoon duo of Aaron Hawley and Mistich might have been their mediocre selves on defense, but they stroked the ball effortlessly at the plate. The real highlight, though, was the home run from LF Andy Tuck (whose newly shaven face might be good luck—despite his worry that he looks like a child) and his "Bash Brother" in arms SS Chris Simons almost hitting another one back-to-back. The lower bar was out of commission on this night, as dumbass college kids and their drug-riddled dance music took over the 123 bar. Sean Kelley continues to be missed. There remains a giant hole in the Chico family that will simply never be replaced. For this deputized-writer-Chico, who oftentimes must translate broken English from a certain person in high office and navigate the sludges of West Virginia politics, this was, unquestionably, his most daunting—but satisfying— assignment to date.—Mistch

2022 SCARS ON THEIR LIVERS

2022 Chico's: (standing) Mark Downs, Nic Crouso, Dave Mistich, Richard Lewis, Aaron Hawley, Dave Lawson, Dave Becker, Walt Sarkees, (kneeling) Shitty Shiflett, Andy Tuck, Bill Ritenour, Jim Antonini, Ken Price, Jeff Goodwin. Photo by Brian Eli.

MAY 12—CHICO'S (0–2) VS PLEASANT DAY CARE Chico's Bail Bonds stumble out of the gate before being pushed down the stairs, dropping both ends of a doubleheader on the most beautiful of opening nights in softball action. The highlights on the field were few as the Bondsmen were overmatched 21–6 in game 1 and 12–1 in game 2 by rival Pleasant Day Care (now stacked with ringers). The highlights were reserved for the postgame reunion and celebration where the Chico team members drank whiskey and cheap beer late into the night. The Bonders welcomed back veteran outfielder David Becker into the fold. He'd been on the disabled list for nearly two years to have a growth (e.g., devil's tail) removed from his lower back. I could have sworn that the hole left behind winked at me during the exceptionally long 1st inning in game 1. In the parking lot after the game, I think I saw the hole in his back mouth the words in a slow-motion drone, "…Meatball is dead…"

Game notes: Game 1 MVP – Dave Becker. The Chico family welcomed back Bondsmen legendary 1B Greg Leatherman and newcomer Scott "Shitty" Shiflett. It's early but Chico utility infielder Chris Evans still leads the league in half-smoked cigarettes during a game. Game 2 MVPs – a tie: Mark Downs, Bill Rittenour. Last Chico Standing – Jeff Ryan.—JA

MAY 27–CHICO'S (0–4) VS FOUNDRY CHURCH Chico's relegated to laughingstocks of BOPARC softball league after doubleheader drubbing. It would not be the Bonders night as they were outmatched and outclassed against undefeated Blue League upstart and juggernaut, Foundry Church, by scores of 15–1 in game 1 and 17–3 in game 2. Despite the disappointing result, the Bondsmen battled their hearts out against a much younger but more physically fit, cleaner living, bible beating, and teetotaling team. There were highlights though for Chico's. Chris Simons delivered a dramatic bases-clearing inside-the-park-home run in game 2. The fielding was mostly stellar in both games, led by shortstop Jim Antonini (Game 2 MVP) who played as if he drank from the fountain of youth, leaping several feet into the air to stab hard hit line drives as well as cover everything batted on the ground between Mississippi Avenue and Darst Street. Outfielders Andy Tuck (Game 2 co-MVP) and Jeff Goodwin made many diving and rolling catches of hot shot low line drives. 2B Chris Evans (Game 1 co-MVP) won the dirt man, bloodiest Chico award, diving for multiple grounders, leaving pieces of skin, unsmoked cigarettes, and pieces of prosciutto and Irish cheddar behind him everywhere.

Game notes: Play of Game – dramatic controversial home plate tag by catcher Ken Price. Last Chico Standing – pitcher Richard Lewis.—JA

photo by Dave Carson

JUNE 15–CHICO'S (0–8) VS PURE COLLECTIBLES Too hot, too many innings, too long. The Bonders' aging lineup was not built for the current heat wave (heat index of 110° F, 36° C) as they melted against friendly rival Pure Collectibles (2–6) and forced to play two complete 7-inning games. The Bonders sadly and embarrassingly lost both ends of the nighttime doubleheader. I've been scolded continually over the years that these Chico write-ups dwell too much on small penis size, poor base running skills, misjudged fly balls, bobbled grounders, poor pitch selection, alcohol overuse, and no idea of what a strike zone is. So, after tonight's debacle, there is nothing left to say—because it was all those things in the doubleheader and more.

Game notes: Andy Tuck has been placed on the 10-day disabled list with an injured groin[1]. Because of his poor performance at the plate and in the field and so many misjudged fly balls, OF - David Becker has been demoted to the AA minor league Chico affiliate in Grafton. Chico slugger Chris Simons left early in game 1 with bruised ribs. Game MVPs – Richard Lewis who went 4–4 in game 1 and OF Jeff Goodwin who had 5 hits, several nice catches, and mowed 6 lawns on the day. Last Chico Standing – Jeff Ryan.—JA

photos by Dave Carson

JUNE 23–CHICO'S (1–9) VS MEGA CORP Chico's dominates game 1 beating Mega Corporation 14–8 in BOPARC softball laugher. But after blowing wad in game 1, the old, tired, and somewhat drunken Bondsmen dropped game 2 of the twin-bill in disappointing fashion by a score of 9–1. Game 1 was all about the battery of substitute pitcher—Ken Price who was forced onto the mound by circumstance and the normally late-arriving David Lawson was needed to catch behind the plate. Pitcher Price did not disappoint hurling seven strong innings that included six strike outs and one beautifully turned double play. Catcher Lawson set a Chico catcher team record, recording six putouts in game 1 that included catching two pop-ups and

1 Groins. The groin has been the most pulled muscle (whether by accident or on purpose) among the Chico players through the years. Other commonly pulled muscles have included hamstring and calf. Broken fingers and head injuries have also regularly occurred. Hangovers are not considered an injury.

throwing runners out at both 1st and 3rd bases. Game 1 was not without hitting stars: 1B Dave Mistich, 1B Aaron Hawley, SS Jim Antonini, and OF Andy Tuck all delivered multiple hits and drove in several runs. Pitcher Price and OF Tuck delivered the final game-winning blows with bases clearing 3-run hits late in game 1. In game 2, the Bondsmen failed to show up, losing to their unassuming opponent in an embarrassing manner. Game 2 MVP was OF Tuck. He scored the lone Chico run and was the only outfielder not to make an error. Despite the disappointment of game 2, happy Chico team members and scores of fans partied late into the night in celebration of their first win of the season. The happy chants of KEN-V-P, KEN-V-P, KEN-V-P from the 123 bar could be heard as far away as the Kingwood Pike. For this night, Chico's were officially winners.

Quote of the night: "Chico players have more scars on their livers than years Mega Corp players have been alive," observed Jon Vehse in the postgame; Last Chico Standing (a tie) – David Lawson and Ken Price.—JA

JUNE 30–CHICO'S (1–11) VS JRC HEATING AND COOLING

Bonders hit rock bottom (I mean bloody-fucking rock bottom) losing both ends of doubleheader against winless doormat JRC Heating and Cooling who pick up their first two wins of the season. I've played over 200 games for Chico's over 15 years and game 2 was the worst display of Bonder softball I've ever witnessed in the team's long and glorious history—and that's saying a lot. Knowing the Bondsmen had a golden opportunity to move up the BOPARC Blue League standings going against their night's beleaguered, downtrodden, and winless last place opponent, a makeshift and compromised but eager and earnest Chico squad of only 11 team members limited due to vacation, injury, and rock-n-roll gigs, roared to an early game 1 lead behind the hitting of Aaron Hawley, David Lawson, Nic Crouso, and Eric Ramón and the pitching of Ken Price. But the highlights ended early as the Bonders were embarrassed due to shoddy outfield play, errant throws, bad pre-game habits (too drunk), and poor lung capacity (too old, too many cigarettes), dropping game 1 by the score

42

KEN PRICE

CATCHER, TEAM MANAGER

BATS: RIGHT **THROWS:** RIGHT **SEASONS:** 8
HOBBIES: FORMULA ONE, WVU FANBOY, CURLING, STEELERS
WALK-UP SONG: "BADMAN" BY GANJA WHITE KNIGHT

Ken is affectionately referred to as KEN-V-P by other Chico players; became team manager in 2024; started his managerial career by winning his first game before losing 36 in a row; has been shushed during a 123 comedy show after a Chico game because of his dangerously loud laugh; is known for his opposite field hitting.

of 18–11. Game 2 was a complete and utter disaster. Chico's lost by the 20-run mercy rule 23–3 in only 3 innings to an opposing pitcher who just had a hip replacement and hobbled on a prosthetic right leg. The game was highlighted by numerous Chico drops of routine fly balls in the outfield and too many base-on-balls allowed by Bonder pitchers. Chico outfielders dropped at least eight very easy, catchable fly balls as well as let numerous slow rolling outfield grounders go through their legs. It was a very sad showing, so bad that right centerfielder Richard Lewis personally removed himself in the middle of an inning because of his very own poor play—a Chico first, retreating to the safety and sanctuary of the beer coolers in the parking lot. Left fielder David Becker has not been the same player since he had the devil tail removed from his lower back in 2020.

Game notes: KEN-V-Ps on the night were David Lawson who delivered 3 hits in game 1 and Aaron Hawley who had 4 hits and 5 RBIs in game 1. Chico Outfield Errors Counts – Richard Lewis (4), Chris Evans (3), and David Becker (9). Last Chico Standing – Ken Price.—JA

JULY 8–CHICO'S (1–13) VS FOUR HORSEMEN COMICS

The sun set on Chico's Bail Bonds as they dropped two hard fought games against a superior and younger Four Horsemen Comics squad in a twilight doubleheader. The Bonders failed to show up in game 1, delivering a lackluster performance before falling 12–1. The Bonders battled hard in game 2 though, letting a victory slip away in the final innings of a tight 9–7 loss. There are so many Chico's players to highlight: OF Andy Tuck made several great catches and throws as well as a big triple off the top of the right field fence in game 1. OF "Bill-Bill-Bill-Bill" Rittenour had the hit of his life with a bases-clearing double to the fence in game 2. Left fielder Dave Mistich ran his ass off, chasing down many fly balls to left. Catcher Eric Ramón had two-line drive singles along with a beautiful tag of a runner at a close play at home plate. Chico veteran Jon Vehse played a flawless first base and led an important Chico team meeting as they assessed the future of the organization in the postgame. Chico SS Jim Antonini made a highlight reel, sprawling diving catch as well as delivering a deep, deep, deep drive to left field to burn the young mullet-proud overrated fielder who tried to play left field for the Four Horsemen (his jersey number was '69'—of course). But pitcher of game 2, Richard Lewis was the star of the night. He kept the Horsemen batters off balance and hit what would have been an inside-the-park-home run if it wasn't for a ground rule ruling that made it a double.

Game notes: 2B Chris Evans didn't bring his normal energy or zest.

He must be injured or got really old, really fast. Pitcher Lewis took the hardest of line drives off his right thigh. He is questionable for the next game. Last Chico Standing – David Lawson. —JA

JULY 21–CHICO'S (1–15) VS LADDER BOYS

The curtain is closing fast on the 2022 Chico season. The ugly season continues as the Bonders dropped both ends of a doubleheader against middling opponent Ladder Boys 12−4 in game 1 and 20−2 in game 2. The Bonders buried themselves deep in the hard Whiston Field infield dirt early in both games, falling behind 11−2 after the 1st inning in each. There's not much good to report: Game 1 MVP OF Chris Simons provided the only highlight in the first game with a deep line drive over the left field fence for a home run. In the night cap, Game 2 MVP OF Dave Becker hustled out a two-run triple for the only significant play. Chico SS Jim Antonini broke his middle right finger (again—for the third time as a Chico) as well as delivered 4 hits on the night. The doubleheader turned out to be the battle of the "Shittys"—the Bonders had Scott Shiftlett "Little Shitty" and the Ladder Boys had an outfielder they called "Big Shitty." Chico Injury Update: veteran catcher Jon Vehse is out for two weeks and lucky to be alive with the deepest of ass bruises after falling off a cliff in southern West Virginia. Last Chico Standing – Ken Price.—JA

JULY 28–CHICO'S (1–17) VS CITY PLUMBING & HEATING

Bonders lose both games of a doubleheader to City Plumbing & Heating on a beautiful late July night—clear, blue skies as far as the eyes could see. The Bondsmen had fun running the bases HARD, making SPECTACULAR plays in the field, and filling the skies with the HARDEST of line drives. But the Bondsmen unfortunately fell short in the scorebook, dropping to a ghastly 1 win and 17 losses on the season. But it's okay, Chico team members partied hard into the night, enjoying each other's company, and rocking to the best live music in the world at the beloved 123 bar. Chico MVP was Scott 'Little Shitty' Shiftlett who turned a spectacular unassisted double play at second base as well as threw out runners at third base and home plate. MVP Runner-ups were Jon Vehse who enthusiastically led the post-game Chico team meeting to heights never before reached, and OF Chris Simons who did not back down from the opponent's mammoth catcher as well as hit multiple extra base hits. Last Chico Standing (a tie) – Dave Mistich, Aaron Hawley, Ken Price, Richard Lewis, Andy Tuck, etc etc etc…

AUGUST 8 SAD NEWS TO REPORT

Olivia Newton-John, Australian singer and pop idol from the 1980's. She was 73 years old. The famed Olivia Newton-John trophy will live forever at the 123 bar. Rest In Peace, Queen Olivia.—JA

photos by Dave Carson

August 19–Chico's (2–20) vs Ford-Lincoln

Anatomy of a Chico Night in August

-The Bonders are scheduled to play a doubleheader at 8 PM & 9 PM at twilight on the unforgiving green pasture of Whiston Field on the most beautiful summer Thursdays ever.

-Several key Chico players are out—slugger Chris Simons is hiking in the mountains of Oregon; pitcher Jeff Ryan is fishing in the surf of the Atlantic Ocean in Florida; Eric Ramón is kicking some stupid asshole's ass somewhere in the tri-state area; and 2B and team spark plug Chris Evans is on the injured list—his tiny left groin is achy.

-Chico manager and shortstop Jim Antonini is stressed—he arrived at the field 1-hour early—the Bonders have played poorly during the current 15-game losing streak—really, really poorly. He chugs a 16-ounce PBR waiting for other Chico players to show up. He hasn't heard from OF Bill Rittenour or Chico star utility player David Lawson.

-Chico players start to arrive. Opponent players for arch-rival Ford-Lincoln also start to show up. It looks like they'll be missing some key players. Antonini is feeling better.

-All of the Chico infield is present at 7:30. None of the Chico outfielders have arrived yet. Word is that some will be late. Antonini is stressed again—he drinks more PBR. Lawson suddenly appears out of the White Park woods near the softball field complex on foot. Lawson appeared 'happy', 'very happy', almost too happy. And Dave Becker hurries from an auxiliary parking lot hyped up on diet Red Bulls and shots of Wild Turkey. He also appears 'happy' (but a different kind of happy from Lawson). Pitcher Richard 'Big Sexy' pulls into the Whiston Field lot and doubles parks. Antonini is feeling much better about the night.

-The earlier BOPARC softball game before the Chico game is running late, going into extra innings as the Bonders warm up. Fourteen Bonders have shown up. Only nine of their opponents have made it. Antonini was feeling optimistic about the night—the losing streak will end he predicts.

-Game 1 against Ford-Lincoln began 25 minutes late. By the 2nd inning, Chico's is already losing 13–0. The aging Bonder players struggled with the poor lighting of the antiquated lights of Whiston Field under the yellow skies at dusk, losing fly balls in the field as well as pitched balls at the plate. Antonini is ready to quit. He starts to doubt himself, thinking his best days are behind him. But the Bonders surprised him, battling hard for the next four innings before falling by a respectable score of 16–10. **Game 1 MVPs** were Scott 'Shitty' Shiftlett who turned in some fine plays in the field as well as knocked some deep drives to left field. 1Bs Dave Mistich and Aaron Hawley each had big hits as the Bonders rallied late in the opener.

-There was hope for game 2 as the skies darkened, and visibility improved under the inadequate field lights.

-Game 2 was a tightly contested game that came down to the last inning. The game was tied 9–9 in the bottom of the seventh. Chico's needed only 1 run to win and end the miserable losing streak that has haunted them since late May.

-Chico veteran 2B Walt Sarkees led off the inning with a hustling single. Following a brilliant tactical move by Chico management, Chico speedster David Lawson was inserted as a pinch runner for Sarkees and later scored on mad dash home on a walk off fielder's choice to second base hit by Chico star OF Andy Tuck. Lawson was wearing a beautiful black and orange feather boa around his neck as he crossed home plate. The Bonders have been known to celebrate win or lose, but this celebration was like no other. Multiple

Chico players (as of the writing of this night's recap); Ken Price, Richard Lewis, and David Lawson were still vying for the coveted Last Chico Standing Award for the night after last call had been made and the sun was about to rise).

-Game 2 stars were many—Chico MVPs were Lewis who had 7 hits on 7 at bats for the night as well as made several nice plays in the field at the mound and Tuck who hit a 3-run home run early in the game. Lead-off hitter and OF Jeff Goodwin also delivered several key line drive hits on the night.

-The post-game celebration started in the Whiston Field parking lot. One case of PBR was quickly consumed by the excited Chico players in the darkness as the MVP robes of the night were presented.

-The celebration continued at the 123 bar as cans of cheap beer and shots of Irish whiskey flowed.

-A random young patron at the 123 bar asked how he could become a Chico—he was told he had to attend a hitting, fielding, and beer drinking tryout/clinic at Whiston Field in March 2023 then fail a drug test. He wasn't confident about the softball skills tryout, but he assured Chico management that he could fail the drug test as early as the next morning if needed.—JA

AUGUST 26 CHICO'S (2–22) VS FOUNDRY CHURCH If you're staying up to read the Chico re-cap, go to bed. Chico's did nothing on the dusty Whiston Field diamond worth writing about. After a base on balls, 3B Scott 'Shitty' Shiflett pulled his groin walking (I repeat, WALKING) to first base early in game 1. It was all downhill after that. 2B Walt Sarkees shined in the field with several nice plays at the keystone. That's it! Go to sleep! Last Chico Standing (a tie) – Jim Antonini and Jeff Ryan.—JA

SEPTEMBER 9–CHICO'S (2–24) VS FORD LINCOLN When the MVP for the night is pitcher Jeff Ryan who gave up 34 runs in a doubleheader, your team has some serious problems, now a sad 2–24 on the year. There's nothing else that needs to be reported for the second week in a row—no details, no stats, no scores. Last Chico Standing (tie) – David Lawson and Richard Lewis.—JA

SEPTEMBER 30—CHICO'S (2-26) VS PICKLED NIMRODS It is said every year— "This was the greatest Chico season ever." And it seems true every year. For the night, Chico's fell in the first round of the playoffs to their greatest rival Pickled Nimrods 13–3 in a hard-fought softball game on the most beautiful cool fall nights. The Bonders played their best, but it wasn't enough. As the team celebrated Chico legend Andy Tuck's 44th birthday, the 2022 season-ending awards were handed out.—JA

2022 Season Awards:

Chico MVPs – Andrew Tuck, Christopher Simons

Chico Rookie of the Year – Shitty

Speedy Baserunner of the Year – Nic Crouso

Big Sexy Award – Richard Lewis

Little Sexy Award – David Lawson

Utility Player Award – Ken Price

Chico Most Eco-Friendly – Jeff Ryan & his electric bike (biking to games saved him $96 in gas this season)

2023 Chico's: (standing) Eric Ramón, Chris Simons, Brieve Morrison (Hooligan), Shannon Davy, Aaron Hawley, Andy Tuck, Richard Lewis, Chris Evans, Fred Baer, Walt Sarkees, Dave Lawson, Jon Vehse, Jeff Ryan, (kneeling) Ken Price, Jeff Goodwin, Dave Brown, Jim Antonini

MAY 11–CHICO'S (0–2) VS CITY PLUMBING & HEATING

"Touch him! Touch him!" Chico 2B Chris Evans yelled from his knees as he crawled in desperation from his position in the dirt to second base with a menthol cigarette dangling from his mouth. "Touch him!" he yelled again.

The City Plumbing & Heating runner slid into home plate as Chico pitcher Jeff Ryan flipped the ball to catcher Ken Price.

"Touch him!" Evans hollered again as the umpire called the runner out.

"It's okay," shortstop Jim Antonini said to Evans. "It was a force out. We got him!"

That was how it started on a glorious opening spring night of the 2023 BOPARC softball season. It was so good to get the team back together again. But a distracted and compromised Bonders team bumbled their way through two winnable games that sadly but predictably ended in defeat—17 to 4 in game 1 and 11 to 0 in game 2 to league juggernaut City Plumbing & Heating. The

Bondsmen were doomed by too many walks and a lack of timely hitting. It was noted how well the Chico squad played defensively for both games.

"That's not what I saw," said Chico game 1 outfielder and game 2 pitcher Richard Lewis.

"Yeah," Evans said. "I made four errors in the third inning of game 1 alone."

An overly prepared Bondsmen team backed by computer files of complex historical and analytical data compiled by assistant manager Price expected a positive change to start the new season after a decade of disappointment. And it worked initially, as newly installed leadoff hitter and left fielder Andy Tuck started game 1 with a deep line drive to the right field

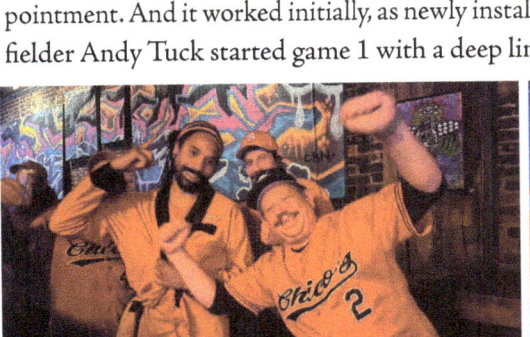

fence. He was quickly knocked in by outfielder Jeff Goodwin (Game 1 MVP). But that was the lone Chico highlight of the night. Bonder power hitter Chris Simons pulled a rib muscle and was removed early in the first game. And it was downhill after that. Many of the Bondsmen showed up drunk and out of shape. Game 2 was highlighted by the strong defensive play of second baseman Walt Sarkees (Game 2 MVP) and rookie Chico first baseman Dave Brown.

During an at bat early in the second game, Chico outfielder Nic Crouso and the home plate umpire were distracted as Lewis loudly asked as the pitched ball approached home plate, "What was the name of that West Viriginia linebacker from years ago who cut his dick off down by the Mon River?"

A laughing Crouso ended up being called out on strikes.

Game notes: Evans played three positions in the two games and began his defense of leading the league in half smoked cigarettes—partially smoking six in the second game. Last Chico Standing – Rookie Dave Brown.—JA

MAY 19—CHICO'S (0–4) VS KEGLER'S

Bonders sleepwalk through humiliating doubleheader loss to bloated and overrated Kegler's Sports Bar from that despicable side of town called Suncrest. Like a fragile elderly man after a long deep nap, the Bonders bumbled and stumbled around the green pasture of Whiston Field, appearing unsure of the time of day, and even worse, what day of the week it was. It was a disappointing and embarrassing display. The offense generated only one run over two games – a mad speed dash by the suddenly svelte and slimmed down first baseman Aaron Hawley. On the season after four games, Chico's has only scored 5 runs.

Game notes: . OF Andy Tuck may have made the play of the decade with a long, running, reaching, diving catch of a deep drive to left centerfield. The over-under for oft-injured, utility player Chris Evans is seven games before he injures himself so bad that he is out for the season. The safe and easy bet after tonight was definitely under as he pulled both quads in the first inning of game 1 after sucking down four afternoon gin and tonics, smoking one tightly rolled joint, and falling down after chasing a routine fly ball in the outfield. It took three Chico OFs to get him up off the ground.

Quote of the night: From a random Kegler's player to Nic Crouso, "You must get a lot of pussy in that outfit," referring to Crouso's trademarked checkered shorts, his proudly displayed evil "666" jersey number, a seventies style porn-stache, and his long wispy hair style. Game MVP David Becker who brought a cooler full of Jäegermeister and banana bourbon airplane bottles. Last Chico Standing (a tie): Dave Brown and Ken Price. Disclaimer- the author of this feature was completely intoxicated during its inception. Chico management is not responsible for the content of this information. The views are solely those of the author. Some of the commentary about the fine neighborhood of Suncrest may not really be true or accurate.—JA

JUNE 2–CHICO'S (0–6) VS O P W It was said by Vehse (aka Jonny Siesta) at 123 bar, "Chico softball brings us together and that's all that matters." The night ended at the bar with the most spectacular team meeting. In the tight stairwell above the bar, ten Chico's lovingly squeezed together. There was a rap battle between Tuck and "Big Sexy" Lewis, beat boxes by Chris Simons provided the back-up, unknown squatters, strangers signing apartment leases, spilled whiskey, and the tightest of rolled joints. A few short minutes after the team meeting commenced, pitcher Jeff Ryan (the true critic of all that is free) busted into the mostly empty downstairs bar and proclaimed, "Worst team meeting ever!" But the next nine Chico's who followed him many minutes later vehemently disagreed.

Second baseman Chris Evans said, "This team meeting was so fabulous, Vehse and I are already reminiscing about it. And it's only been five minutes."

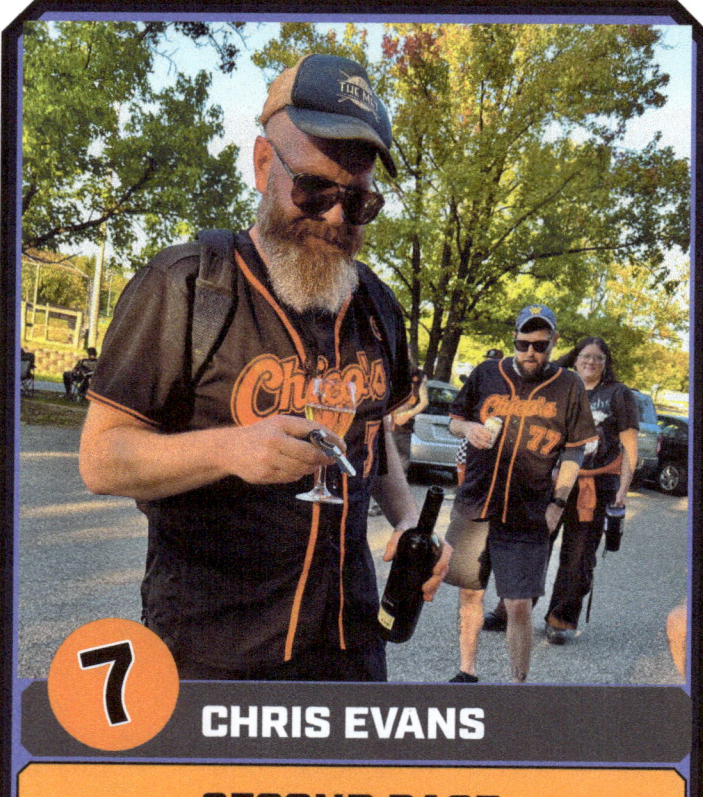

7
CHRIS EVANS

SECOND BASE

BATS: RIGHT   THROWS: RIGHT   SEASONS PLAYED: 5
HOBBIES: FAST TIMES, FINE WINE, CIGARETTES, BILLIARDS
WALK-UP SONG: "MY WAY" BY FRANK SINATRA

Chris is the co-owner of the historic Met Pool Hall in downtown Morgantown; is always hurt but never injured; enjoys fine Portuguese reds from the early 1990s and raspberry White Claws from 2021; is the BOPARC softball league leader in half-smoked cigarettes during games; oftentimes needs a handler; is the leader and heart and soul of the Chico postgame Team Meetings.

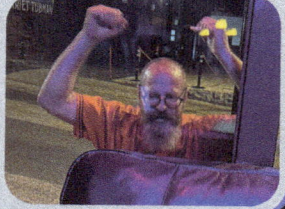

Despite the late-night revelry, it can't be forgotten that two softball games were played, apparently only as a formality. Chico's (0–6) lost both to O.P.W. by the scores of 16–6 in the first and 14–1 in the second. Despite the disappointment, it was a glorious evening that will be talked about forever as the Chico players partied long into the night, drinking the cheapest beer and the strongest whiskey.

Several players, most notably, team assistant manager Price said, "I'm not going home. First Friday is only a few hours away. Why should I leave now?"

As a brief recap of the actual games, the Bondsmen faded in the heat on the dusty desert-like concrete playing surface of Liberatore Field. Jeff Ryan scampered home all the way from first base on a double hit by Price.

Ryan noted, as he huffed and puffed his way to the bench, looking for a cigar and a tin cup of homemade spo-dee-o-dee, "That's the most I've run in over 15 years."

Game notes: Chico MVP was utility player Aaron Hawley who had multiple hits on the night and provided even more exemplary defensive plays at third base—his most brilliant, a diving stab of a line drive to his right happened at the exact same time as his young daughter getting stung by a bee on the sidelines. Chico 1B Dave Mistich forgot his cleats. He played in slippers in the field for both games. 2B Chris Evans increased his league lead in half-smoked cigarettes by a large number during the game with seven on the night. Despite the drubbing of Chico's and bashing six home runs over the fence on the night, O.P.W. team members took batting practice long into the night after the doubleheader as Chico players drank beer for several hours postgame in the Liberatore Field parking lot. It's not surprising then that O.P.W. leads the BOPARC Blue League in Slugging Percentage, whereas the Bonders lead the league in Chugging Percentage. Last Chico Standing – Dave "the bruise" Brown. What a fun night it was.

As Vehse said before leaving for his long trek to Fairmont, "If there wasn't a softball game scheduled tonight, none of this would've ever happened. And that would have been such a shame. There can't be too many people in this world who had more fun than we did tonight. And we got slaughtered in two softball games.".—JA

JUNE 9—CHICO'S (0–8) VS PURE COLLECTIBLES

It was a bad night to be a Jeff. Chico's dropped two hard fought games against the younger Pure Collectibles team 18-3 in game 1 and 21–6 in game 2. Despite the ugly score differentials, the Bonders' bats came to life late after the most dismal start in game 1, led by deep drives from Game 1 MVPs David Lawson and "Shitty" Shiflett. In the first inning of game 1, pitcher Jeff Ryan got drilled by a screaming line drive to his lower body. He collapsed in the heavy dust of Liberatore Field pitching mound. Everyone feared the worst. Fortunately, the ball hit his knee and not his penis. Nearly unable to walk, he toughed it and completed the game. Also, outfielder Jeff Goodwin got beaned in his left shoulder by an errant throw as he raced to third base. Unable to throw the ball after his injury, he exited the game and headed to a local hospital for X-rays. As of this writing, there was no update on his status, but it must be serious. His personal tattoo artist had been summoned.

In game 2 and looking for a spark, Chico assistant manager Ken Price (who also had to replace the injured pitcher Jeff Ryan) called out, "I need a lead-off hitter!"

Chico third baseman Chris Evans, and Game 2 MVP, answered, "I'm your man."

And boom, it was immediately 1–0 as he drove a deep majestic shot to left centerfield into the hazy night sky, scoring in a cloud a dust at home plate—an inside-the-park home run! At the time, it should have been a MIC-DROP moment—"so long suckers, the Bonders are going to the 123 bar!" But the Chico

squad hung around and got thoroughly humiliated. Pitcher Price gave up 21 runs in three short innings, bloating his ERA to an astronomical and almost unheard of 93.00. Dejectedly, with their heads held low and their gaze locked on the ground, the Bondsmen retreated to the parking lot for postgame beers and whiskey shots.

Shortstop Jim Antonini commented, "Damn, 0–6 hurts."

Chris Evans corrected him, "No dude, we're 0–8."

Game notes: Dirtiest Chico (a three-way tie): Chris Evans, Dave "the Bruise" Brown, and Ken Price. Last Chico Standing (a tie) – Jeff Ryan and David Lawson (Dave Brown's streak is broken). —JA

153

JULY 7–CHICO'S (2–10) VS LADDER BOYS Olivia Newton-John is dead. Sorry David Becker. Throw the new winless trophy in the trash. The Bonders ended a nearly yearlong winless drought. Chico's Bail Bonds softball squad defied all odds on the muggiest of nights in BOPARC softball history, dominating the Ladder Boys in the most majestic doubleheader sweep in years. The Bonders bested their archrivals 21–15 in game 1 and 14–7 in game 2. Chico scorekeeper and catcher Eric Ramón had writer's cramp by the end of it all. Chico's had over fifty hits in the two games. It had been decades since that had happened. Chico legend Ravi Shibley smiled down from the heavens after this beautiful display of softball offensive efficiency and power. The Chico heroes are too many to mention. Everybody hit, and everybody scored.

Game notes: Chico MVPs were Dave Brown for second week in a row. He bashed line drives to centerfield for two hours, and Chico rookie Shannon Davy debuted in spectacular fashion, knocking 7 hits in the two games. Antonini turned in his strongest defensive performance in years for both games that proved vital in the two victories. His unassisted double play ended game 2 in dramatic fashion. The final Chico MVP on the night was catcher and assistant team manager Ken Price who went four-for-four in game 1 and constructed the winning lineups for both games. After a celebratory hour in the postgame parking lot, Chico team members hurried to the 123 bar with their victory penises erect.

Quote of the evening: Ladder Boys asked if they could use multiple courtesy runners per inning due to injury.

Ken Price said, "Yes!" because it was good karma, and he knew we'd beat their asses both games with the way we were playing no matter what.

Chico 2B Chris Evans disagreed, "No, no, no!" he loudly objected. "We got a shortstop who eats from the senior citizen menu at restaurants, and he can't get a courtesy runner every time he gets on base.".

Andy Tuck Postgame Math Night: The average age of the Chico roster is 44.3 years of age. Collectively, the Bonders have spent 700 years on the earth. Chico average penis length is 5.8 inches (without Richard "Big Sexy" Lewis) but 8.5 inches (with him).—JA

JULY 21–CHICO'S (2–14) VS MEGA CORP

In the battle for last place, a depleted Chico's squad of 10 determined souls failed the test. Arch-rival and nemesis Mega Corp (3–13) outlasted the Bonders 16–14 in a marathon 1-hour and 20-minute game 1. The older and short-handed Chico team was no match in game 2 as they wilted in the heat of the humid July night as the younger opponent dominated them 13–4 to sweep the twilight doubleheader. Chico MVPs for the night were OF Chris Simons in game 1 who hit a majestic grand slam home run into the hazy, firefly-filled summer night sky; and pitcher Richie 'Big Sexy' Lewis who in both games battled control issues on the mound but dominated at the plate with run-scoring doubles and triples; and Jeff Goodwin who almost turned a triple in game 2 into an inside-the-park home run, only to be tagged hard at a close play at the plate.

Game notes: . OF Nic Crouso had one of his best hitting nights as a Chico, bashing two-line drive base hits. 3B Aaron Hawley leaped high into the air at the third base line to snag a line drive. Folks in the crowd swore that his feet never actually left the ground. There were more Chico's in the team meeting than on the field of play.

The postgame team meeting atmosphere was described as intense, crowded, not the best, having a shortage of oxygen, and the comment, "Good thing Jeff Ryan wasn't there". Dirtiest Chico –1B Shannon Davy; Last Chico Standing–utility player and leadoff hitter Dave Brown. As the Bonders disappeared to the 123 bar seeking solace and comfort in whiskey and jukebox music, the rains and the thunder and lightning came—an end-of-the-world type of rain[1]. Rain so heavy it pushed all the stupid orange construction cones that have populated the streets of Morgantown that summer to the bottom of the hill in front of the 123 bar.—JA

---

1 End-of-the-world type of rain. Chico's have played in all types of weather- oppressive heat, wind storms, downpours, thunder and lightning storms, and even snow showers. The Bonders have had over 82 games canceled through the years due to weather. In 2017, Chico's were rained out 7 games in a row.

AUGUST 24–CHICO'S (2-18) VS WATERFRONT URGENT CARE

The regular BOPARC softball season ended for the beloved Chico's Bail Bonds. The good news—the Bonders did not finish in last place. The bad news—they finished with a despicable record of 2-18. Chico's thanked the Ladder Boys for their own historically dismal season and last place debacle. On the night, the Bondsmen lost to 1st place Waterfront Urgent Care 18-3 in the opener and 18-1 in the nightcap. If you're keeping score at home, the Bonders have been outscored 77-9 in the past two doubleheaders. The highlights on the night were few. Chico first baseman Dave Mistich had a two-run base hit in the 1st inning of game 1. Outfielder David Lawson had a run-scoring triple in game 2. Chico MVP on the night was shortstop Jim Antonini who had one of his best defensive games in the field in years and delivered multiple line drive hits on the night. Last Chico Standing: C/assistant manager - Ken Price. The Bonders begin the postseason playoffs next week. Word has it they will face their arch nemesis Four Horsemen Comics. The Bondsmen are doomed.—JA

AUGUST 30–CHICO'S (2-19) VS FOUR HORSEMEN COMICS

In the first round of the playoffs, Chico (2-19) plays valiantly but fall 12-9 in a heartbreaker in the last inning to BOPARC Blue Division's best team and offensive stalwart Four Horsemen Comics. Chico's overcame an almost insurmountable deficit of 9-2 to tie the game with a seven-run comeback going into the last inning 9-9. The Bonders played a perfect game in the field by not committing a single error (hard to believe but true). Left center fielder Jeff Goodwin and second baseman Chris Evans provided the entertainment for the packed and boisterous Whiston Field crowd, each making acrobatic circus catches. Right fielder David Lawson and shortstop Jim Antonini were flawless in the outfield and infield, respectively, making the hard plays look routine. It also was the best pitcher Jeff Ryan had looked on the mound in years, despite being squeezed by the home plate umpire's tight strike zone. The hitting stars were many – catcher Eric Ramón had two big hits; Antonini was a clean three for three (all line drives); Ryan also contributed two hits; third baseman Aaron Hawley had two hard hit singles; outfielder Chris Simons had two hits including a deep double off the fence in the first; back up first basemen Shannon Davy delivered a two-out RBI single in the Chico seven-run comeback inning; and clean-up hitter and left fielder Andy Tuck added two important hits on the night. However, the big blow in the game was delivered by utility player Walt Sarkees who knocked in Dave Mistich with a bases-clearing double that tied the game at 9-9 in the opening half of the last inning. But the Bondsmen couldn't close it out, succumbing to the younger and more talented Four Horsemen team in the bottom of the last inning. Chico MVP – everyone. Last Chico standing – Dave Lawson. Chico unsung heroes – Assistant coach Ken Price who devised the stacked line-up; 1B Dave Brown who had to man third base, a position he never played before; and OF Nic Crouso who rallied the team when it looked like it would be a short night.

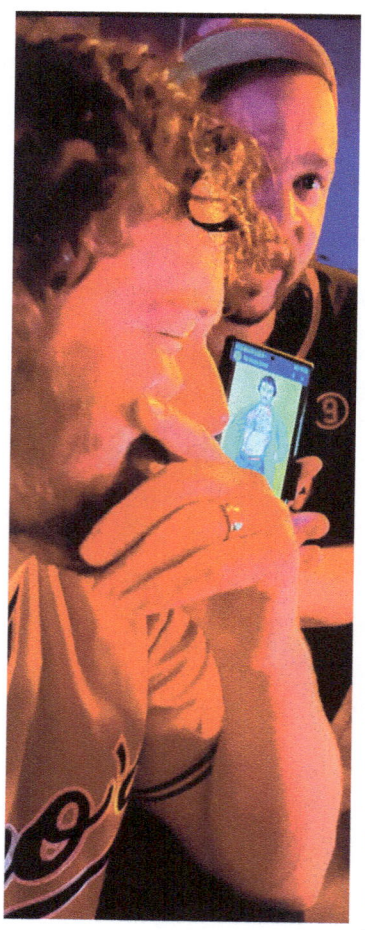

Despite the loss and the record, it was one of the most enjoyable seasons ever for most Chico team members.—JA

2023 Season Awards:

Chico Rookie of the Year – Dave Brown

Chico Most Eco-Friendly – Jeff Ryan & his magic electric bike

Chico Gold Glove – David Lawson

Chico MVP – Chris Evans

Chico Ironman – Jim Antonini

2024 A NEW ERA FOR CHICO

2024 Chico's: (standing) Devin Williams, Andy Tuck, Chris Simons, Richard Lewis, Eric Ramón, Aaron Hawley, Jeff Ryan, Dave Mistich, Dave Lawson, Nic Crouso, Fred Baer, Chris Evans, (kneeling) Jeff Goodwin, Jim Antonini, Ken Price, Dave Brown

MAY 9–CHICO'S (1–0) VS MEGA CORP In the mud, the blood, and the gore of sloppy Liberatore Field, a fresh Chico's Bail Bonds squad (a little sleeker and a little younger than previous seasons) opened the new campaign. In a rain-shortened and dramatic game 1 victory, the Bonders outlast Mega Corp by the score of 8–6, despite Mega Corp's illegal use of 13 hitters and 15 players in the field.

The heavens then opened and canceled game 2 of the doubleheader and the postgame parking lot celebration with a thunder and lightning end-of-the-world type of storm. As hail and wind-blown branches and leaves rained on the victory party, the Bondsmen quickly retreated to the safety, comfort, and whiskey of the 123 bar. Catcher and newly appointed full-time manager Ken Price started his career 1–0 in his coaching debut—if previous seasons are any indication, he probably should retire at this point while his head is still above water.

Nearly every Chico in the lineup contributed to the first game win. Richard 'Big Sexy' Lewis pitched the Bonders to victory with a sassy and sterling three-strikeout performance. The six runs he allowed, in which only two were earned, lowered his career ERA to a still unsightly 27−23. Outfielder David Lawson played a solid right centerfield with multiple long-running catches. New shortstop Devin Williams brought the juice and fresh legs, greatly expanding the range of what the last old and tired shortstop couldn't supply. Right fielder Aaron Hawley had a solid game, delivering two run-scoring hits and throwing out the last runner of the contest at second base while a lightning bolt exploded overhead, canceling the rest of the season opener. Slugger Chris Simons drove in two runs on multiple hot shot line drive singles over third. Chico old timer and new third baseman Jim Antonini delivered three singles and drove in three runs. Designated hitter Dave Mistich was on base all three times he came to the plate despite not hitting a ball hard or out of the infield. Last Chico Standing – to be determined but probably David Lawson. Chico Sombrero MVPs[1] – 3B Jim Antonini, P Richard Lewis, RF Aaron Hawley, vuvuzela-blowing and bartender Brieve Morrison. Dirtiest Chico – Ken Price and surprisingly not Dave Brown. It's a new era for Chico softball. The Bonders might actually win most of their games this season and shock the BOPARC softball world.—JA

MAY 16–CHICO'S (1–2) VS PICKLED NIMRODS In week 2 of the new softball season, Chico's Bail Bonds returned to earth after a stellar opening week, dropping both ends of a doubleheader to rival[2] and overrated Pickled Nimrods (2−0). The Bonders controlled game 1 behind the dominating pitching performance of Big Sexy Lewis. Chico's led 7−1 late into the game until the wheels fell off in ONE BAD INNING. Lewis had struck out a personal record seven batters in the early going. It was downhill soon after—errors, poor pitch selections at the plate, heavy in game alcohol use, and no juice in the Bondsman bats, spirit and tired legs led to an epic downfall as they dropped the opener 9−8 in heartbreaking fashion.

Chico's zombie-walked in game 2, losing 16−6 in a pitiful shortened 6-inning mercy rule 10-run game. There were bright spots on the night however – left fielder Andy Tuck broke out of his two-year slump with four hits and two triples on the night. Right center fielder Chris Simons hit the Bonders first home run of the season over the fence. He also delivered four other hits. Right fielder David Lawson turned in the defensive play of the night with his running-diving-tumbling grab of a line drive catch in game 1. The other defensive stalwart on the night

---

1 Sombreros. Starting in the 2024 season, the game MVPs would wear an orange sombrero in the parking lot during the postgame.
2 Rivals. The teams considered Chico's greatest rivals through the years are Boaz, Honest Abe's, Morgantown Sober Living, Pickled Nimrods, and Mega Corp. The Bonders have a losing record against each of them.

was second baseman Chris Evans who made every play (nearly 714 of them—Chico legend Meatball would've been proud) in game 1 that included underhanded and overhanded throws as well as multiple 'touch him' plays at the keystone. Sombrero MVPs – P Lewis; hitters – Tuck and Simons;

defensive stars – Lawson and Evans. Dirtiest Chico – Dave Brown. Chico shoutout of the night— longtime friend and 123 legend, Casey R Williams who was gifted his customized 808 black Chico jersey postgame. Injury report – Chico old-timer and pinch hitter Dirty Fred blew out his hamstring after his only at bat on a laser line drive to left field. He fell in a heap of dust on the first base line. Efforts to resuscitate him failed. A memorial service has been planned. He ended his Chico career batting a perfect 1.000 for the season.—JA

MAY 23–CHICO'S (1–4) VS CITY PLUMBING & HEATING
Weak bats, tired legs, and empty souls. Chico's Bail Bonds, the world's most lovable softball team, shit the bed in the most lackluster of early season performances ever. The Bondsmen pitifully dropped both ends of a twilight doubleheader to City Plumbing & Heating (4–0) by the embarrassing scores of 9–1 in game 1 and 15–0 in game 2. The Bonders didn't deserve a postgame writeup after scoring only one run in two slow-pitch softball games. If you didn't know, in slow-pitch softball, a big round ball is slowly and gently lofted in the air from 45 feet away to a batter who holds the hardest, most technologically advanced metal composite bat—hard enough to drive the slow-pitched ball to outer 'mother fucking' space—something that did not come close to happening for Chicos on the night. Sombrero MVPs – Defense, Shortstop Devin Williams, who made numerous spectacular plays in the middle of the

infield; Offense – OF Aaron Hawley who delivered three hits in game 1. The MEATBALL Award went to 2B Chris Evans who smoked 7 cigarettes during the two games, drove in the only run on a weak fielder's choice groundout to shortstop, dropped an easy infield fly pop up, and stepped up in the postgame to lead a beautiful team meeting upstairs of the 123 bar.—JA

JUNE 6–CHICO'S (1–6) VS ALLISON'S FINE JEWELRY A brash, bold, and drunken Chico squad stupidly went to Jared. In return. Allison's Fine Jewelry jokingly took Chico to the woodshed and spanked the Bonders' asses, humiliating the Bondsmen 11–3 in game 1 and 10–0 in game 2. It was brutal – you can't even imagine how bad. A drunk, high, and compromised Bonders team sadly showed up NOT ready to play. It was painfully pathetic – Chico's have scored only four runs in the last four games. The Bondsmen are at the crossroads. They need the younger players to step up and carry the veterans on their shoulders before the season spirals away. Sadly, Chico MVP was pitcher Big Sexy who was higher than an Oregon pine tree and any other normal human should ever be. Defensive MVP was David Lawson who made multiple highlight-reel catches and roamed left centerfield not seen since the days of Chico legend – the Silver Fox, Rob B. For the fourth week in a row, Chico second baseman, Chris Evans won the MEATBALL AWARD—he drank a margarita, a gin and tonic, two watermelon White Claws, and a PBR, as well as smoked four Marlboros in the pregame and then hustled from third base to second to tag out a runner who was already standing on the bag.—JA

JUNE 13–CHICO'S (1–8) VS KEGLER'S "We've seen a lot of bad Chico teams over the years, but this one might be the worst," muttered a high ranking, longtime BOPARC softball officials. The Bonders were humiliated in both ends of a doubleheader against rival Kegler's on the hottest night of the summer yet. Chico's lost game 1 by the score of 17–5 in uninspiring fashion. There was nothing of note to highlight in the first game Chico debacle. The Bonders even made an error on a foul ball in the parking lot. Bondsmen 1B Shannon Davy stands 6 feet and 8 inches tall and may be one of the tallest players in BOPARC softball league history. Yet, Bonder infielders Chris Evans, Jim Antonini, and Devin Williams continually made errant throws over his head. Game spectators couldn't determine if Chico's were too high, too drunk, too tired, or all the above.

Game 2 was a little different in that the Bondsmen competed for 4 innings, even holding a 2–1 lead before the wheels came completely off. Chico's ended up losing 15–4 in a game not shortened by the 10-rule mercy rule but by Bonder second baseman Chris Evans who had seen enough. The umpire agreed awarding the early victory to Kegler's with two innings still to go. Chico team members were so angry with Evans, they made him walk the one mile from Liberatore Stadium to the 123 bar.

This was the most popular issue in the magazine's history, according to publisher and editor-in-chief, Jason Coleman

In the postgame however, the team's anger soon dissipated as Evans bought shots and led a rousing team meeting in the 123 Green Room. The team meeting was so spectacular, Chico team members were texting SOS help messages to the more sober Bonders who remained in the bar down below.

Game Notes. Sombrero MVP – SS Devin Williams delivered the highlight of the night—a mad dash unbelievable inside-the-park-home run. Beaten Egg Award – pitcher Richard Lewis who was drilled with line drives off both his foot and shoulder. Beaten Egg runner-up – 2B Evans who took a stinging hot shot line drive off the wrist. Dirtiest Chico – Devin Williams. Last Chico Standing (a tie) – David Lawson and Ken Price. Best Defensive play of the night – LF Chris Simons with a long running catch of a deep fly ball. Worst Defensive play – RF Nic Crouso who missed a fly ball so bad, it dropped between his legs and rolled behind him all the way to the fence. With each passing week of the young summer, Chico's continued to fall deeper into last place. It may be a long time before the Bonders recover from the free fall – but there's 13 games left, and because of that there is hope—but just a glimmer.—JA

JUNE 20–CHICO'S (1–10) VS CROCKETT'S LODGE An over-matched but determined Chico's softball squad battled for two hours in the harshest conditions against bloated and boring rival Crockett's Lodge before finally wilting in the hot, humid and sweltering 95-degree heat and dropping both ends of a BOPARC softball doubleheader. The Bonders slept walked through game 1, losing by the score of 13–3. Many of the Chico players were too worried about the heat than actually playing the game. Second baseman and team spark plug Chris Evans set a disappointing and losing tone by insisting on playing in the shaded right field of Whiston stadium as opposed to his natural position in the hot and dusty infield. Game 1 MVP was Chico veteran third baseman Jim Antonini who went a perfect 3 for 3 at the plate, including his first double of the season and perhaps his last of his career due to aging knees and a tired soul. It was a different story in game 2 as the Bondsmen fought for all seven innings only to lose a heartbreaker 18–13. Despite giving up 18 runs, Jeff Ryan pitched one of his best games in years. Rookie Shortstop Devin Williams led the offense with an inside-the-park home run for the 2nd week in a row. He nearly gave Jeff Ryan a heart attack, chasing him all the way home. Chico outfielders Chris Simons and Andy Tuck both had strong nights at the plate. But it doesn't get any better for Chico's. They return to the diamond next week as upstart rival Ford Lincoln awaits and this summer's apocalyptic heat wave is forecasted to persist. Game Notes. Regular LCF Jeff Goodwin was out with a bad back. Dirtiest Chico – Dave Brown. Out of concern for safety, Chico manager and birthday boy Ken Price waived long-time but almost crippled softball

journeyman Dirty Fred before the game. Fred's antiquated wooden knee braces and 42-ounce 1959 wooden softball bat were mailed to Poughkeepsie, New York after the game for eventual enshrinement in the Landlord Hall of Fame.

JULY 11–CHICO'S (1–14) VS ALLISON'S FINE JEWELERS Chico's has been bad before. Very bad. They even had a winless season (0–23; the Olivia Newton-John trophy debacle) in 2015. But they have never been this bad. Ever. The Bonders (1–14) lost game 1 by the score of 21–2 to Allison's Fine Jewelry (10–4).

After the 1st inning of the doubleheader versus Allison's Jewelry, Chico second baseman and energetic spark plug Chris Evans asked, "What's the score?" The umpire laughed, "14 to nothing." "That's much worse than I thought," Evans mused.

> **"SELL THE TEAM!! LOUIS GIULIANI IS RUNNING THIS FRANCHISE INTO THE GROUND!!"**
> **—NIC CROUSO, 7-1-24**

Unlike previous weeks, Chico started off energized and refreshed after the July 4th break in the schedule. But giving up 14 runs in the 1st inning of the 1st game of a doubleheader has a way of draining what little soul the Chico team members had left – which wasn't much. Game 2 of the doubleheader didn't get any better. It got worse. Much worse. The Bonders melted in the heat, lasting only three innings and dropping the night cap by the outrageous and ugliest score of 25–0 to Crockett's Lodge (14–1).

Game note: Dirtiest Chico – Dave Brown. Reported injuries – catcher Nic Crouso, bruised balls; OF Jeff Goodwin, bruised balls. Sombrero MVPs – Ken Price, scorekeeper game 1; Eric Ramón scorekeeper game 2.

"Bitch, girl!" OF David Lawson teased. "Those two had a lot of work to do keeping up with all those runs scored against us!"

The season is quickly slipping away. The Bonders have six games left to right the sinking ship of a season. If Chico's can win four of those games, infielder Jim Antonini will get Chris Evans' face tattooed across his back.

"He used to be my favorite Chico, but now he's about 7th on my list," Antonini was heard saying in the postgame.

After 15 games, the Chico offense has scored a grand total of 53 runs. It doesn't get any worse than that…—JA

JULY 19–CHICO'S (1–16) VS PICKLED NIMRODS It was a great night to be a Chico. Despite two heartbreaking losses in the final inning of both games of a twilight doubleheader on the most beautiful of Morgantown summer nights, it felt like two victories as Bonder team members partied late into the night at the 123 bar. It was one of the longest and hardest but most enjoyable of team meetings ever in the history of 123 postgames. A shorthanded Bonders (1–16) squad of just 11 eager players without several

55
AARON HAWLEY

FIRST BASE, THIRD BASE

BATS: RIGHT   THROWS: RIGHT SEASONS PLAYED: 13
HOBBIES: PHISH, PHISH, GOOSE, PHISH, PHISH, GOOSE
WALK-UP SONG: "BIG POPPA" BY THE NOTORIOUS B.I.G.

Aaron loves being a Chico maybe more than any other Chico. His kids' favorite Chico was 3B Shitty; has proven to be a versatile team member, having played first base, second base, third base, and outfield during his Chico career; enjoys conversation; is the mastermind behind Gene's Beer Garden's annual Townie X-Mas.

key members, including sluggers Andy Tuck and Chris Simons as well as others battled their asses off before falling 11−10 in the final fucking inning to archrival and overrated Pickled Nimrods in the opener. The Bondsmen stranded the bases loaded in the top the last inning, leaving the score tied. The Nimrods closed out the game with a deep drive to left centerfield over converted infielder Chris Evans' head in the bottom of the inning to walk off the win. Chico's delivered an even more heroic effort in game 2, taking the younger and more athletic Ford Lincoln team to their final at-bat. The game was tied 8−8 in the final inning before the wheels came off for Chico's as they gave five runs in the final frame, dropping the contest by a final score of 13−8. The Bonders played two games for an unprecedented two hours and thirty minutes. Each Chico batter had at least eight at-bats on the night.

Game notes: Every Chico contributed positively on the night. Game 1 Sombrero MVP was Dave Lawson who drove in six of the Chico runs and made several spectacular plays in left field. Game 2 Sombrero MVPs were numerous – pitcher Jeff 'ELVIS' Ryan played his best and most energetic game in over a decade with the finest of pitching performances and his hustling base-running exploits. Second baseman Walt Sarkees looked a younger version of a different man, making great play after play in the infield in game 2. Young Chico first baseman Shannon Davy had his most complete night as a Bonder, playing a solid first base and delivering several clutch hits. Dirtiest Chico – so many: C Ken Price, SS Devin Williams, P Jeff Ryan, OF David Lawson, 2B Walt Sarkees. Defensive play of the night - tie: Devin Williams diving line drive catch at shortstop and Richard 'Big Sexy' Lewis bobbling double bounce running catch in right field. Last Chico standing – a tie: Chris Evans and David Lawson.

BOPARC softball transactions 07/19/2024 - Chico's OF Andy Tuck cut; Chico's OF Chris Simons cut; Chico's 1B Aaron Hawley cut; Chico's C Nic Crouso cut; Chico's C Eric Ramón cut; Chico's 2B Chris Evans returned to Chico's from Allison's Fine Jewelry along with a bottle of Yukon Jack and note that read, "No, thanks! He's all yours." —JA

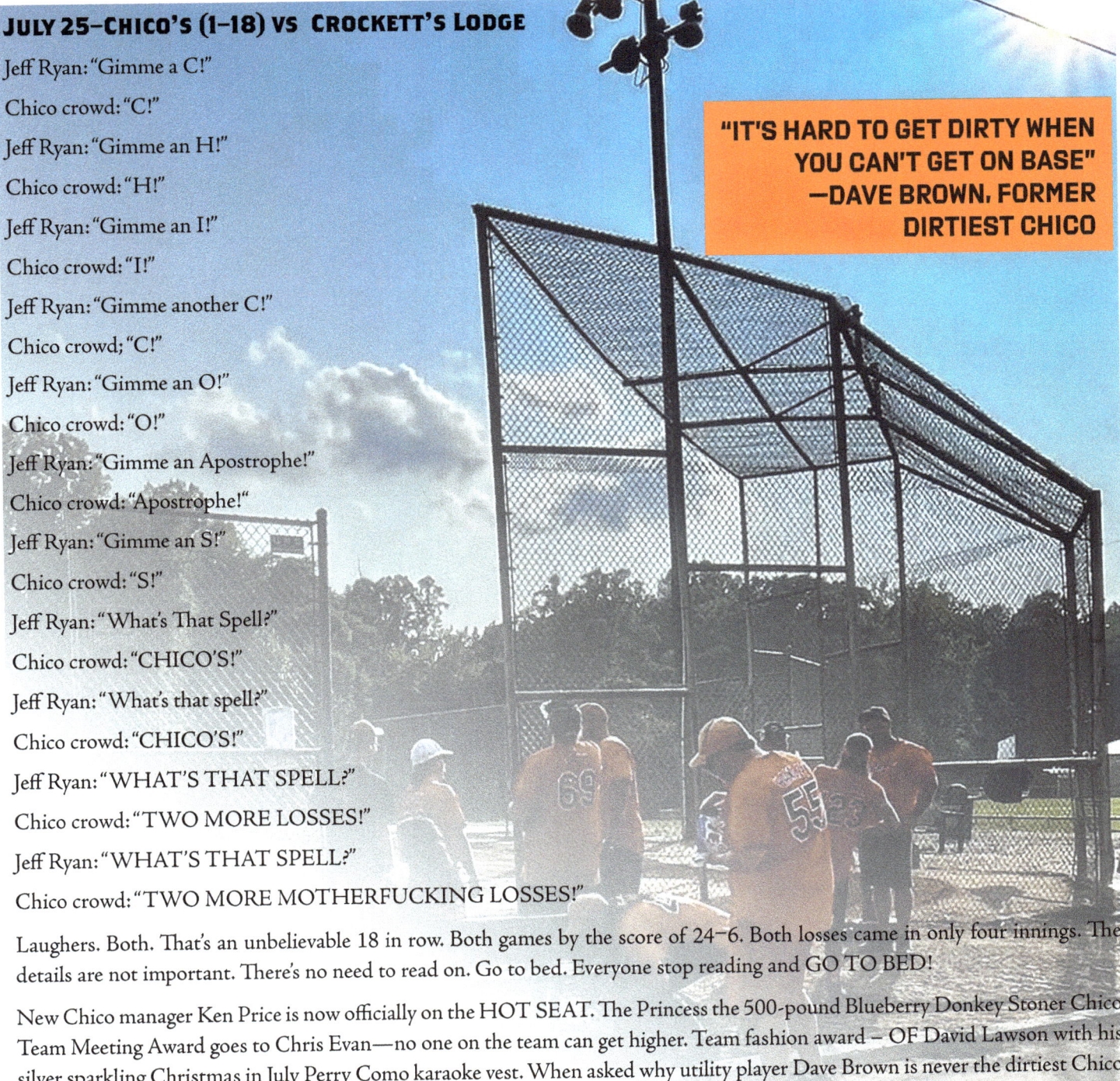

JULY 25–CHICO'S (1–18) VS CROCKETT'S LODGE

Jeff Ryan: "Gimme a C!"

Chico crowd: "C!"

Jeff Ryan: "Gimme an H!"

Chico crowd: "H!"

Jeff Ryan: "Gimme an I!"

Chico crowd: "I!"

Jeff Ryan: "Gimme another C!"

Chico crowd; "C!"

Jeff Ryan: "Gimme an O!"

Chico crowd: "O!"

Jeff Ryan: "Gimme an Apostrophe!"

Chico crowd: "Apostrophe!"

Jeff Ryan: "Gimme an S!"

Chico crowd: "S!"

Jeff Ryan: "What's That Spell?"

Chico crowd: "CHICO'S!"

Jeff Ryan: "What's that spell?"

Chico crowd: "CHICO'S!"

Jeff Ryan: "WHAT'S THAT SPELL?"

Chico crowd: "TWO MORE LOSSES!"

Jeff Ryan: "WHAT'S THAT SPELL?"

Chico crowd: "TWO MORE MOTHERFUCKING LOSSES!"

"IT'S HARD TO GET DIRTY WHEN YOU CAN'T GET ON BASE" —DAVE BROWN, FORMER DIRTIEST CHICO

Laughers. Both. That's an unbelievable 18 in row. Both games by the score of 24–6. Both losses came in only four innings. The details are not important. There's no need to read on. Go to bed. Everyone stop reading and GO TO BED!

New Chico manager Ken Price is now officially on the HOT SEAT. The Princess the 500-pound Blueberry Donkey Stoner Chico Team Meeting Award goes to Chris Evan—no one on the team can get higher. Team fashion award – OF David Lawson with his silver sparkling Christmas in July Perry Como karaoke vest. When asked why utility player Dave Brown is never the dirtiest Chico anymore (an award he consistently won last season) Brown quietly mumbled "It's hard to get dirty when you can't get on base,"—JA

Standings

2024 Mens Black

Team	Won	Lost	Tie	Win %	Streak	RF	RA
City Plumbing & Heating (Black)	20	1	0	.952	Won 13	249	90
Crocketts Lodge	15	6	0	.714	Won 1	245	136
Allison's Fine Jewelry	13	8	0	.619	Lost 1	202	179
Ford Lincoln of Morgantown	12	9	0	.571	Lost 1	232	180
Keglers Sports Bar	11	10	0	.524	Won 4	183	193
Pickled Nimrods	7	14	0	.333	Lost 6	194	261
Mega Corp Logistics	5	16	0	.238	Won 1	184	247
Chico's Bail Bonds	1	20	0	.048	Lost 20	90	293

AUGUST 9–CHICO'S (1–20) VS MEGA CORP "Did the Chico's win?"

Man, If I had an ice cold PBR and a shot of Jameson every time someone asked me that, I'd never get home alive. I always reply, "What do you think?" When you you see a wall of Orange at Chestnut Brew Works as we support our brother, or the sea of Orange and Black at 123 Pleasant Street on a random Thursday night... Do you think the Chicos's won? The truth is that every single Chico that has put on the Orange is a winner. Everyone that has cheered for the Bondsman is a winner.

Did the Chico's win a softball game? SOFTBALL?? We are talking about SOFTBALL?!?!? Are you kidding me?!?!? Who the hell cares about SOFTBALL?

All I care about are my guys, 20 amazing mofos that I can't imagine my life without. I can assure you each and every one of them is a winner.

If you must know the Chico's scored 3 runs, the other team scored way more than that. If you were expecting a different outcome... well that's kind of on you, I don't believe we've done anything this year to make you think otherwise. Game MVP - Nic Crouso, he had an RBI, good enough. Honorable Mention - Devin Williams who scored 2/3 of our runs. Last Chico standing... as I started the long walk up the hill, Devin, Casey, and Lawson were looking strong. Winner will most assuredly be decided by a monkey knife fight to the death in international waters or of Big Times, whichever is closer.—Ken Price

AUGUST 23–CHICO'S (1–23) VS FORD LINCOLN Chico's died. Under the lights of Liberatore Field. On the most beautiful of summer nights. It's over. All team members are dead. No fireworks. No explosions. No three-headed fiery horses appearing from the sky. No crop-killing cloud of locusts. No salvation. No funeral. No tributes. No memorials. No savior. Chico is done. No heaven. No hell. An eternity of disappointment. Purgatory. Errant throws forever. Base running blunders. Never-ending. Batted balls between the legs. Tired heavy legs. Wounded souls. Always. Pitiful. Sad. Everlasting. Second baseman Chris Evans. Injured. Achilles burning. A cigarette is lit. On the grass. Short right field. Just out of his reach forever. No more puffs. No more nicotine highs. Never again. His eternal sacrifice. A suffering. Like no other. Slugger Chris Simons. Deep majestic high flies to left field. Every time. Warning track power. The fences taller. Just short. A flyout for eternity. Caught. A routine out always. He rounds first base. Drops his head. Forever. Richard Lewis. Pitches flat. Pitches short. Pitches deep. Base on balls after base on balls. The bases are always loaded. No outs. No infield flies. The runs walk in. And walk in. And walk in. No defense. No strikes. Never. Forever and ever. Pitcher Jeff Ryan paces the parking lot. The delectable smell of Great Wall teriyaki chicken on a stick is everywhere. But no chicken. Never. The takeout bag he carries. Empty. Always. The all-encompassing aroma of fried cheese won-tons. Steamed pork dumplings. It's everywhere. But not. Shot glasses at the postgame. At the 123 bar. Empty. For eternity. Parched tongues. Dry. Sober. Worse than hell. Purgatory. An eternal treadmill to nowhere. Nothing. It was the worst of nights. The Bondsmen were embarrassed in both ends of the twilight doubleheader to the gentlemanly (and somewhat overrated) Ford-Lincoln squad by scores of 15–3 and 13–0. Despite the pitiful showing, three Chico's donned the MVP sombreros in the postgame- OF/1B Dave Mistich who delivered the only two hits in game 1. OF Jeff Goodwin who was tuned in to pregame scouting reports and made several stellar plays in left centerfield with perfect positioning. And Chico infielder Walt Sarkees who smacked two clean solid line drive singles to left field in game 2. Last Chico Standing – just about everyone. It was a late and soul crushing night for many Bonder team members. Some who may never be heard from again. Dirtiest Chico – SS Devin Williams. Cleanest Chico (and a shocker) – Infielder Dave Brown. RIP Chico's Bail Bonds softball. It's been a good run. An unprecedented three team meetings were held in the postgame—all led by Chris Evans.—JA

<u>2024 Season Awards:</u>

Chico Slugger – Andy Tuck

Chico Rookie of the Year – Devin Williams

Chico MVP – Dave Lawson

Chico Gold Glove – Dave Lawson

Most Loyal Chico – Ken Price

Chico Team Meeting MVP – Richard Lewis

Chico Please Touch Me Award – Chris Evans

My Favorite Chico – Dave Brown

"WE WOULD HAVE TO PLAY 420 GAMES TO HAVE AS MANY WINS AS CITY PLUMBING AND HEATING" —CHRIS SIMONS, 8-16-24

169

2025 **THE FUTURE IS ORANGE**

2025 Chico's: (standing) Andy Tuck, Chy Meking, Noah Geogerian, John Casey, Richard Lewis, Shannon Davy, Aaron Hawley, Chris Evans, Walt Sarkees, Devin Williams, Nic Crouso, (kneeling) Chris Simons, Jim Antonini, Jeff Goodwin, Ken Price, Jeff Ryan, Dave Brown

MAY 15—CHICO'S (0–2) VS PICKLED NIMRODS They closed the streets of First Ward. Crowds lined each side from West Virginia Avenue to Mississippi Street to Liberatore Field—orange as far as you could see. Pom poms, bottle rockets, and balloons. The first 500 fans received Chico schedule magnets. It was the start of a new softball season, and Chico Nation was ready. The skies were blue and clear. The air was comfortably warm and dry. A perfect night for a celebration. There were middle school marching bands, creepy politicians in sports cars, crying babies in strollers, beauty queens throwing candy, and softball royalty (many in wheelchairs) from days gone by. The best day of spring.

Seventeen Bonders, some veterans, some rookies, roared onto the lush green grounds of Liberatore to make history on the 27th opening day of Chico softball. But in true Bonder fashion, the buildup, the pomp and circumstance, was bigger than the actual product on the field. The Bondsmen were doomed from the start—walks, poor infield play would be their downfall. Opening day pitcher Jeff Ryan walked the first three Pickled Nimrod batters he faced in Game 1, causing manager Ken Price to remark, "This isn't good

but seems about right." Chico's fell behind early and never could dig themselves out of the hole, battling for seven hard-fought innings to lose 12–7 to their longtime rivals. The season's first team meeting was held in shallow center field as four Chico players collided behind second base on a lazy fly ball. RCF Christopher Simons nearly killed the Chico waif of a SS Devin Williams. Simons chipped a tooth, and Williams broke a finger.

The Bonders were better in game 2. Pitcher Richard Lewis brought stability as the Chico's offense came alive with several clutch hits and scored nine runs, only to fall 14–9 in the nightcap. The night was highlighted by the play of 2B Chris Evans, who predicted that there would be 'a whole lotta Evans' for the twinbill—and it was true. Evans was called out for baserunner interference for wildly flailing his arms to distract the Nimrod 1B causing him to drop a routine pop, was caught off second on an infield fly rule pop out (first time I've ever seen that), was viciously run over at a close play at second base, and was the supposed target at 2B for numerous errant throws of a Chico infielder who shall not be named.

Game notes: Chico MVPs were 3B Aaron Hawley (nice plays in the field, a 2-run double), 1B Shannon Davy (2 triples), and RF Dave Brown (4 hits, 4 runs scored). Other stars included LF Andy Tuck, who led Chico's with 5 hits, and rookie Noah Geogerian, who delivered three hits in his Chico debut. Dirtiest Chico - Dave Brown, Devin Williams. Last Chico Standing - all the way from Beckley, David Lawson. Team meeting MVP - John Casey.

Despite opening night losses, the Bonder team members celebrated hard into the early morning hours. It was good to see everyone again after a long, hard offseason.—JA

MAY 22–CHICO'S (0–2) Chico's rained out. Chris Evans wins Subway gift card and shows injured butt to crowded 123 bar. Casey Williams is lucky to be alive. Jeff Ryan endures. Sometimes, it's just good to be postponed. Best rainout ever.—JA

MAY 29—CHICO'S (0–4) VS MUNDY'S An earnest and unfettered Chico's Bail Bonds (0–4) roared into the 2nd week of the early BOPARC season in search of their 1st win only to drop two to the gentlemanly squad (3–1) from Mundy's neighborhood bar. The Bonders held their own in game 1, jumping out to an early 8–3 lead before falling in dramatic fashion 10–8 in the last inning to the very big, big bats of their rivals. Chico heroes included Big Sexy Lewis, who pitched a near flawless game (asking Mundy sluggers where they want it in terms of pitch selection), 3B Noah Geogerian for his hustle and heart, and dirty Dave Brown who knocked three hits and played a flawless right field. Game 1 MVP was "a whole lot more of Evans." Chris Evans was on base four times and made a spectacular catch in front of 2nd base, despite restraining himself to only 2 menthol cigarettes for a long night of fun. He exited game 1 with more bruises than he started the night with, and thus was unavailable for game 2.

In expected Chico fashion, the Bonders laid the biggest egg in decades in the nightcap, before being humiliated 21–2 in a late-night laugher. Game 2 stars were Chico's newbies - birthday boy John Casey and catcher Nic Crouso, who drove in both Chico runs. Outfielder Jeffrey Goodwin made several fine running catches of deep flyballs hit in the dark.

Game Notes: Dirtiest Chico Award: (tie) Dave Brown, Devin Williams, Noah Greogerian. Chico trifecta MVP - John Casey (game 2 MVP, Team Meeting MVP, Last Chico Standing). New Chico jersey alert- Ira Wile (NOTWOLF) finally got his 940 Chico jersey. Injuries- Chico star outfielder Christopher Simons left game 2 with a significant lower leg injury. His availability for the months of June and July is in doubt.—JA

JUNE 5–CHICO'S (0–6) VS FORD-LINCOLN OF MORGANTOWN

Chico's swept in a doubleheader to rival Ford-Lincoln of Morgantown to fall 0–6. It's been a dreadful start to the season. Sometime in the middle of game 1, a random Chico fan arrived late and asked, "How's Ford-Lincoln? Are they any good?" Chico pitcher Richard Lewis answered, "They've loaded the bases three times already." "What about Chico's?" The fan asked. "Chico's? They showed up loaded," Lewis said, "especially Chris Evans ." The Bonders dropped both games by the combined score of 34–6. In the postgame 123 party, Chico manager Ken Price lamented, "I hope we don't have to add another rung to the Olivia Newton-John No Win trophy of 2015. As it looks now, we may not win a game." It's become that bleak so early in another softball season that is spinning downward. The highlights for the Bondsmen were few. Chico MVP Jeffrey Goodwin made scores of fine running catches of deep, majestic drives by rival hitters. It was a Chico first for rookies Chy Menking and Braxton Lewis who picked up their first hits as Chico team members. Game 1 pitcher Lewis also struck out 6 Ford-Lincoln hitters.

video by Cyclone Cord using a Sony CCD-TR7

Game notes: Chico slugger and star outfielder Christopher Simons is out for 4–6 weeks with a calf injury. 2B Chris Evans was doubtful for the start of game 1 with an acute flare-up of prostatitis (not to be confused with prostitutitis). After several minutes of deep tissue massage and sustained Irish whiskey shot therapy, he was available for the first pitch in game 1 and played both ends of the doubleheader. The highlight of the night was the return of Chico legend and hall of famer—Meatball. Chico players were entertained in the postgame by the exceptional music by Weary Space Wanderer, The Tuck Band, and a set by Chico rookie and speedster Noah Geogerian.—JA

173

JUNE 12–CHICO'S (0–8) VS KEGLER'S Chico's may bring Olivia Newton-John back from the dead. The dreadful Bonders team (0–8) sadly may not win a game this season, matching their awful 0–23 winless 2015 season. It has gotten that bad. Where's is Dave Becker? We may need a second trophy to document this most pitiful version of Chico softball. The Bondsmen dropped two games in swampy bayou conditions against an upstart and more energetic Kegler's squad who was more prepared than Chico's. Advanced scouting reports had the Kegler outfielders perfectly positioned all evening as well-hit Chico batted balls fell harmlessly into easy outs. On the other hand, the entire Bonder scouting and analytics team was fired in the very tense postgame at the 123 bar. Chico fielders were lined up out of position all night, leaving them to chase each other around the chaotic outfield like a Benny Hill spoof. The first game of the night was competitive as the Bonders lost 8–3 behind the solid

pitching of Richard Lewis. Game lowlights included shortstop Devin Williams trying to illegally bunt for base hit—the most unforgivable sin in slow-pitch softball when the goal is to mash a gently lofted big yellow ball to outer space with the hardest of plutonium-uranium double-walled composite bat. After the game, Williams was later placed on waivers (not for trying to bunt but because of his 11 throwing errors in the two games. He overthrew the 6-foot-8-inch 1B Shannon Davy three times). His mentor, 2B Chris Evans, was blamed for Williams' poor performance. As Pitcher Lewis noted, "there are no bad students, only bad teachers." As of press time, no other BOPARC softball team has yet to claim Williams from waivers. In the second—a game that Chico Nation wants to forget, the Bondsmen fell in an embarrassing laugher 25–3 to Kegler's. It was so bad that Richard Lewis went from heckling the opponent to heckling his own team. Chico fans shouted encouragement to the team, "It's all right. You can't get up until you've been down." Lewis countered, "Unless you're a Chico, when we get down, we stay down."

Game 2 was so bad, the Chico team cinematographer Cyclone Cord, who filmed both games on a camcorder, was driven to the Westover Bridge and forced to toss the tape of the two-game debacle into the muddy waters of the Monongahela River below. The star of the game was Kegler's redheaded, muscle-bound slugger in the clean-up spot, who hit two over-the-fence home runs. By the middle of game 2 on the hot, steamy night, he had removed his jersey and faced struggling game 2 Chico pitcher Jeff Ryan topless, leading Chico agitator Lewis to comment, "Yeah, leave it to the redhead to get naked after the sun goes down." The comment led to a break in play as the redheaded batter, Chico catcher Eric Ramón, and the gentlemanly BOPARC umpire busted out into hysterical laughter that caused a long delay in the nightcap.

Game notes: Game 1 MVP - pitcher Richard Lewis, who struck out 7 Kegler's batters. Game 2 MVP - 3B rookie Braxton Lewis, who smacked 3 hits and made a spectacular line-drive bobble-bounce double play in the field. Postgame MVP - Sydney Walker for buying the spent and undernourished Chico players six pizzas. The Fred Baer Base-running Award - Chris Evans, who fell face first in the batter's box after hitting a slow roller to third. Although his Chico teammates tried not to laugh, audible snickers could be heard as far away as the Dorsey Avenue. Last Chico Standing- beleaguered pitcher Jeff Ryan; honorable mention- beleaguered Chico manager Ken Price, beleaguered 2B Chris Evans, nearly crippled Chico designated hitter and veteran Jim Antonini. For the third week in a row Chico Team Meeting MVP was John Casey "JC3". Chico slugger Christopher Simons remains on the injured list. The Bonders welcomed the return of longtime Chico outfielder Ethan Wells who looked a little rusty in game 1 but recovered in game 2.—JA

JUNE 26–CHICO'SS (0–10) VS SCORERS OG In a dismal performance in both ends of a doubleheader on a stormy and steamy summer night versus Scorers Og, the 2025 version of Chico softball is reminding folks too much of the dreadful 2015 team—the only winless team in Chico history. The current Bonders team is now an awful 0–10 on the season, dropping the night's opener 13–3 before falling in the nightcap 17–1 in three short pitiful innings. The Bonders

have now lost an incredible 32 straight games since opening day in early May 2024 last season. The highlights were few: game 1 MVP was 1B Shannon Davy who entertained with an earth-shaking, dirt-eating slide into third base after a triple to deep left centerfield. In appropriate Chico offensive futility, he was stranded at third base and did not score. Game 2 MVP was RCF Noah Geogerian who used his incredible speed to make numerous great defensive catches in the outfield. Other than that—nothing. Chico team members were sadly and constantly observed yelling at each other during and after the debacle. Embattled Chico manager Ken Price nearly turned in his resignation after a contentious and mutinous team meeting. One bright spot, Bonder veteran and longtime infielder Jim Antonini made his season debut in the field at second base, just six short months since his right leg amputation surgery. Chico Chicas - Sydney Walker and Meg Beatty were awarded their very own Bonder jerseys. Dirtiest Chico - Shannon Davy. Team meeting MVP - Dave Brown. Late Chico Standing - probably Chris Evans (who was fresh after an inadequate and less than spirited performance in game 1). The damaged second baseman is doubtful for the next Chico game two weeks away on July 10. —JA

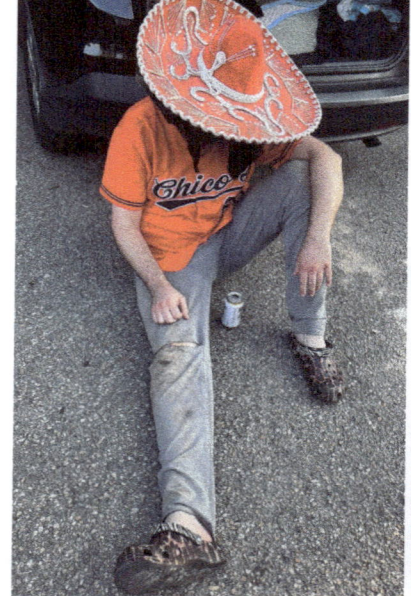

JULY 10—CHICO'SS (0–12) VS MEGA CORP Chico manager Ken Price described the night's debacle best, "I didn't find my shortstop of the future, and my current second baseman (Chris Evans) belongs in the past." Chico's were dominated, humiliated, spit on, cummed on, and overmatched against a young and rejuvenated, hard-charging Mega Corp, losing 19–1 in game 1 and 18–3 in game 2, goddamn! In this version of the BOPARC

Futility Bowl, the Bondsmen were more than futile—they sucked like they've never sucked before. The Bonders are now a dreadful zero wins and twelve losses on the season. The 14-month, 34-game losing streak that stretches into last season goes on. This has to end. But it won't—worse Chico team ever, maybe—on the playing field. (But not in the postgame—greatest 123 Thursday ever). Chico game MVP - Shannon 'smoke stacks still not tall enough' Davy. Chico team meeting MVP - John Casey . Last Chico Standing - captain Jim Antonini, suckers…—JA.

Today 3:42 PM

Chicooooooo. You coming tonight? Hope so!

Today 6:57 PM

Fuhsho

So, we already lost both games. Heading to 123 in like 20.

Read 8:22 PM

Man, I fucked up, nic told me 8 last night, I should've looked at the schedule myself

👍

I'll be there soon

177

Gary "Meatball" Nehls 1966–2025

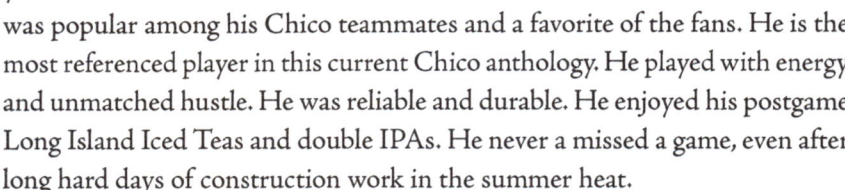

Sadly, beloved Chico Gary "MEATBALL" Nehls, 59, unexpectedly passed away on July 16, 2025 from complications after a heart attack.

Meatball was known for his big heart and even bigger laugh. He was a tireless worker with a strong work ethic. He brought energy and humor wherever he went. And, he was always available to help a friend in need.

He was the longest tenured Chico, having played 23 years before his retirement from softball in 2021. He

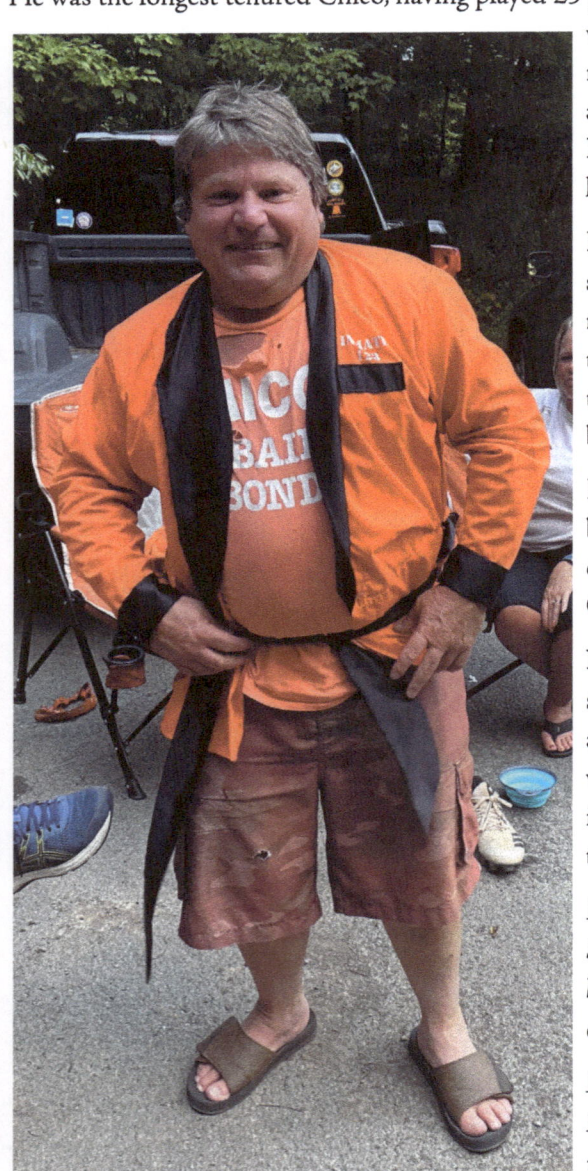

was popular among his Chico teammates and a favorite of the fans. He is the most referenced player in this current Chico anthology. He played with energy and unmatched hustle. He was reliable and durable. He enjoyed his postgame Long Island Iced Teas and double IPAs. He never a missed a game, even after long hard days of construction work in the summer heat.

He holds the Chico Ironman Award, having played an incredible 171 straight softball games – a record that will never be broken. He also holds Chico records for most seasons played and most games played. He is a member of the Chico All-Time team. Word has it that BOPARC will soon announce their selections for the area's first softball hall-of-fame team of which Meatball will be an inaugural member.

Fortunately, Meatball showed up for a visit during a Chico game a few weeks before he passed away. It was the first time in year or two that many of the current Chico players had seen him. It also was the first time the newer Chico players had ever met him.

No tribute would be complete without telling a "Meatball story." There were so many—from the humorous to the touching to the sometimes illegal to the almost unbelievable. One of the favorites is the "summer school story." This story was told to Chico players in the postgame parking lot by a member of an opposing team who grew up with Meatball in Suncrest. Meatball was present during the telling of this story and chuckled the whole time. The story goes as follows:

Meatball was failing English class one year during his time at Suncrest Junior High School. Even though Meatball was performing poorly in the class, he had endeared himself to the teacher. She even called him Meatball, instead of Gary like all the other teachers in the school.

During the telling of the story, Meatball chimed in "I wasn't performing poorly. I wasn't performing at all. The class was right before lunch. I would act up so she would send me to the principal's office. On my way to the office, I would check all the unlocked lockers for lunches. I would take the ones that looked good."

Because she had a soft spot in her heart for Meatball, she decided to give him one last chance to pass the course and not have to attend summer school. She would give him a final exam. If he passed the final exam, he would not have to report to summer school. Meatball was the only one to take the exam. He had to take it during the last week of school and in front of the entire class.

The teacher handed Meatball the test. He sat down at a desk in the middle of the room and immediately started working on it. His classmates surrounded him, watching with interest, excitement, and anticipation. Could Meatball pass the final? A buzz filled the crowded the classroom. For many students, it was liking watching a sporting event—Man vs. English Composition.

For over thirty minutes, Meatball leaned over the piece of paper without looking up, appearing to feverishly answer the questions. The other students were amazed. They couldn't believe Meatball was actually completing the exam.

Finally, the teacher stood.

"Time's up, Meatball."

He put his pencil down, slow-walked the completed exam to the front of the room, and handed it to the teacher. The teacher studied it a moment and showed it to the rest of the class.

Instead of answering the questions, Meatball had drawn a picture of the school with a drawing of himself standing on the steps in front. In the drawing, he was waving his arm, like he was saying, "goodbye, Suncrest Junior High." In the word bubble next to his mouth, he had written in large capital letters the now infamous line, "MEATBALL AIN'T GOING TO SUMMER SCHOOL!"

His teacher was quick to reply, "I'll see you in July, Meatball."

Of the Chico players in the postgame parking lot on the night the story was told, they all immediately looked to Meatball after the story was over. He blushed a little and nodded. Soon after, a playful grin filled his face. Then he laughed. The story was true. If you ever hear other Meatball stories, they also are all true. RIP Meatball. There will never be another like you.—JA

GARY "MEATBALL" NEHLS

THIRD BASE 12

BATS: RIGHT THROWS: RIGHT   SEASONS PLAYED: : 23
FAVORITE NUMBER: 714
HOBBIES: CLASSIC ROCK, BUFFETS, INTERSTATE COMMERCE, HARD WORK
WALK-UP SONG: "I FOUGHT THE LAW" BY THE BOBBY FULLER BAND

Meatball holds the Chico Ironman record for playing in 171 straight games; played one season under house arrest; is always quick to take his shirt off after the last out in a game; was once nearly traded to the Reno, Nevada softball league in 2012.

Gary "Meatball" Nehls: From a Friend's Perspective:

The Man

Gary was well known for being a happy, friendly guy who made friends with ease. I first met Gary when we were 15 years old on a camping trip. The rest of us were already at the campsite, a fire glowing and beverages flowing, when out of the darkness appeared Meatball carrying nothing but a 12-pack of Stoney's. I asked him if he brought a sleeping bag or a tent. He replied, "Don't need one," and cracked open a beer. I knew instantly that this was someone I wanted to hang with.

Gary was a baller. Whether it was football, basketball, or baseball/softball. He played football with ferocious determination, had a beautiful jump shot, and the Chico's crowd can attest to both his ball skills and his all-in attitude as a teammate. He was also an accomplished skier, hitting the steep and deep with the best of us. On one unforgettable ski trip, we were way out on the backside of Copper Mountain when a friend broke a ski. Gary immediately insisted on trading skis so he would be the one skiing on a single ski. A testament to not only his athletic skills, but more importantly, his character.

I had the pleasure of working alongside Gary for over 30 years and on more than 400 projects - from one-day jobs to major bridge construction. He was a rock-solid all-around builder, with especially excellent skills as a finisher and tile setter.

Gary was a complex guy. He didn't know the word "quit." He was tough as nails, and to this day I've never met a man who could out-shovel him. He was a great problem-solver, had solid math skills, and was a deep thinker. He showed up to every job, big or small, with a scrap of paper filled with bold print explaining how we should proceed, even if we already had engineered prints. He put great thought and time into his drawings, earning him the nickname "The Professor." It was never a dull moment working with Gary.

Though he wasn't a man of many words, we had many great conversations. Sometimes about obscure things he'd recently read, but more often about life as it unfolded. And when he talked about his granddaughter, his whole face lit up with pure joy.

The Myth

Many people only knew Gary as an old-school, hard-working man, and badass baller. But he was also a truly sweet and generous soul. He'd help neighbors shovel snow so they could get out, and he was always there for a friend in need.

He was quite a cook and knew good food (although quantity was also important). A foodie in his own way, with an undeniable affinity for coleslaw. We ate at hundreds of places, and he always ordered coleslaw! He liked giving waitresses a friendly hard time, but always cleaned his plate and tipped generously.

The Legend

Gary was a friend to all he met, and if you were his friend, you were for life. The world is a better place for having kind souls like Gary. I am a better man for having known him.

Until we meet again,

Geoff Kemp

JULY 17–CHICO'S (0–13) VS OG SCORERS & CHICO'S (0–14) VS MEGA CORP Meatball would have been proud. In tribute, the Bonders played their two best games of the year. Despite losing both ends of the doubleheader to still remain winless (0–14) on the 2025 season, the Bondmen took two of BOPARC Black Division's best teams to the limit, playing a full game in each.

In Game 1, Chico's held an 8–5 lead with one inning to go against league juggernaut OG Scorers before succumbing to the dreadful one 'not so bad' inning, giving up six runs in the sixth inning before losing a heartbreaker 11–8.

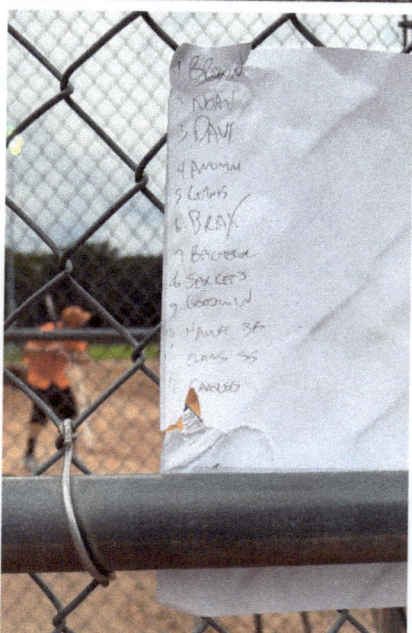

In game 2, the Bonders briefly held a 2-run lead against rival Mega Corp before dropping the night cap 12–4 in seven hard fought innings. Sadly, Chico's again (as always) were undone with one bad inning where their rivals scored eight unearned runs in the fifth.

The stars for Chico's on the night were many: SS Chris Evans and LF Dave Brown may have made the defensive plays of the

season each with an over-the-shoulder tumbling acrobatic catch. Aging and somewhat out of shape Evans remarked afterwards, "that maybe was my last great catch of my career." After viewing photos of the catch, he made note that he didn't realize how big his belly was. OF Noah Geogerian dazzled the crowd with his elite speed on the base paths as well as his solid defensive play in the outfield. Veteran Jim Antonini delivered 5 hits on the night, which included legging out a double (which may be the last of his career due to failing knees). Pitcher Big Sexy gave up 'only' 23 runs on the night, remarkably lowering his league worst earned run average. He also hustled out two triples and drove in 5 runs on the night. Catcher Nic Crouso had his best offensive performance of the season, knocking three line drive singles. 1B Shannon Davy shined both at the plate with multiple hits and in the field with several scoops of errant bouncing throws to first. The Bonders enthusiastically welcomed back Chico legend Thomas Batchelor who manned a solid second base for each game. Chico veteran Walt Sarkees also made his first appearance of the year, smacking multiple hits, including a perfectly placed double down the third base line. Sombrero MVPs - Chris Evans (defense), Shannon Davy (hitting, defense), Big Sexy (pitching, hitting). Team Meeting MVPs (tie) - Dave Brown, Sydney Walker . Last Chico Standing - Ken Price. RIP MEATBALL - you will be missed.—JA

JULY 24—CHICO'S (1–15) VS LADDER BOYS The nightmare 37-game losing streak is over! Finally! Chico's ENDURE! On the muggiest night of the summer, Chico's (1–15) win game 2 in epic 90-minute softball thriller 24–20 against Ladder Boys. Embattled Chico manager Ken Price said it best, "It felt like we lost that game five times. I don't know how we won." The Bonders won game 2 with youth and speed, coming back from several multi-run deficits to secure victory. The big decisive blow of the night came from the bat of Christopher Simons (just activated from the 6-week injury list) who smashed a bases-clearing triple off the left field fence in the game 2's final inning. The recent youth movement in the transformation of the Chico roster is finally paying dividends. The sombrero MVPs on the night were all Chico youngsters. OF John Casey knocked three hits and scored three runs as well as played a flawless right field. Shortstop Devin Williams ignored the YIPS that have plagued him all season and turned in his best performance since early last season, delivering multiple hits and scoring numerous runs along with one of the best defensive plays of the year. Chico rookie, spark plug, and jitterbug Noah Geogerian scored 9 daring and dashing runs (that's 9 runs in one game) to lead the Bondsmen to victory. Slugger Simons went six for six on the night with three doubles and one triple. But there were others heroes - LCF Jeffrey Goodwin

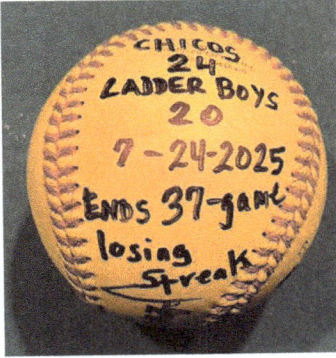

made several fine running catches in the outfield, catcher Nic Crouso delivered several clutch hits, pitcher Jeff Ryan stayed focused, hurling the Bonders to victory by limiting walks and striking out six Ladder Boy hitters. Ryan also gave the capacity, mostly female Whiston Field crowd a thrill by exposing his voluptuous man boobs from the mound on two different occasions. Chico's lost game 1 by the score of 14−3 to rival and suddenly resurgent 2nd place Pickled Nimrods (13−3). The Bondsmen welcomed back Chico veteran Dave Mistich who bashed one line-drive single and scored one run in game 2. Dirtiest Chico (a tie) - Devin Williams, Noah Geogerian. Team meeting MVP - Jon Vehse. Last Chico Standing - 2B Chris Evans (who literally pulled a fielded ball out of his ass and threw the runner out at second). This win was for MEATBALL.—JA

185

2025 Season Awards

Chico MVP – Richard Lewis

Chico Gold Glove – Chris Evans

Ravi Shibley Chico Slugger Award – Shannon Davy

Chico Rookie of the Year – Noah Geogerian

Most Improved Chico – Nic Crouso

Most Loyal Chico – Jeff Goodwin

David Lawson Chico Fashion Award – Nic Crouso

Chico Team Meeting MVP – John Casey

Chico Meatball 714 Hustle Award – Chris Evans

My Favorite Chico – Chris Simons

APPENDIX

ALL-TIME CHICO TEAM

All available postgame write-ups and box scores from the past 26 years were uploaded into an advanced data analysis software package (JMP Statistical Discovery, Cary, NC USA) in an attempt to name an all-time Chico team. Not only was the performance on the field evaluated in the determination of the Chico all-stars, but the activities off the field after the games were considered as well.

FIRST BASE	LEATHERMAN, PORTERFIELD, SHILLING, HAWLEY
SECOND BASE	BATCHELOR, EVANS
THIRD BASE	MEATBALL, BUTLER
SHORTSTOP	ANTONINI, CARNEY
OUTFIELD	TUCK, SHIBLEY, ROB B., GUILIANI, BECKER, SIMONS, LAWSON, RAESE, GOODWIN, KOICUBA, KURKENDALL, KELLEY
CATCHER	VEHSE, MCGINLEY, PRICE
PITCHER	FOREMAN, KROVICH, RYAN, LEWIS
DESIGNATED HITTER	MISTICH, MARCH

CHICO'S STATISTICS

MOST SEASONS	MEATBALL
MOST GAMES PLAYED	MEATBALL, ANTONINI
OLDEST CHICO TO APPEAR IN A GAME	NELMS, MANILLA
MOST GAMES PLAYED IN DENIM JEANS	MCGINLEY, KOURY, GRADY, D BROWN
MOST GAMES PLAYED WEARING BOOTS	MARCH
DIRTIEST ON FIELD CHICO	D BROWN, DOWNS, MEATBALL, VEHSE
MOST POSTGAME TEAM MEETINGS ATTENDED	VEHSE, RYAN
MOST POSTGAME TEAM MEETING MVPS	LEWIS, EVANS
MOST CAREER IN-GAME WHOLE CIGARETTES SMOKED	VEHSE, PORTERFIELD
MOST CAREER IN-GAME HALF CIGARETTES SMOKED	EVANS
MOST OFTEN INJURED CHICO	PORTERFIELD, KROVICH, ANTONINI, SKINNY, SIMONS
HIGHEST CAREER WHISKEY CHUGGING PERCENTAGE	VEHSE, PORTERFIELD

HITTING RECORDS

MOST CAREER OVER-THE-FENCE HOMERUNS	SHIBLEY, TUCK, SIMONS, KURKENDALL
MOST CAREER RUNS BATTED IN	LEATHERMAN, TUCK
HIGHEST CAREER SLUGGING PERCENTAGE	SHIBLEY, TUCK
MOST CAREER HITS	ANTONINI
MOST CAREER WALKS	GUILIANI
MOST CAREER RUNS SCORED	KROVICH
HIGHEST CAREER BATTING AVERAGE	SHIBLEY, TUCK

PITCHING RECORDS

MOST CAREER WINS	FOREMAN, KROVICH
MOST CAREER LOSSES	FOREMAN, KOURY
BEST CAREER EARNED RUN AVERAGE	KROVICH
WORST CAREER EARNED RUN AVERAGE	RYAN, KOURY
MOST CAREER STRIKEOUTS	FOREMAN
MOST CAREER WALKS ALLOWED	RYAN, KOURY

year	wins-losses
1998	10-12
1999	4-14 (summer), 7-9 (fall)
2000	9-11 (summer), 2-6 (fall)
2001	6-14
2002	3-16
2003	13-10
2004	14-9
2005	12-11
2006	12-10
2007	9-10
2008	8-11
2009	4-16
2010	8-8
2011	2-16
2012	5-17
2013	3-17
2014	4-19
2015	0-23
2016	3-20
2017	3-22
2018	3-22
2019	4-16
2020	4-20
2021	4-24
2022	2-26
2023	2-19
2024	1-22

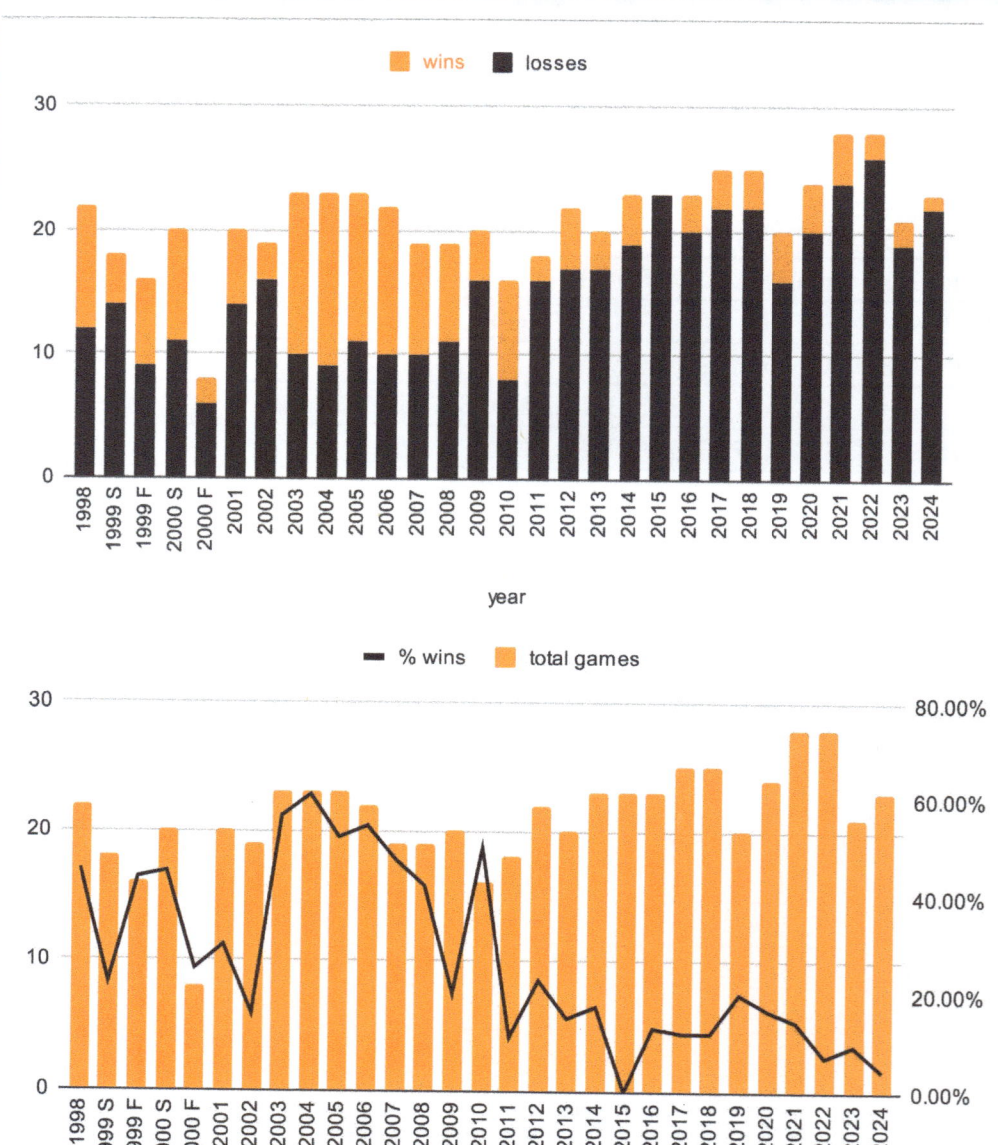

Games played 611

Overall team record (26 years) 161 wins – 450 losses

Winning percentage 26.4%

Average yearly record 6 wins – 17 losses

MARK DOWNS

CHAD KOURY

AARON HAWLEY

BILL, BILL, BILL

KEN PRICE

ERIC RAMON

DAVE MISTICH

TYLER GRADY

In 2018, photographer Jesse Wright and Chico Ken Price collaborated to make Topps-style baseball cards for each player, using Jesse's excellent photos (many of which appear throughout this book). The cards were displayed at the Chico's art show and each player was given their card to keep.

MEATBALL

JEFF GOODWIN

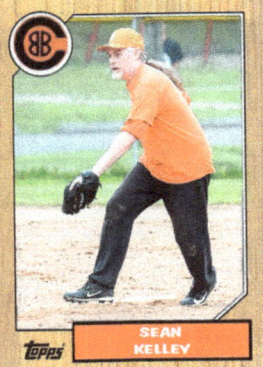

SEAN KELLEY

DAVE LAWSON

JIM ANTONINI

CHICO'S AND MUSIC

Chad Koury

From the start, the Bonder softball roster was filled with many musicians from Morgantown. Through the years, select nights at 123 Pleasant Street, usually at the end of a softball season, were solely dedicated to bands that featured Chico team members. On a few occasions, the proceeds collected at the door would go to a local charity. Other times, the Chico music night served as the end-of-the-year softball party for the players and their legion of loyal fans. And two times, a Chico team member preformed the national anthem before a game at Whiston Field. In 2014, Chad Koury played the anthem on electric guitar, and in 2019, Dave Lawson performed it on clarinet. Both times, the team members for Chico's and the opponents (IDK in 2014; Pickled Nimrods in 2019) lined the first and third base lines, respectively.

Dave Lawson performs the Star Spangled Banner on clarinet

One Man Gaga 4 Gaga: Dave Krovich

Andy Tuck

Chico's Bail Bonds
Benefit Show

all proceeds benefit the Mountain People's Co-op

featuring performances from:
One Man Gaga For Gaga
Andy Tuck
Jet Set Vapour Trails
Goodwolf
Aaron Hawley & the Foul Tips

Fri. May 15th 9pm $5
123 Pleasant St.

Greg Leatherman

Dem Donkey Boys: Dave Lawson, Tom Batchelor

The following is a list of Chico's (and at least one of their affiliated bands) who have significantly contributed to the local music scene (we apologize for any omissions):

Tom Batchelor: Rasta Rafiki, Tom Batchelor Band, Dem Donkey Boys

Bob Butler: Brain Police, Weedhawks

John Casey: Randy, Golden Horseshoe

Raj Chandran: Born Again Hindus, Love Me Knots, Buddha Thunkit, R.U.L.E.

Matt Cross: Treasure Cat, NYC, Kashmir, Ponderosa

Nic Crouso: Vulgar Royalty

Shannon Davy: Vulgar Royalty

Donnie Duppee: Granny's 12-Gauge, Ogua, Stonewall Jackson 5ive

Eddie Freedom: Hogblast

Noah Geogerian: Stupidhead

Tyler Grady: Goodwolf

Jeff Goodwin: Law Biting Citizens, Ghost Road, Jet Set Vapour Trails

Aaron Hawley: 85 Flood, The Border States

Tom Batchelor Band: Tom Batchelor, Jon Vehse

The Border States: Dusty Hays, Jeff Wiles, Aaron Hawley, Walt Sarkees. Photo by Emily Dillman Sarkees

The Dick Tuck Band: Andy Tuck, Richard Lewis

Stonewall Jackson 5ive: Donnie Duppee, Jeff Hindal, Dave Krovich, Jeff Ryan

CHICO'S $ BAIL $ BONDS $

End of Season Party & Rock Show
Fri. Aug. 12 - 9pm
123 Pleasant St.

Ghost Road
Tom Batchelor & Friends
The Border States
Born Again Hindus

All proceeds benefit WV Flood Relief
& United Way of Greenbrier Country

Noah Geogerian

Tyler Grady, still from the Goodwolf music video, "Selfie"

Ghost Road: Jeff Goodwin

Dusty Hays: 85 Flood, The Border States, Dead All Along

Jeff Hindal: Ogua, Stonewall Jackson 5ive, The Darbys

Dave Lawson: Lords of Lester, Dem Donkey Boys, The Tuck Band

Sean Kelley: Bearded Clams

Chad Koury: Chad Koury All-Stars

Dave Krovich: One Man Gaga 4 Gaga, Stonewall Jackson 5ive, Ish

Greg Leatherman: The Flying Listravians, Sugarcamp

Tom Moore: Velez Manifesto, Elephant Typewriter, Plow, Jet Set Vapour Trails

Andy Pintus: the traveling harmonica man

Brian Porterfield: Love Me Knots, Cheap Trucker's Speed

Robert Raese: Kashmir, Ponderosa

Jeff Ryan: Stonewall Jackson 5ive

Walt Sarkees: Dead All Along, The Border States

Jeff Shilling: Moon, Granny's 12-Gauge

Andy Tuck: The Greens, Power Forward, The Tuck Band

Jon Vehse: Tom Batchelor Band, The Mannekynz

Jeff Wiles: The Ramps, Diabolo Sandwich, The Border States

Jon Vehse, Chad Koury

JSVT: Jeff Goodwin, Tom Moore

Randy: John Casey

Vulgur Royalty: Nic Crouso, Shannon Davy. Photo by Brian Dye.

CHICO'S INSPIRES ART

What other softball team in the history of the world had an art opening celebrating its existence? None.

On July 27, 2019, A Chico's Bail Bonds Retrospective and Art Show was held at 123 Pleasant Street. The show highlighted all things Chico—a celebration of a brotherhood of magical misfits. Featured work included Chico-inspired paintings from Malissa Baker (see pages 78 and 200) and prints from Brian Pickens.

In years since, Chico's has inspired digital artwork by Chico Dave Mistich, a paper-mache portrait marionette of Jon Vehse by Chico Jeff Ryan (at the jukebox, page xiii, at the beginning of this book), bobbleheads of Jeff Ryan and Ravi Shibley (see page 111, Ravi by Chico Ethan Wells), the famed CHICO painting by Billy Federer and the 2025 season schedule poster art by Chico Nic Crouso.

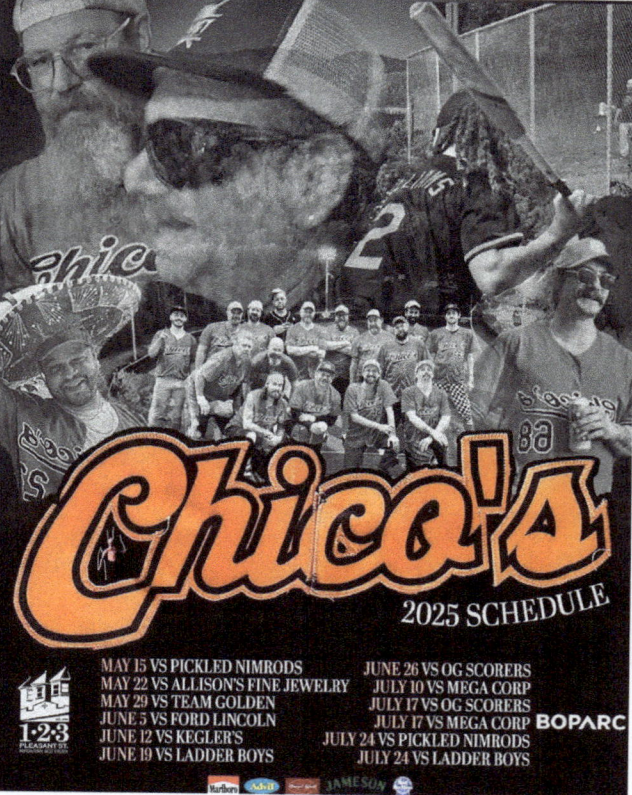

2025 Season Poster design by Chico Nic Crouso

Jeff Ryan bobblehead crafted by Chico Eric Ramón

Meatball digital figurine by Chico Dave Mistich

Chico's tattoo design by Brian Pickens, ink by Wild Zero, body of Chico Jeff Goodwin

Poster design by Brian Pickens

...I fell in love with the team reading [Antonini's] side splitting accounts of the athletic misadventures of this local softball team who brings the entertainment value of the Globetrotters combined with Win/Loss record of the Generals. Tattooed freaks, bartenders, bouncers, dreadlocked guitar players, and computer nerds displaying flashes of athletic brilliance between groan inducing ineptitude and endearing buffoonery...

—Billy Federer

**"CHICO" by Billy Federer
mixed media on card stock**

CHICO'S INSPIRES STYLE

Through the years, Chico's uniforms have evolved from t-shirts and orange ball-caps to pro-style jerseys, accessorized with custom hats, pants, socks, and even neck gaiters, specifically designed for the 2020 pandemic season. A smoking jacket and prison jumpsuit also have been created for the Bonders' squad. And love of the team has led players to purchase custom license plates for orange cars, uniform-up their dogs, and trick-out their electric bikes in Chico-orange.

CHICO'S INSPIRES BEER

AUGUST 8, 2019 CHESTNUT BREW WORKS RELEASE – ONE BAD INNING LAGER

This refreshing beer was crafted by Josh Taylor and Chico Bill Ritenour, inspired by Chico's Bail Bonds, the area's most beloved and infamous softball team. Classic meets contemporary with German Pilsner malts complementing American Mosaic hops. The beer is light, crisp, wonderfully balanced, and perfect for those last warm evenings as summer fades into fall. One Bad Inning Lager is ideal for a football tailgate or after a hike on your favorite mountain trail. And unlike the softball team for which it was inspired, this beer will never let you down. It's always a winner! At the taproom starting August 8! Cheers! ABV 5.1%, IBU 25.

Inset painting by Melissa Baker, 2019

200

September 18, 2020 Chestnut Beer Works Release – Chico's Two Game Win Streak Kolsch

Dedicated to the short but still notable win streak during the glorious 2020 softball season. This popular beer by Chestnut Brew Works has been referred to as a "softball game beer", "lawn mowing beer", "dad beer", and "porch-drinking beer." Chico's Two Game Win Streak is a Kolsch-style late-hopped ale with Mosaic hops—a simple and easy-drinking fermented barley ale.

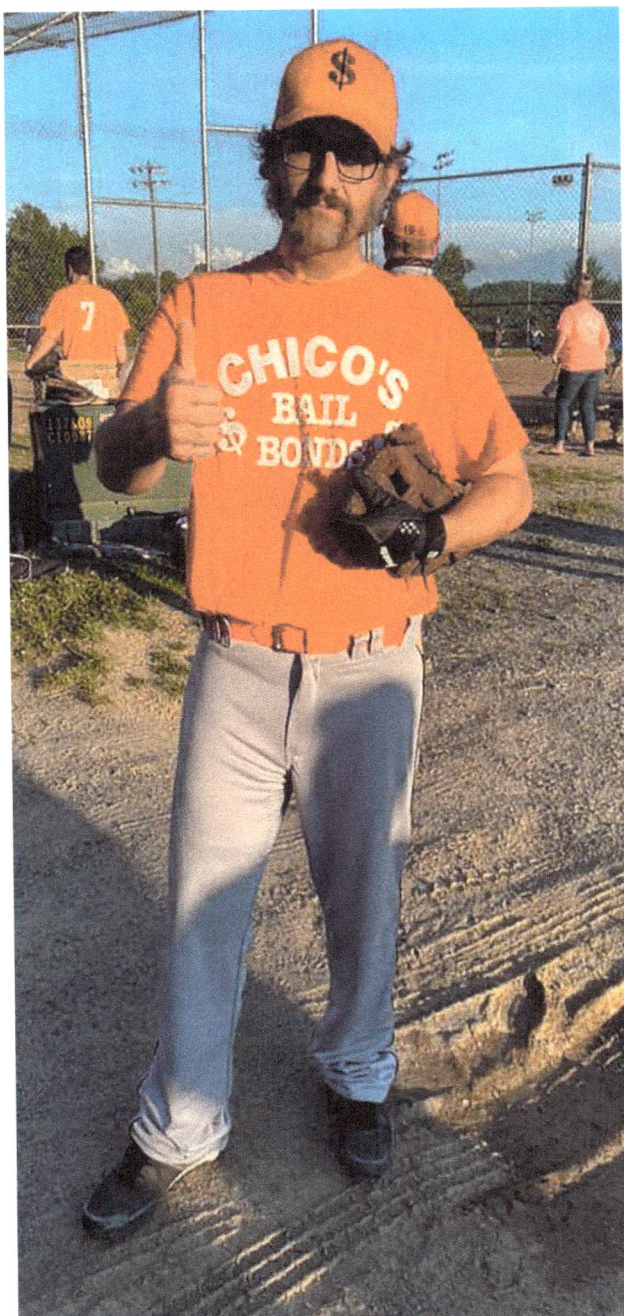

CBW Owner and Chico Bill Ritenour

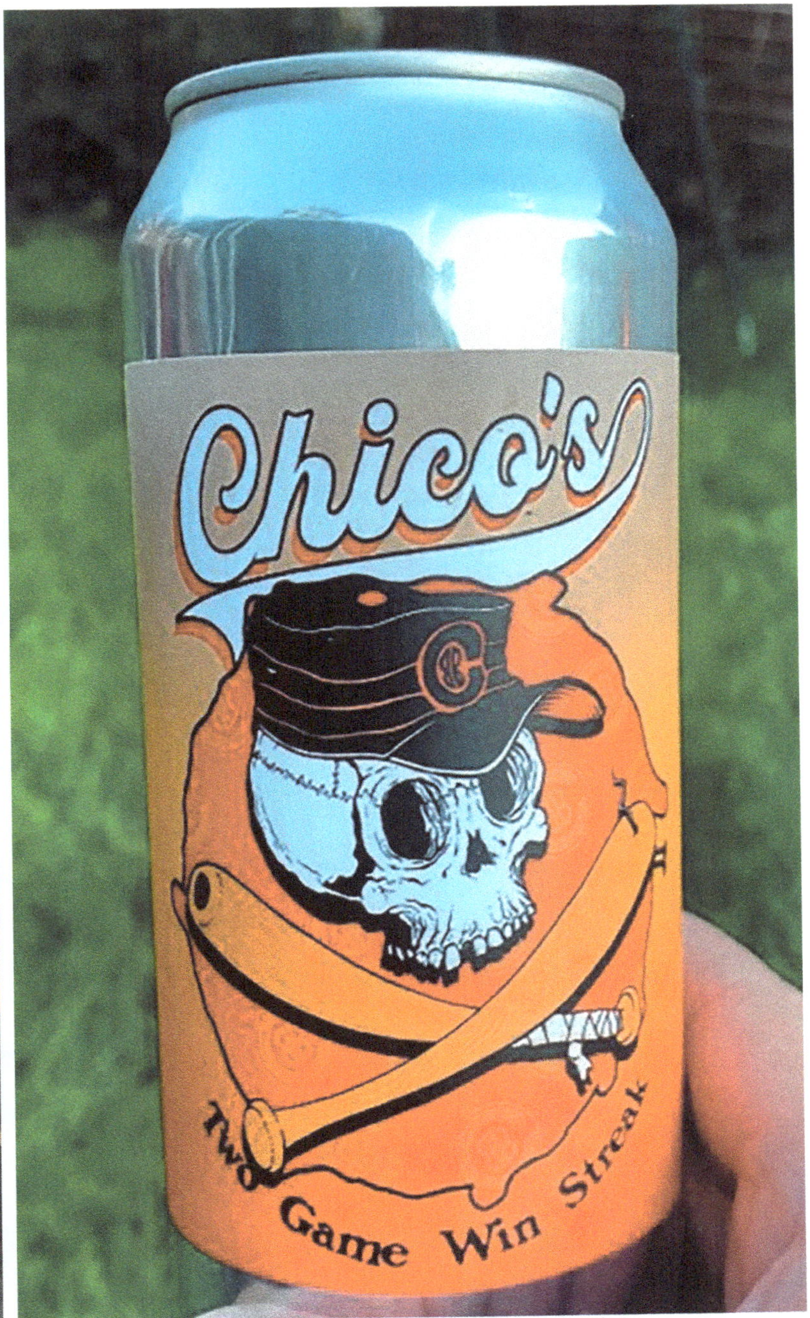

Two Game Win Streak can artwork by Brian Pickens

CHICO'S INSPIRES PAIN

The only other thing as common to Chico's softball as losing is injury. And through the years, Chico players have had all types from bumps, bruises, cuts, broken bones, concussions, contusions, punctures, as well as muscle pulls, strains, and tears. And all body parts have been affected, including the head, face, shoulder joint, shoulder blade, collarbone, back, elbow, wrist, hand, fingers, ass cheek, groin, hamstring, knee, calf, ankle, heel, foot, and toes. But no pain is enough to diminish the spirit that drives Chico's.

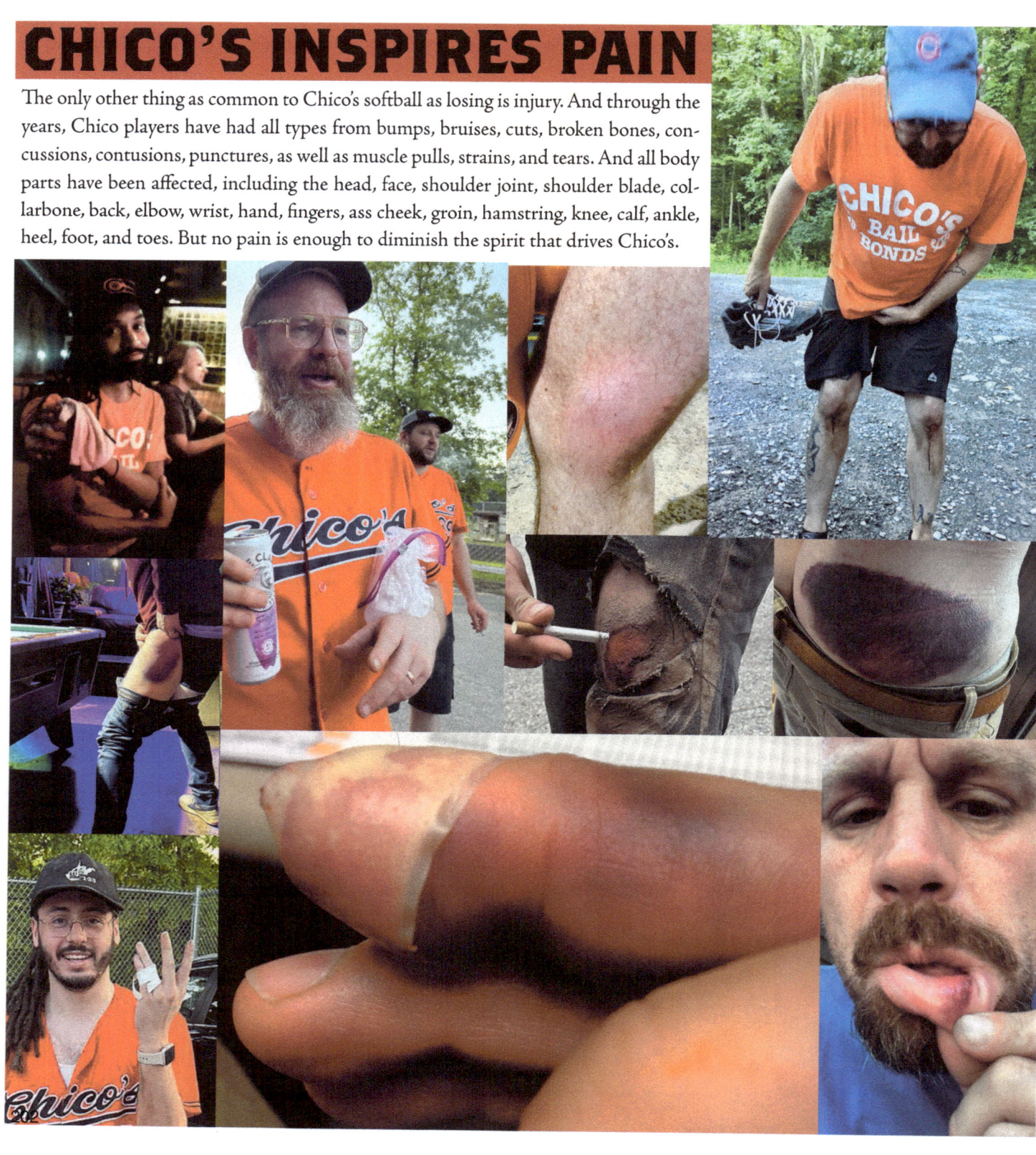

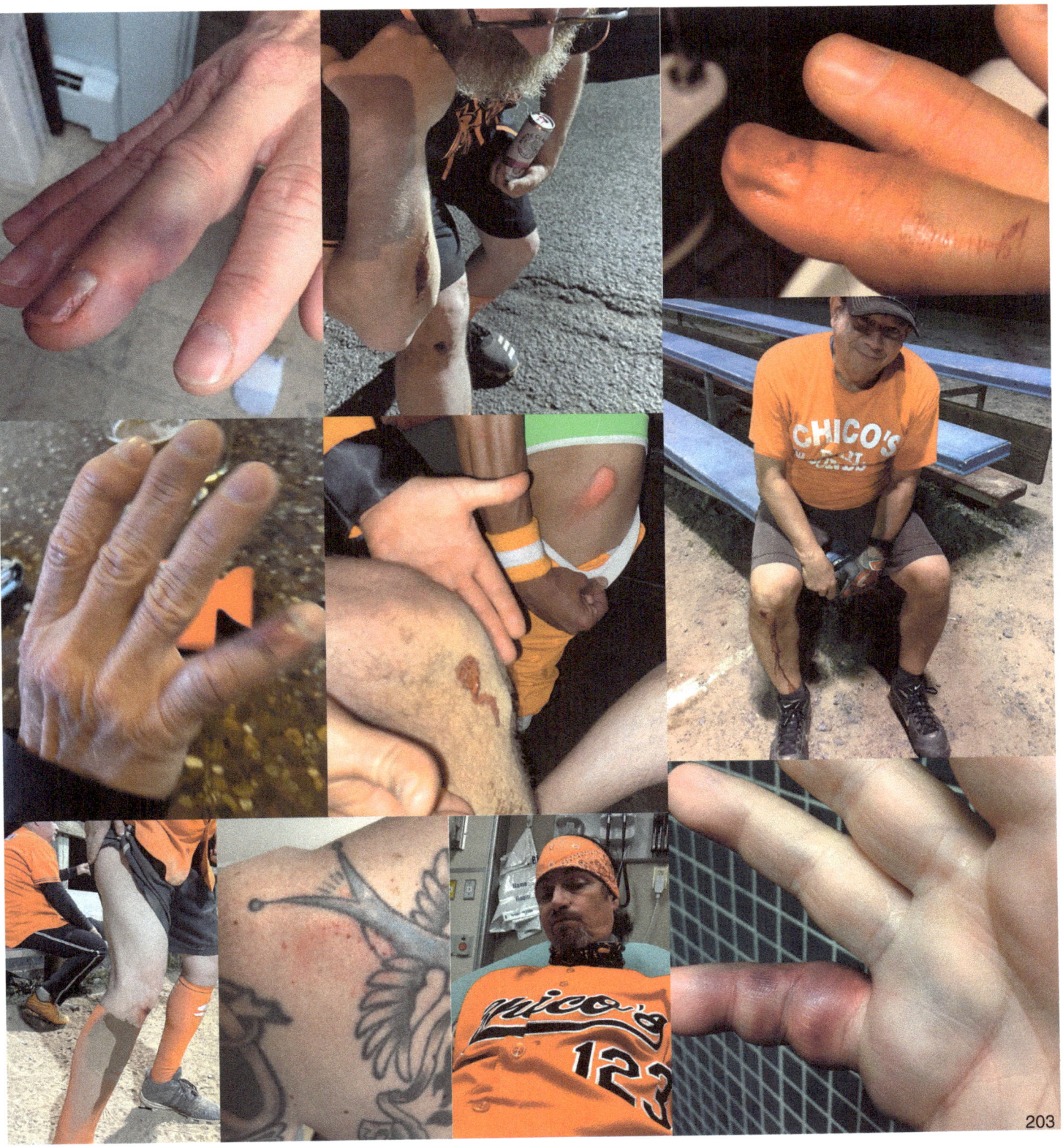

203

Jim Antonini is an award-winning author from West Virginia who has four novels published by Pump Fake Press: *Bullets for Silverware* (2020), a gritty, murder-mystery thriller set in the backwoods of West Virginia and a finalist for the Appalachia 2020 Best Appalachian Book of the Year; *Like Falling from an Airplane* (2021), a romantic, urban drama set on the downtown streets and back alleys of San Francisco; *Wild Bill Rides Again* (2023), about a socially awkward middle-aged family man who steals one million dollars and goes on an unforgettable joyride across the country; *The Butcher and the Butterfly* (2024), about a wearied boxer who turns his back on a chance at a world championship to search for his estranged brother in the French Quarter of New Orleans, where he discovers love, friendship, and heartbreak. Jim also co-wrote *The Hot Dog Diaries* (2024), a book about Gene's Beer Garden—Morgantown, West Virginia's oldest and most beloved neighborhood bar.

All five books are available online at www.jimantonini.com

Suzanne Reynolds is pursuing her MSW and does graphic design and industrial engineering consulting on the side. She lives out in the country with her spouse Mark and their dog. They play music and have fun.

www.ingramcontent.com/pod-product-compliance
Lightning Source LLC
Chambersburg PA
CBHW041113120626
46547CB00019B/2688